What Manner of Woman Are YOU?

What Manner of Woman Are YOU?

by

James Ivey

What Manner of Woman Are YOU?

All scripture quotations are from the *Holy Bible, King James Version,* public domain. Word definitions marked "Vines" are from *Vine's Complete Expository Dictionary of Old and New Testament Words* (Nashville, TN: Thomas Nelson Publishers: 1996). Word definitions marked "Strongs" are from *Strong's Exhaustive Concordance of the Bible* (Gordonsville, TN, Dugan Publishers, Inc.: no date.)

Published by:

McDougal & Associates
18896 Greenwell Springs Road
Greenwell Springs, LA 70739
www.thepublishedword.com

McDougal & Associates is dedicated to spreading the Gospel of the Lord Jesus Christ to as many people as possible in the shortest time possible.

ISBN 978-1-950398-23-2

Printed in the U.S., the U.K. and Australia
For Worldwide Distribution

Dedication

For Maricel:

Many daughters have done virtuously, but you truly have excelled them all.

Thank you for being my wife.

Acknowledgments

The Lord gave the word: great was the company of those that published it.
Psalm 68:11

My thanks to my mother, Apostle Charlean C. Ivey, my son, Gideon Ivey, and the entire congregation of Miracle House Ministries for their prayers and support in helping to bring this vision to pass.

CONTENTS

Finally, brethren, whatsoever things are true, whatsoever things are honest, whatsoever things are just, whatsoever things are pure, whatsoever things are lovely, whatsoever things are of good report, if there be any virtue, and if there be any praise, think on these things.

Philippians 4:8

PREFACE
(FINDING YOURSELF)

For it is God which worketh in you both to will and to do of his good pleasure. Philippians 2:13

The master key that unlocks the door to a life of purpose, meaning, joy, and contentment is understanding the role that you were born to play in this world and in the world to come. Throughout the long ages of this planet's history, human beings have walked the earth, from one phase of life to another, in the great celestial theater. They have been born as babies, grew into children, matured into adulthood (with jobs and careers), and produced offspring of their own, continuing the cycle. And, while multitudes of peoples have taken on the roles and the parts that come with the program of life, many have passed from the cradle to the grave having never reached their highest potential. This sad reality has occurred because the majority travel the wide highway of life wandering aimlessly, as opposed to following the narrow path that leads to everlasting, abundant life.

Truly one of the great moments in the annals of cosmic history took place when Almighty God, the Father of Creation, stepped out of eternity and spoke creation into existence. With the sound of His all-consuming and authoritative voice, He spoke the universe into being. The stars, the planets, and all the firmament of heaven that is far beyond the stars of our own galaxy were all fashioned by the voice of the Great I Am. Not only did His voice create the cosmos, but He spoke living creatures and sentient spirits into being. And, in His infinite wisdom, as a part of His grand plan for the ages, He made human beings to share in His creative symphony. Then, like a great conductor or master playwright, He gave to each being, not only life, but a role to play on His stage with a script that would be the guiding light for their lives.

Then, however, darkness crept onto the stage, and wicked spirits worked their influence and produced wicked men and women, who, instead of evolving in pursuit of the high calling of God, fell by the wayside of life. Instead of taking on the nature and character of the Divine, hearts became evil and took on archetypal roles, roles that God never intended for us to have. But, thanks be to God, He made a way, through His Son Jesus, to save us from the evil that sweeps across our world. More than that, He has made provision for us to know His will, to do His will, and to understand that this takes place by becoming the person He has ordained us to be. The book that you hold in your hands is a tool to help you to become that person.

The title of this book is *What Manner of Woman Are You?*, and it is a manifesto to help women of all ages, ethnicities, cultures, and backgrounds to become the God-ordained woman that God wants you to be. In a day and age in which the woman question is being re-examined and redefined in our collective culture, a message such as this is needed and must be brought forth. Our collective cultural conscious is seeking to empower women in a way that we have not really seen in such zenith in the modern era. Society is hoping to change standards and mindsets that have kept women in a kind of second-class status that has, in turn, produced many hurts and wounds to her on an emotional level. While these efforts are laudable and worth implementing, the issues that confront us will never be truly resolved unless and until they are examined from the viewpoint of the Source of absolute truth, the Word of God, contained in the Holy Bible.

I have felt stirred in my spirit to approach this subject from the foundation point of the word *manner*, hence the title of the book. In our modern vernacular, when that word is spoken, the meaning of social grace or a certain code of conduct often comes to the mind of the hearer. While those ideas are consistent with the meaning of the word, I would like us to examine it from a biblical point of view and from there draw out a much deeper understanding.

When the Bible was translated from the original languages of Hebrew, Greek, and Aramaic, along with previous English translations into the King James Version of the Bible, the scholars of that day thought about the word *manner* in a more exhaustive context than we do today. When they chose that word to use for certain scriptural passages, they were choosing a word that conveyed a certain character type, a character type that, based upon that personality, lived a specific way of life. The Bible speaks for itself in explaining this in this passage found in the gospel according to Matthew:

> *And when he was entered into a ship, his disciples followed him. And, behold, there arose a great tempest in the sea, insomuch that the ship was covered with the waves; but he was asleep. And his disciples came to him, and awoke him saying; Lord, save us; we perish. And he said unto them, Why are ye fearful, O ye of little faith? Then he arose, and rebuked the winds and the sea; and there was a great calm. But the men marveled, saying, What manner of man is this, that even the winds and the sea obey him!* Matthew 8:23-27

Here we read of one of the outstanding miracles in the life and ministry of Jesus. As we take joy in the wonder of this happening, we also notice something very important in the text concerning the disciples. The followers of Jesus who were with Him on the boat that day saw this great event, and, as a result, asked among themselves a particular question. They did not ask how He did what He did or even why He did what He did in the way that He did it. They asked quite simply, "What manner of man is this that even the elements of nature obey Him." That word *manner,* in the original Greek, is defined as "a certain way of life," and "a particular character type." Based upon that question, we see that the success Jesus had in His life and ministry was a direct result of the character type He was in the role He inhabited and the way in which that role resulted in His way of life.

In the Old Testament, there is another example of the use of this word that speaks directly to this issue. The event of which I speak deals with Rebekah, the wife of Isaac. When Rebekah became pregnant, she was carrying twins, and those twins fought within her. When she enquired of the Lord regarding the reason for this struggle, God answered her in this way:

> *And the LORD said unto her, Two nations are in thy womb, and two manner of people shall be segregated from thy bowels; and the one people shall be stronger than the other people; and the elder shall serve the younger.* Genesis 25:23

Once again we are confronted with this word *manner* in relation to two distinct individuals and the destiny for their lives. In the original Hebrew, that word *manner* not only implies a specific character personality type, but also refers to a particular course in life. From these two verses, we can begin to connect the pieces together to understand what God is trying to say to us. The success or failure your life will become is directly connected with the manner of woman you are. Jesus mastered life and fulfilled His divine destiny because He took on the role and became the character He was meant to become. His personality type and way of life was so in-line with the will of the Father that He lived a life of abundant productivity. The two children who came out of Rebekah's womb lived two different lives—one of victory and the other of heartache—because of their personality types, which affected the course of their lives. The child Jacob grew into a man who pursued the blessings of God, while his brother, Esau, became a man whose personality and character held no regard for the blessings afforded to him as a descendant of Abraham.

The Bible speaks of three distinctive personality types of women: the strange woman, the silly woman, and the virtuous woman. Every female on this earth, whether they realize it or not, is in one of these categories. In this book, I will define and explain each personality type so that you can identify yourself, and if you discover that you are in one of the first two categories, then you can make the necessary change and become the virtuous woman God has purposed for you to become. You must understand that the quality of your life or the lack thereof is a result of the kind of woman you are.

Why is it that certain women consistently attract a certain type of man and are only looked at by men as objects for pleasure? Why is it that some woman are drawn to men who have weak minds and weak spirits, but put on a facade of masculinity and call it being a "bad boy?" Why do certain women struggle with balancing career and family life, all the while wondering if it is even possible to fulfill all these roles? Why do so many women have negative images of themselves instead of seeing from the viewpoint of God, the Creator, Who makes all things beautiful in His time? This book will answer these questions and many more, so that by the time you are finished reading, you will have a greater perspective of how God wants you to live your life.

Throughout the lexicon of common phrases and sayings that are used in our collective vernacular, the phrase "finding yourself" is one that comes up over and over again. Often we hear a person saying, "I found myself in college," or "I found myself when I moved to such and such a place." Of course, what they are saying is that they achieved an awareness of the person that brings them the most fulfillment, and they became that person. This concept is a good one, and one worth merit. However, if it is only approached at the shallow end of the waters, then the benefits that will spring forth from it will only be fleeting because it does not come from a fountainhead of revelation. If a person is to truly find themselves and become the person they were born to be, they must approach the issue the way our Lord Jesus did. The Bible declares to us:

> *Looking unto Jesus the author and finisher of our faith; who for the joy that was set before him endured the cross, despising the shame, and is set down at the right hand of the throne of God.* Hebrews 12:2

The Word of God declares to us that Jesus is the example of the life we should aspire to live. He lived in such a way that He faced and overcame the tests and trials that came His way and achieved a victory that made it possible for Him to reposition Himself in His eternal seat of authority. If we want to overcome as Jesus overcame and live in a place of walking in the authority of the believer, we must discover our role in the plan of God as Jesus did. This then begs the question: how did Jesus do this? It is worth noting that the very first words the Bible records as coming forth from the lips of Jesus was something He told His parents as a youth.

After Jesus had gone missing at the age of twelve, Mary and Joseph found Him among the great learned men of His day, engaging and fellowshipping with them. Out of their concern, as parents, they confronted Him and asked Him why He had separated Himself from their company. Jesus answered this way:

> *And he said unto them, How is it that ye sought me? wist ye not that I must be about my Father's business.* Luke 2:49

Even at that young age, Jesus had an understanding of Who He was and knew that, as the Son of God, He must discover the full nature of His mission. Although He was God in the flesh, He was still a human being Who had to grow in wisdom and knowledge, and this was why He was with the scholars, asking them questions. We also know that the answers to His purpose and His eternal destiny were found in the Holy Scriptures, for we are given this account by Luke:

> *And Jesus returned in the power of the Spirit into Galilee; and there went out a fame of Him through all the region round about. And he taught in their synagogues, being glorified of all. And he came to Nazareth, where he had been brought up; and, as his custom was, he went into the synagogue on the sabbath day, and stood up for to read. And there was delivered unto him the book of the prophet Esaias. And when he had opened the book, he found the place where it was written.*
>
> *The Spirit of the Lord is upon me, because he hath anointed me to preach the gospel to the poor, he hath sent me to heal the brokenhearted, to preach deliverance to the captives, and recovering of sight to the blind, to set at liberty them that are bruised. To preach the acceptable year of the Lord.*
>
> *And he closed the book, and he gave it again to the minister, and sat down. And the eyes of all them that were in the synagogue were fastened on Him. And he began to say unto them, This day is the scripture fulfilled in your ears.*
>
> Luke 4:14-21

Here we find something truly remarkable. The Man called Jesus had just returned to His hometown and entered the local synagogue. He took His place at the center of attention and opened to His text from the words of the great prophet Isaiah. He read words that spoke of a Deliverer Who would come and not only proclaim a message of freedom and healing, but also usher in a new age of the hope of a better world based on better promises. Then, at the climax of the lesson, He closed the book, returned to His seat, and, with every eye totally focused on Him, said, "This day is the fulfillment of that prophecy." And from that moment until His ascension back to glory, Jesus fulfilled His destiny by finding His course of life and Who He was in the Word of Almighty God. This is what we, too, must strive for. If we want to become our best selves, then we must realize that the ideal person we are looking for is in the Bible. The Bible contains the entire blueprint for who we need to be and how we need to live. If we do as Jesus did and find our identity in the Scriptures, we will also succeed. As you continue to read this book, I pray that it will help you on your journey to be the living epistle of God's glory He has called you to be—both now and forever.

Introduction
(The Wisdom of Solomon, the Exhortations of Paul, and the Message of Jesus)

Approximately three thousand years ago, before the Common Era, the sun had begun to set one day on the city of Gibeon. This thriving metropolis was, even at that time, a city that was ancient and rich in history. Great events had taken place there, dating back to the early conquests of the children of Israel, up until the days of the reign of Israel's first king, a man named Saul of the tribe of Benjamin. Gibeon was one of the most prominent places of worship at that moment in history, not only serving as the location for the housing of the Tabernacle of Moses, but was also the city in which "the great high place" altar was built, where so many sacrifices and offerings were made to the Great I Am. At this particular moment in time, another great event was about to take place which would result in the world being able to feast upon the wisdom of one of the greatest minds of all time. Earlier that day, the young man had made a great sacrifice before the altar to honor the God he served. While others may have sacrificed there before, the man who made this offering came to this hallowed spot having recently been entrusted with the fate of an entire nation.

The man's name was Solomon, and we are told in the Scriptures that he made a great sacrifice to the Lord. The sacrifice he made was so great because the need in his life was great. Solomon had only recently been anointed King over Israel, to serve his people after the passing of his father. Solomon's father had not been just any man; he was David, one of Israel's greatest heroes: David, the youth who had slain Goliath; David, the man known as the sweet singer of Israel; David, the king who came to the throne and united all the tribes of his people into a kingdom that was strong in power and prestige. This was the man who had closed his eyes and was now asleep with his ancestors, leaving the young Solomon, who described himself as being, "but a little child who knew not how to go out or come in." One does not have to use too much imagination to understand the desperation of this moment for Solomon. How could he step into this awesome role and not only maintain all that his father achieved, but carry it to a greater level?

Later that evening, after Solomon had made his sacrifice, he retired to his chamber to sleep. In a moment of what might have been an anxious slumber, as he dangled between the place of rest and worry, the Lord appeared to him in a dream and asked him the simple question that we would all love to hear God ask us. God asked Solomon quite simply, "What do you want me to give to you?" It was perhaps the greatest moment in Solomon's life, and it was happening on that very spot there in Gibeon. God Himself, the Almighty, the Maker of all things and the One Who had the power to do anything had just asked this young man to write his own ticket to the future. He could have asked for anything, and, more than likely, he would have received it. But, out of all Solomon could have asked for that night, he sought for the most important resource in all creation. He answered the Lord:

> *Give therefore thy servant an understanding heart to judge thy people, that I may discern between good and bad for who is able to judge this thy so great a people.* 1 Kings 3:9

This young man understood something that is extremely profound. He had enough spiritual insight to realize that the greatest tool God could give to a human being is the ability to perceive clearly and distinguish between right and wrong and good and evil, not only regarding situations, but also as it relates to people. From that point on, God began not only to expand Solomon's kingdom, but also to give him revelation regarding and perception in judging the thoughts and intentions of others. It is the revelation that God gave to Solomon regarding the Strange Woman that will be the fountainhead upon which we will build our study of this particular character type.

A thousand years after Solomon reigned in glory and honor, history once again moved forward, marching on to other actors who would take the stage. Empires rose and fell, and kings came and went, until there arose a mighty eagle that soared above all of the empires that had once filled the skies of the culture of humanity. The great power that I speak of is the Roman Empire. The eternal city of Rome shined as a beacon of industry, exceptionalism, and absolute authority that stretched across the entirety of the ancient world. Along with its glory, however, came corruption and decadence that sowed the seeds for its eventual decline and downfall. At the height of this empire, there arose a man who would be used by God to travel all through that vast empirical expanse and help establish a new movement that was birthed on a hill far away with a old rugged cross and a Man Who died on that cross crying out, *"It is finished!"*

The Man Who died on the cross, of course, was Jesus, and the other man I spoke of was the apostle Paul. Paul was profoundly changed by the Man called Jesus, for He did not stay dead on the cross but rose again and appeared to Paul (then Saul) and called Him to a life of service that would change the course of history. Throughout the life and ministry of Paul, he worked with unending devotion to spread the Gospel to the nations. Not only through his oratory, but also through his writings, we can see the fruits of a life devoted to the will of God and to walking in obedience to the heavenly vision. Along with that vision came revelation pertaining to a understanding of the problems and the needs of the human condition. Out of the plenitude of profundity that sprang forth from this man's writings, there is a verse that focuses on our subject. It says:

> *For of this sort are they which creep into houses, and lead captive silly women laden with sins, led away with divers lusts.* 2 Timothy 3:6

In this one verse, so rich in wisdom and containing such an abundance of revelation, Paul opened to us the subject of the Silly Women, and we will use this as our golden text as we examine what the Word of God says concerning this type of woman.

Finally, I want to return now to the Man Who died on that old rugged cross that I referenced earlier. The Bible records that this Man did not remain dead. He vanquished the sting of death and conquered the grave. He now sits at the right hand of the throne of God the Father, where He will remain until He returns to this planet again in His second coming. This Man known as Jesus Christ, the Son of the Living God, did once walk this earth and was anointed by the Holy Ghost to transform the lives of the people He was called to minister to. On one occasion, when He was on His way to meet the need of another person, a woman who saw Him passing by made the decision that she would get a miracle from the Lord as well. This woman had an incurable blood disease which had totally depleted her financial resources, as she sought medical help to relieve her of the malady. Despite her best efforts, all of her attempts to seek natural aid had failed, and her condition not only did not improve; it grew worse. But even in the midst of her darkness and despair, a beacon of hope was raised up in her heart, and she determined that if she could get to Jesus and simply touch His clothes, she would be made whole.

The woman's resolve to get to Jesus was just as great as her revelation that Jesus could heal her. Despite facing a sea of people who were surrounding the Master, thronging Him and lavishing such emotional frenzy upon Him (no human being has ever faced such adulation), she pressed her way through. Her desperation for His impartation propelled her forward until she was close enough that she could stretch forth her hand and touch His clothes. At the moment she touched His garment, her faith came into contact with His anointing, and a miracle took place. What is most fascinating about this miracle is what the Bible records after she touched Him. Here is what the Scriptures say:

> *And Jesus, immediately knowing in himself that virtue had gone out of him, turned him about in the press, and said, Who touched my clothes?* Mark 5:30

The Word declares that virtue had gone out from Jesus, and that virtue was transferred to the woman. This word *virtue,* in the original Greek language, means "the manifestation of His divine power as expressed in His moral goodness." Hence we see the power of a virtuous life. The moral excellence of the character and nature of Jesus, combined with the indwelling anointing of the Holy Spirit and joined with this woman's faith, produced a miracle that cured her of her blood disease. The spiritual application to this account shows us that if you reach out for the power of God and allow His anointing to minister to you, you will become the virtuous woman that God has called you to be. His virtue will deposit virtue into you, freeing you of every disorder in your life, and transforming you into the woman who is complete in spirit, soul, and body.

It is from this foundation—the wisdom of Solomon, the exhortations of Paul, and the power of Jesus—that I have constructed for you a divine pattern to follow to become a true woman of power and destiny. I will show, through many other scriptural references from throughout the Bible, what steps you must take to achieve this goal. And just as the woman who reached out to touch Jesus so many years ago, if you embrace the message of this book based on the principles of God's Word, you, too, will be made whole. In the final analysis, God's desire is that every woman rise and take her place in the plan of the ages and in the center of His love. As you continue to read, may you be blessed and changed.

James Ivey
Fort Washington, MD

Part One

The Strange Woman

CHAPTER 1

THE SEED OF THE WOMAN

While the earth remaineth, seedtime and harvest, and cold and heat, and summer and winter, and day and night shall not cease. Genesis 8:22

All that was made in the beginning of creation and all that exists now in this time came into being through the agency of a seed. The seed is the instrument God used to infuse the universe with the raw materials of life. From the seeds that God sowed in the time before time, life came forth and continues to produce that which is necessary to sustain all things. The first chapter of the book of Genesis records how God caused everything to be seeded and for seeds to yield after their own kind.

Even as mankind grew wicked in thought and action, and God was forced to destroy all that was made, He still preserved a seed. He called Noah and told him to take himself, his family, and two of every living creature and build an ark to save them all from the coming flood. After that Great Flood had ended and the world was made new, God established a principle that was to remain as long as this world lasted. You read the verse at the beginning of this chapter, and the interpretation of the verse is this: As long as planet Earth remains in existence, there will always be a time of sowing seed and a time of reaping a harvest from that which has been sown.

When we approach the Bible, seeking to understand the meaning behind the message, we must realize that very often God will use natural things to express a spiritual principle. From that standpoint, it is helpful to have at least a basic understanding and appreciation of the natural example in order to fully grasp the spiritual application. This is especially true in reference to the message of seed and harvest.

Very often, in Christian circles, this message is mainly used in reference to the area of finances. While that is a true application, there is a deeper understanding that is worth exploring. The greater meaning behind the message of the seed and the harvest is the depositing of the Word of God into our lives. For example, The apostle James wrote:

> *Wherefore lay apart all filthiness and superfluity of naughtiness, and receive with meekness the engrafted word, which is able to save your souls.*
>
> James 1:21

According to *Vine's Expository Dictionary of Old and New Testament Words*, a source I will quote frequently throughout this book, the word *engrafted* means "to implant." *Vine's* goes on to say that the metaphor is used in connection with a seed rooting itself in a person's heart. Jesus also used seed as a metaphor for the teaching of the parable concerning how the Word of God is received by humanity. The Bible declares.

> *And when much people were gathered together, and were come to him out of every city, he spake by a parable. A sower went out to sow his seed; and as he sowed, some fell by the way side and it was trodden down and the fowls of the air devoured it. And some fell upon a rock; and as soon as it sprung up, it withered away, because it lacked moisture. And some fell among thorns; and the thorns sprang up with it, and choked it. And others fell on good ground; and sprang up, and bare fruit an hundredfold.*
>
> *And when he had said these things, he cried, He that hath ears to hear, let him hear.* Luke 8:4-8

Jesus made this statement and then gave the explanation of the parable:

> *Now the parable is this. The seed is the word of God.* Luke 8:11

Based upon these references, we can infer that, metaphorically and spiritually speaking, when the Bible refers to seed, it is speaking of a deposit of something that someone has either within them or in their possession. This deposit, whether it be money, a talent, or the Word of God, will ultimately produce a harvest once the seed is planted, whether for good or for evil. The ground or the soil, which the Bible constantly refers to, is speaking of where the seed is planted. It cold be a situation, a person, or something else. The point is this: when that deposit is placed in any given situation, it produces a certain result.

God has placed within humanity seeds, or deposits, of greatness. If used properly, these will bring blessing upon individuals, peoples, and nations. This is especially true in the case of women because, while God shows no partiality based on gender, He does understand the special quality that women possess to fulfill His divine purposes. This point is made clear to us from the very first book in the Bible. The book of Genesis informs us that when God created Adam and placed him in the garden, He bequeathed to him a special commission to have dominion over His created order. But, God saw that within this framework something was lacking. Adam, in spite of all of his abilities, was still missing a component that would help him fulfill the plan. The Word of the Lord declares:

> *And the LORD God said; It is not good that man should be alone; I will make him an help meet for him.* Genesis 2:18

God, in His wisdom, saw that in order for His divine plan for the earth to come to pass in full manifestation, Adam needed a helper to aid him. On his own, he lacked what was needed to carry out the plan. So, because it was God's intention for Adam to have dominion over the earth, not only did Adam need the woman, but the earth needed her as well. The earth would benefit as a result of sound leadership.

Satan understood this because we are also told in Genesis that when he attempted to initiate the fall of man, he first approached the woman. Down through history many male theologians and prognosticators have used this as a prerequisite for expressing the idea of female inferiority. However, there is a scripture that gives some interesting insight and provides a more concrete interpretation:

> *No man can enter into a strong man's house, and spoil his goods, except he will first bind the strong man, and then he will spoil his house.*
>
> Mark 3:27

Satan had a plan to destroy the house that God had built by causing man to sin. Based upon the principle of this scripture, he understood that in order to destroy the house, he would first have to get a grip on the strongest person in the house. Therefore, he did not approach Adam; he approached his helper, Eve. Based on what we have just read from the gospel of Saint Mark, Eve must have been the strongest of the two. Let us look at the context and see what it says:

> *Now the serpent was more subtitle than any beast of the field which the* Lord *God had made. And he said unto the woman, Yea, hath God said, Ye shall not eat of every tree in the garden?*
> *And the woman said unto the serpent, We may eat of the fruit of the tree of the garden. But of the fruit of the tree which is in the midst of the garden, God hath said, Ye shall not eat of it neither shall ye touch it, lest ye die.*
> *And the serpent said unto the woman, Ye shall not surely die. For God doth know that in the day ye eat thereof, then your eyes shall be opened, and ye shall be as gods, knowing good and evil. And when the woman saw that the tree was good for food, and that it was pleasant to the eyes, and a tree to make one wise, she took of the fruit thereof, and did eat, and gave also unto her husband with her and he did eat.* Genesis 3:1-6

The devil, or, as he is referred to here, *"the serpent,"* attempted to poison humanity with sin. In other words, we could say that he attempted to destroy the house which God had built. Like any master tactician, he probably observed his prey before he chose to attack. The Bible tells us that the devil walks about like a roaring lion seeking whom he can devour. We also know from the Scriptures that his intention is to devour all of humanity. In order to get to the whole house, he, just as Jesus said in Mark, must first get to the strongest. Although both Adam and Eve were blessed by God with seeds of greatness, the stronger of the two must have been Eve, because Satan chose to approach her first.

Far too often our culture and society measure strength based upon physicality or bravado. However, true strength is the ability to influence people and situations to respond in the way that you want them to. Eve must have had this in greater measure than Adam, because Satan approached her first. And it took some convincing on Satan's part to trick Eve, while Adam apparently just went along with whatever was put in front of him.

It is also interesting to note that after sin had entered into the human race and God had to address the issue with Adam, Eve, and the devil, He informed them of the plan that would take place to redeem mankind from the powers of darkness. He made a prophetic declaration:

> *And I will put enmity between thee and the woman, and between thy seed and her seed; it shall bruise thy head, and thou shalt bruise his heel.*
>
> Genesis 3:15

The first prophetic word recorded in the Scriptures was an utterance that God spoke to Satan himself concerning how he would be defeated. God said that from the agency of a woman a seed would come forth that would war against the seed of the adversary. While the devil's seed would bruise the heel of the woman's seed, hers would bruise his head. This prophetic word was referring to Jesus. He came into the world through the womb of a woman named Mary, and He came to war against and destroy the works of the devil. The bruising of the heel refers to the death of Jesus on the cross, while the bruising of the serpent's head speaks of the triumph of Jesus when He cried out and said, *"It is finished,"* thus destroying the power of sin over humanity and making a way for anyone who so wished to receive salvation.

I pointed out to you earlier the passage in which Jesus said that the seed is the Word of God. Throughout the Scriptures, Jesus is also often referred to as the Word of God. I want you to take note of the truth that God chose to bring redemption through the agency of the female vessel. I am not seeking to institute a false doctrine based on some idea that women are somehow greater than men or that they hold a higher status in divine affairs. I am making the point that, in spite of the efforts of forces (both spiritual and natural) to oppress women throughout the centuries, the Bible provides us with the information it does to show that not only are women special; they are also powerful. God has placed within women seeds of greatness that can influence all levels of society. Even the devil understood this, because he sought to destroy the house by first binding the strong man (who just happened to be a strong woman).

It is important that we see and understand the power of the seed, because a seed, in the spiritual sense, is a deposit that has the potential to produce a result. We also see that, throughout history, there has been a contention between that which God wishes to deposit into humanity and that which the devil wishes to deposit into humanity. In the New Testament, the teachings of Jesus are recorded for our learning, to help us understand the things pertaining to the spiritual world. Many times Jesus spoke in parables, using natural examples to help the people grasp how the unseen world works. One of the most significant parables is recorded in the gospel of Saint Matthew:

> *Another parable put he forth unto them, saying, The kingdom of heaven is likened unto a man which sowed good seed in his field. But while men slept, his enemy came and sowed tares among the wheat, and went his way. But when the blade was sprung up, and brought forth fruit, then appeared the tares also. So the servants of the householder came and said unto him, Sir, didst not thou sow good seed in thy field? From whence then hath it tares?*
> *He said unto them, An enemy hath done this.*
> *The servants said unto him, Wilt thou then that we go and gather them up?*
> *But he said, Nay; lest white ye gather up the tares; ye root up also the wheat with them. Let both grow together until the harvest; and in the time of harvest I will say to the reapers, Gather ye together first the tares, and bind them in bundles to burn them: but gather the wheat into my barn.* Matthew 13:24-30

Here Jesus was describing the supernatural world that He called the Kingdom of Heaven and comparing it to a sower scattering seed in a field. He went on to give the interpretation of the parable:

> *Then Jesus sent the multitude away, and went into the house, and his disciples came unto him, saying, Declare unto us the parable of the tares of the field.*
> *He answered and said unto them, He that sowed the good seed is the Son of man. The field is the world; the good seed are the children of the kingdom, but the tares are the children of the wicked one. The enemy that sowed them is the devil; the harvest is the end of the world; and the reapers are the angels. As therefore the tares are gathered and burned in the fire; so shall it be in the end of this world. The Son of man shall send forth his angels, and they shall gather out of his kingdom all things that offend, and them which do iniquity; and shall cast them into a furnace of fire; there shall be*

wailing and gnashing of teeth. Then shall the righteous shine forth as the sun in the kingdom of their Father. Who hath ears to hear, let him hear.
Matthew 13:36-43

In the interpretation to the parable, Jesus presented a clear and concise exegesis of not only the future, but also the day and the hour in which we are living right now. We are also confronted once again with the principle of the seed. Here Jesus said that there was a field that represented this world. Within this field were two sowers—one the Son of Man (referring to Jesus) and the other the enemy called Satan. Jesus has sown good seed into the ground, into those who have heard the Word of God and had it planted into the soil of their hearts, while Satan has sown tares. Tares look similar to good seeds, but they are corrupted and cause harm. The tares represent those who have allowed the plans of the wicked one to enter into their hearts and lives. Jesus said that at the end of the age there would be both a gathering and a separation of the good and the wicked from the harvest. Every person in this world, whether they know it or not, is in one of these two categories. This is important for every person to understand, but particularly so for women. Why is that?

Among the billions of human beings who populate this planet, the majority are of the female gender. There are more women than men in the workplace, on college campuses, and in what is now commonly known as "the social scene." Women are the heart of the family unit, because more often than not, the mother is the first teacher a child will have, and she is often the one who sets the tone for how the dynamics of a home are structured. The current population ratio of more women than men in society, just as a numbers issue alone, tells us that God is trying to say something, in an area we might consider to be unimportant.

In the book of Genesis, God gave Adam authority to name His creation and to oversee the garden. That seed, or deposit, was placed within him. God gave Eve the ability and the power of influence, and whatever she presented to Adam, he immediately partook of. She had the ability, the seed of greatness within her, to influence and move authority in a certain direction. That was the reason Satan approached her first. There is a deep message here if we will allow the Lord to open our eyes to see it.

Women have a God-given ability to be influential in every arena of society. Whether they are in a leadership position or behind the scenes supporting their husbands, there influence can carry great weight, and this can be either for blessing or for destruction. Not only does God know this (because He placed that within her), but the devil understands it too. As the adversary looks out on the field of the world, he realizes that if he can sow enough bad seeds, otherwise known as "tares," in the majority demographic of the human populace, then he can corrupt an entire vineyard. Women, you must understand not only your ability, but also the potential for that ability to be perverted and used in a harmful way. God's desire is that His program of how you should live your life, based upon the tenets of the Scriptures, be ingrained within you, and that you live them out day by day. Satan also desires that his program and pattern of how he wants you to live your life be ingrained within you and that you will live that idea out day by day. You have to take heed to ensure that you align yourself with the image that God has set before you.

It is fascinating to note that in the parable Jesus gave about the seed, He said that the enemy came and sowed the tares while the people slept. Remember that Jesus is giving a natural illustration to express a spiritual application. When a person is sleeping, naturally speaking, they are not conscious of what is going on around them because their senses are not active. When the Bible refers to sleep in a spiritual sense, it is speaking of a person or persons who are not spiritually aware of what is going on around them. They are so desensitized to their environment that when things are deposited into their spirits, they are not aware of what is happening. This is often how television and movies influence our lives. These mediums so often influence how we dress, how we act, and how we communicate. They put up images which subconsciously try to say what is beautiful, what is appealing, even what type of mate we should look for. Because we are usually in a mode of relaxation when we consume their programs, we are not spiritually sensitive to how we are being brainwashed to base our way of life on what we see on the screen. This is very dangerous because, more often than not, what we see is not from godly influences. This is the primary way Satan enters our minds to corrupt our thinking, and we must be diligent to base our value and our image of what is appealing and successful, not on what this world says, but on what God says.

I want to return now to the power of influence. As I stated earlier, God has given women the extraordinary ability to have influence, not only in their individual lives, but also in the lives of others and in situations that could bring great blessing or cause terrible destruction. The key for you is to be aware of what seeds you are allowing to take root in your mind and your spirit regarding what kind of a woman you should be. Will you pattern your life, your self-image, and your social values on the pattern of the Word of God? Or will you allow the images, ideas, and values of this perverse society to dictate to you what is your worth? The choice will affect every part of your life in ways you could never imagine.

There are two references in the Scriptures that validate the point I wish to convey here. The first comes from the Old Testament book of Esther. The Bible records that at the time in which the events of that book took place, the Jewish people were under the rule of the Persian Empire, displaced from their homeland and under foreign domination. The Jews also faced a man who had devoted himself to seeing their entire race exterminated from the face of the earth. His name was Haman.

Haman had devised a plan to have the entire Jewish population eradicated. Fortunately, a godly man named Mordecai obtained knowledge of this scheme. Through the agency of carefully coordinated events, Mordecai's relative Esther was able to rise to the position of Queen of Persia, and this gave her influence with the king. Mordecai instructed Esther to intercede on behalf of her people by asking the king that the wicked plot Haman had devised against the Jews be turned against him. The king agreed, and, because of Esther, a nation was saved. The Bible declares.

> *And Mordecai wrote these things, and sent letters unto all the Jews that were in all the provinces of the king Ahasuerus, both nigh and far. To stablish this among them, that they should keep the fourteenth day of the month Adar, and the fifteenth day of the same, yearly. As the days wherein the Jews rested from their enemies, and the month which was turned unto them from sorrow to joy, and from mourning into a good day; that they should make them days of feasting and joy, and of sending portions one to another, and gifts to the poor. And the Jews undertook to do as they had begun, and as Mordecai had written unto them. Because Haman the son of Hammedatha the Agagite, the enemy of all the Jews, had devised against the Jews to destroy them, and had cast Pur, that is, the lot, to consume them, and destroy them. But when Esther came before the king, he commanded by letters that his wicked device, which he devised*

against the Jews, should return upon his own head, and that he and his sons should be hanged on the gallows. Wherefore they called these days Purim after the name of Pur. Therefore for all the words of this letter, and of which they had seen concerning this matter, and which had come unto them.

Esther 9:20-26

From the reading of this text, we are given a divine portrait of the working of the Holy Spirit in the destinies of nations. God Almighty, working through Mordecai, who was a spiritual type of Jesus, sowed the seed of the good plan into Esther's heart. Then, Esther used her graces and charms as a woman of purpose, power, and godly character, to move the heart of the king to save a nation and render justice upon the wicked. This is the power that God has granted to the woman, used at its most potent level, to fulfill the divine will of the Great I Am.

However, just as there is a counterfeit for every true thing in the world, the seed of the woman can reap blessing, but it can also be a corrupt seed that reaps the whirlwind. There is an account recorded in the New Testament of a young woman, who, while not as famous in the annals of history, did cause a chain of events that had devastating consequences. These events are recorded in the gospel of Saint Matthew:

At that time Herod the tetrarch heard of the fame of Jesus. And said unto his servants, This is John the Baptist, he is risen from the dead; and therefore mighty works do shew forth themselves in him.

For Herod had laid hold on John, and bound him, and put him in prison for Herodias sake, his brother Philip's wife. For John said unto him, It is not lawful for thee to have her. And when he would have put him to death, he feared the multitude, because they counted him as a prophet.

But when Herod's birthday was kept, the daughter of Herodias danced before them, and pleased Herod. Whereupon he promised with an oath to give her whatsoever she would ask. And she, being instructed of her mother, said, Give me here John Baptist's head in a charger. And the king was sorry; nevertheless for the oath's sake, and them which sat with him at meat, he commanded it to be given her. And he sent, and beheaded John in the prison. And his head was brought in a charger and given to the damsel, and she brought it to her mother.

And his disciples came, and took up the body, and buried it, and went and told Jesus. Matthew 14:1-12

This is one of the most tragic stories in the entirety of the Word of God, and like all moving dramas of history, it behooves us to understand how this travesty came to pass. Like Esther, we are here given a picture of another young woman who was in the palace of another man of authority. Unlike Esther, who had the godly counsel of Mordecai, this young woman had the unholy influence of her mother, Herodias. Because of the fact that she was offended by John's rebuke of her marriage to Herod, Herodias was angry with him. Her animosity toward the prophet was so strong that she desired to have him killed, and when Herod celebrated his birthday, she had her chance to fulfill her wicked desire. She had her daughter dance before Herod, and, through the power of her seductive prowess, the man became so intoxicated with thoughts of lust that he was willing to give her whatever she wanted. This is a powerful and sobering thought because it goes back to the power of influence and how a corrupt seed can be used to reap a negative harvest. This young woman used her beauty and her physicality in a fashion that incited unholy passions in this man. Because she was influenced by the ungodly counsel of her mother, which represents the corrupt seeds that the devil seeks to implant in humanity, she used her body as a weapon against a holy man of God.

For his part, Herod was so overcome by this that he offered the daughter of Herodias whatever she wanted. Herodias now had her chance to kill John the Baptist. When the daughter asked for John to be beheaded, Herod felt that he had no choice but to grant the request. In this way, one of the greatest prophetic voices of all time was silenced, as a result of hatred, manipulation, and lust. While, for some, this may be an uncomfortable issue, it is an issue that needs to be addressed all the same. A woman's femininity can be a powerful tool of influence, and that influence can be used for good or evil, depending upon the spirit behind it. In the case of Esther, we are given the account of how God had a woman put in place, and, as a result of her beauty, her charm, and, most importantly, her godly virtue (which radiated without, as well as within), was used to save a nation and fulfill the will of God. As a woman, Esther had influence over King Ahasuerus that Mordecai understood could be used to bring about positive change.

God has placed within women the ability to bring out something within their male counterparts. That something can be of tremendous blessing, as in the case of Esther, or it can be of great harm, as it was with Herodias's daughter. The key is: which seed is inside of the woman? Is it the seed of the Word that produces a godly, wholesome appeal that can bring out the best in others? Or is it the tares of the devil that causes one to use their body, their mind, and their spirit to influence others in ways contrary to God's will? Both Esther and Herodias's daughter had the power of influence, but one had a positive seed planted within her, while the other was motivated by a wicked vessel. She used her femininity as a instrument to incite lust, leading to sin. You must be sober and vigilant in understanding what you allow to be deposited inside you because of your enormous ability to not only influence yourself, but those around you.

Think of it! The way Herodias's daughter moved her body so affected Herod that he lost himself in his carnal emotions, but the words of Esther and the way she conducted herself in the presence of King Ahasuerus caused him to reverse his original decree to give Haman the power to destroy the Jews and turn it so that Haman himself would be destroyed. God is saying something here within these texts. He has granted to women a great ability of influence. Your responsibility is to be motivated and submitted under the Holy Spirit and not a demonic spirit. I will address this further in the next chapter.

Chapter 2

Understanding What Spirit Ye Are Of

Beloved, believe not every spirit, but try the spirits whether they are of God; because many false prophets are gone out into the world. 1 John 4:1

Several years ago, a prominent journalist and astute social commentator wrote an essay addressing a subject that has always seemed to plague the heart of many people. The essay was structured around a question being asked by an agnostic to those who purported to be believers in a Supreme Being. The agnostic asked, "If there is a God who governs and controls everything in the Universe, and if this God is all-loving, all-wise, and totally benevolent, why is it that evil sweeps across the world? How could there be a Supreme Being Who is completely good and has control over a world that is full of venality that manifests itself in every shape and form throughout every sphere of society?" The question, as I said, is not a new one, and it is one of mankind's oldest thoughts, but the journalist who wrote the article mused over the fact that despite his enquiries into the matter, he seemed to never find a suitable answer to the question. However, if one would go to the Bible for wisdom and truly search the Scriptures with eyes to see and a heart to understand, then the answer would be revealed and the problem solved.

The Bible does declare that there is a God and that He is, indeed, all-good and all-powerful. And yet, the Bible also declares that there are other forces in this universe, and, although they are not omnipotent, they do possess degrees of ability that can affect the created universe. One must understand that there are two worlds in creation. There is the natural world that we can see and interact with through our natural senses, and there is also another world, known as the spirit world. While the natural senses of a human being cannot necessarily see the spirit world, that part of creation does exist. Not only does it exist; more importantly, it has a direct influence on this natural world.

Within the spiritual world exists God, the Almighty Maker of Heaven and Earth. Not only is God there and His angels are there, but there are also wicked spirits, the devil and his forces, that exist in the spirit world, working behind the scenes, causing things to happen that affect the natural world. I touched on the fall of mankind in the previous chapter. As a result of the events that took place in the Garden of Eden, as recorded in the book of Genesis, mankind not only lost his fellowship with God, but also his ability to have authority over this world's system. That authority was stolen by the devil. The reason this society is corrupt is that it is under the control of demonic forces. The Bible affirms this fact, when it says:

> *In whom the god of this world hath blinded the minds of them which believe not, lest the light of the glorious gospel of Christ, who is the image of God, should shine unto them.* 2 Corinthians 4:4

Another example of this point comes from the famous account of the temptations that Jesus faced while He was in the wilderness. It is fascinating to read that when Satan sought to ensnare the Lord Jesus, he made Him an offer that seemed to be something he was unqualified to give. Matthew tells us:

> *Again, the devil taketh him up into an exceeding high mountain, and sheweth him all the kingdoms of the world, and the glory of them; and saith unto him, All these things will I give thee, if thou wilt fall down and worship me. Then saith Jesus unto him, Get thee hence; Satan, for it is written, Thou shalt worship the Lord thy God, and him only shalt thou serve.* Matthew 4:8-10

Pay close attention to how this scene is described and the words that were used by both participants. The devil took Jesus to the pinnacle of a certain mountain from which one could see all the kingdoms of the earth and told Him that if He would bow down and worship him, he would give Him all of those kingdoms and their glory. When Jesus rebuked the devil and resisted the temptation, He did not deny that Satan had the authority to give those kingdoms. Why? Because Jesus understood that those nations and their social systems were under demonic jurisdiction. That is why the apostle Paul referred to the devil as *"the god of this world."* While Satan is not all-powerful like God, he does have some power, and this makes him a god. Also, even though this planet belongs to the Lord, the systems that govern the planet are under the influence of Satan, another reason Paul called him *"the god of this world."* This explains crime, poverty, and hate. More importantly, this is why, when you turn on your television set, nearly every program contains immorality. This is why some ninety percent of all advertisements use tactics that appeal to the carnal desires of humanity to sell their products. And this is why you find yourself living the way you do. Satan is not only seeking to corrupt society; he desires for that corruption to totally influence how you think and how you live.

There are two types of people in this world; a person is either saved or unsaved. The person who is saved is someone who has acknowledged that they were a sinner in need of the saving power of Jesus Christ. As a result of this acceptance of their need for salvation, they asked Jesus not only to save them from their sin, but also to be their Lord and Master, thus giving Him total control over their life from henceforth and forever. A person who is unsaved is someone who is not enlightened to the reality of their depraved condition as a practitioner of an ungodly life. That lack of knowledge causes them to be without God, without understanding of their true spiritual condition, and without hope for today or tomorrow. If one thinks I am being hyperbolic in my assessment, then let us look to the Scriptures. This is how the Bible describes the condition of the unsaved person:

> *That at that time ye were without Christ, being aliens from the commonwealth of Israel, and strangers from the covenant of promise, having no hope, and without God in the world.* Ephesians 2:12

And here is a biblical description of a person who is saved and in the state of being known as "the born-again experience":

> *Now therefore ye are no more strangers and foreigners, but fellow citizens with the saints, and of the household of God.* Ephesians 2:19

Despite the differences between the two categories, the saved and the unsaved do have one distinct commonality: they are both influenced by the spirit world. Whether they realize it or not or even understand it or not, the influence is there. The person who is born again lives their life under the compete influence of the inspiration and the guidance of the Holy Spirit. The person who is not born again but is unsaved lives their life under the influence of the powers of darkness. Think about it this way: why is it that certain women feel the need to dress in a provocative and seductive fashion for every social setting? Even in the workplace, why is there a desire to wear revealing clothing or garments that are tight fitting and inspire thoughts of lust in their male co-workers? Why do some women feel the need and have the desire to post risqué photographs of themselves on their social media platforms for anyone and everyone to view? These are natural symptoms that are the result of a spiritual condition. Once again, let us examine what the Scriptures have to say along these lines. The Word of God declares:

> *And you hath he quickened, who were dead in trespasses and sins; wherein in times past, ye walked according to the course of this world, according the prince of the power of the air, the spirit that now worketh in the children of disobedience: among whom also we all had our conversations in times past in the lust of the flesh, fulfilling the desires of the flesh and of the mind, and were by nature the children of wrath, even as others.* Ephesians 2:1-3

In this passage of the Scriptures, Paul was writing to Christians, reminding them of the spiritual condition they were under before they came to a saving knowledge of Jesus Christ. Even though he was addressing Christians, the description he was laying out of the unsaved person is crystal clear. Paul said that the unsaved person is functioning according to the plans of this world's system, and that system is under the control of the devil, who is revealed here are *"the prince of the power of the air."* This dark prince, known as Satan, is working within unsaved peoples through the agency of himself and other malevolent spirits, to carry out his plan of perverting the entire human race.

Now, consider another series of questions as you examine yourself: Why is it that you find yourself consistently gravitating to a certain kind of man who is abusive, either verbally or physically? Why is it that you find a certain type of man appealing, even though this type of man is a individual of little worth? Because he is the exciting bad boy that the corrosive culture says is more interesting, you continue to align yourself with that type of man. Why do you seem to attract only the type of man who is interested in you solely for your outward appearance and for how you may be able to stimulate their flesh, while men who could provide you with fulfillment on every other level want nothing to do with you? Let's go deeper and ask, why is it that you always seem to attract unbecoming attention and receive inappropriate advances from male colleagues and co-workers, even though you are not consciously seeking it? These are hard questions and can come seem to be intended to incite offense or create shock value. I assure you, however, that this is not my intention. The issue is confronting a malady that must be treated, and, in order to treat the problem, we must diagnose the cause of the disease.

As I stated previously, these are spiritual problems that manifest in the natural world. I refer back to Paul's text in Ephesians where he went on to speak of the conversation his readers had in times past. In the original Greek, the word *conversation* simply means "your conduct," or we would say, "how you carry and present yourself to society." How you carry yourself results from how you perceive yourself, and your perception of yourself is based upon the desires within you. If you are walking with the Lord, you will be ruled by the desires of your spirit, which has been born again. If you are unsaved, you will fulfill the desires of your flesh, which is controlled by a corrupt mind. Your very nature is corrupted as a consequence of having not yet been born again. All of these factors result in why you think and act the way you do and why you live the type of life you live.

Understanding the reality of the spirit world and how it affects, not only the natural things of society, but also your individual life as well, is essential for mastery over every circumstance. Often there are occasions in which we are tempted to react to a situation in which we find ourselves in a fashion that may seem to have good intentions, but if the response is contrary to the character and the ways of God as given to humanity through His Word, no matter the good of the intentions, the results will prove to be counterproductive. There is an example recorded in the Bible that speaks to this issue. The incident involved Jesus and His disciples as they were preparing to go into a certain city for their ministerial work. Before I give the exposition of the text, I want to give the full account directly from the Scriptures:

And it came to pass, when the time that he should be received up, he steadfastly set his face to go up to Jerusalem, and sent messengers before his face and they went, and entered into a village of the Samaritans to make ready for him. And they did not receive him, because his face was as though he would go to Jerusalem. And when his disciples James and John saw this, they said, Lord, wilt thou that we should command fire to come down from heaven, and consume them, even as Elias did? But he turned and rebuked them, and said, Ye know not what manner of spirit ye are of. For the Son of man is not come to destroy men's lives, but to save them. And they went to another village.

Luke 9:51-56

Jesus and His party were making preparations to go to Jerusalem, with the intention of passing through a Samaritan village on the way to their final destination. Unfortunately, the villagers in that place would not welcome Jesus because of His plans to go to Jerusalem. As a result of this rejection, the disciples James and John became so offended that they asked the Lord if they should call down fire from Heaven to consume the villagers. They even tried to put a pious facade on their animosity by citing the example of the time in which the Old Testament prophet Elijah called fire down from Heaven. In their zeal, they did not realize that, not only were they taking what Elijah did out of context, but also they were being influenced by a ungodly spirit. They sought to take actions that were contrary to the nature of God. It was for this reason that Jesus corrected them and explained that His mission was not to destroy but to save. The point I want to express to you is this: even though these men were followers of Jesus, and even though they were lieutenants in His ministry, they still came under the influence of a false spirit that sought to pervert the mission of the Master. Every time you allow your thinking and your actions to be dominated by views and concepts that run antithetical to the tenets of the Bible, you have given yourself over to a spirit that is against the knowledge of God. This is why I am taking the time to force you to look at yourself in a more clinical way.

Notice I did not say "critical way," but a more "clinical way." When you examine yourself and take heed to what you allow to influence you, you will not condemn yourself. Rather, you will allow the Lord to minister to those areas in your life that need to be changed.

There is another example from the Word of God that I wish to share with you that will make this principle become even more engrafted into your thinking. It also involves an incident in the life of Jesus. In this account, He was having a conversation with His disciples about His coming death on the cross. I will once again let the Bible speak and then proceed with the explanation:

> *Then charged he his disciples that they should tell no man that he was Jesus the Christ. From that time forth began Jesus to shew unto his disciples, how that he must go unto Jerusalem, and suffer many things of the elders and chief priests and scribes, and be killed, and be raised again the third day. Then Peter took him, and began to rebuke him, saying, Be it far from thee, Lord, this should not be unto thee. But he turned, and said unto Peter. Get thee behind me, Satan: thou art an offense unto me, for thou savourest not the things that be of God, but those that be of men.* Matthew 16:20-23

This is, at once, one of the most fascinating and, taken at face value, one of the most confusing texts in all the biblical Canon, but if we allow the Holy Spirit to shine the light of proper exegesis on these verses, we can see revelation that is clearly understood for those with eyes to see and ears to hear. At this point in the life and ministry of Jesus, He was looking ahead to the approaching hour in which He would face His greatest battle by suffering, dying, and rising again to make atonement for the sin of the world. Like any great leader, Jesus wanted His followers to be ready for that day of trial, so He started to make His disciples more fully aware of these matters. We can imagine the sadness that must have invaded their hearts as they were being exposed to the reality that one day their Lord would no longer be with them.

One of Jesus' disciples, a man named Peter, was so affected by what he had just heard that he took Jesus aside and began to try to correct Him and insist that those things would *not* happen. A person could read this and immediately cast dispersions at Peter, but we need to examine how Jesus dealt with this issue, in order to understand what was really going on in this text. The Bible says that Jesus cast His eyes directly at Peter, but then He addressed Satan and commanded the devil to remove himself from the entire scenario. Even though He physically looked at Peter, Jesus recognized that, at that moment, Peter was allowing His emotions to be influenced by Satan himself in a attempt to abort the plan of redemption to bring salvation to the world. This is why Jesus said Satan was an offense to Him. That word *offense* means "to cause one to stumble," and Satan sought to make Jesus stumble and miss the assignment that was set before Him. Because Peter was emotionally attached to Jesus, Satan could use those emotions to manipulate the man into say things contrary to God's will. In that moment, Peter was not allowing his thoughts to be in subjection to the knowledge of God. Even though he had sincere and heartfelt intentions, because they ran contrary to what needed to happen in order to facilitate salvation, Satan tried to use this man to convince Jesus that what He said should not come to pass. And, as a result of what was being attempted, Jesus had to address the spirit that was seeking to influence the man.

This brings me back to the series of questions that I posed to you earlier. The reason you carry yourself a certain way, the reason you attract certain types of people and situations to yourself, and the reason you respond to things in the way you do can all be traced directly to what manner of spirit you are of. The spirit that influences you and dominates your life causes you to be the manner of woman you are. This knowledge is not given as a license to blame everything on the devil and his forces while taking no responsibility for the part you have to play in all of this. The Bible gives us this very important command:

> *Neither give place to the devil.* Ephesians 4:27

We are also exhorted along these lines by another verse of scripture that says this:

> *Submit yourselves therefore to God. Resist the devil, and he will flee from you.* James 4:7

These passages inform us that it is our role to be aware of the world around us; and to understand the duty that we have to give the devil no space in our lives in which he can come and dominate our inner being. We are also comforted in knowing that as we resist Satan's attacks, he will flee from us. With these foundational stones from the Word of God having been laid in the soil of your heart, I now want to use the next chapters to speak directly about the strange woman. I will begin by presenting a clear definition of what I mean when I use that terminology, and I will expose the demonic spirit that is the dominant influence working in the life of this type of woman.

Chapter 3

The Unclean Spirit

As a jewel of gold in a swine's snout, so is a fair woman which is without discretion. Proverbs 11:22

One of the essential prerequisite for understanding the Bible for all that it is worth is coming to an awareness of the fact that every word in the Scriptures has been put there for a specific reason, to illuminate a spiritual principle. No matter how insignificant a word or a phrase may appear to be, the entirety of God's Word has been recorded for our spiritual enrichment and our moral and physical edification. Once a person comes to understand this principle, they set themselves on a path of grasping the truth that God is seeking to get across to them. Not only is it important to appreciate the value of the words, but also to understand the context and the time and setting in which they were written.

The Bible is an ancient book that speaks to our present age. Even though it speaks to us in the time that we live in, we must have some background of the age and time in which the events of the Bible took place, so that we can get the full picture of how what took place back then speaks to us today. Many casual readers of the Bible are confused by what they read because they do not take the time to understand the cultural and historical context in which the recorded events took place. Some even grow frustrated or become offended by what they read simply because they attempt to impose modernist thinking onto ancient words and context. All of these factors result in one missing the spiritual message that is so richly laid out before them.

I raise this point in order to help you understand that when I use some of the terminology in my exposition, I am using ancient historical words that come from the Scriptures. I intend to define these terms and explain how they correspond to helping you to find yourself. The words and phrases that I will use are not to cause offense, but, rather, to help you discover your true spiritual condition. The only way that can take place is for us to look to the Word of God and allow our thinking to align with what the Word says. Our job, as seekers of truth, is to allow our thoughts to line up with God's thoughts and to understand the ways and the contexts by which He chose to communicate to us His ways. So, once again, I will say that every word in the Bible is put there for a reason. By virtue of the fact that God chose to use the words that He used in His Word, it is incumbent upon us to understand the meaning behind those words, and the cultural background in which they were offered. As we utilize all of these tools, not only will the Bible come alive to us, but it will also change our lives both now and always.

Now that I have established those points, let us examine the strange woman. I want to begin by defining this term and looking at this type of woman through the prism of the life of Solomon.

In the preface to this work, I spoke briefly about Solomon and how God had blessed him with great wisdom and discernment. As a result of the grace that was bestowed upon him, his kingdom grew and expanded beyond the glory of his father, David. Solomon's mental prowess was of such high caliber that rulers and peoples from all across the ancient world came to sit at his feet. He built the greatest temple of worship the world had ever seen until then. His palace, his storehouses, and even his servants had an opulence about them that begged all description. The Bible records that when the Queen of Sheba came to investigate Solomon and his empire, she was so moved by his intellect, his charisma, and the grandeur of his realm that it took her breath away. Solomon was a man who reverenced God and did his best to walk in the paths of justice and righteousness.

For all of his glory, Solomon had one great character flaw. The Bible informs us that even the little foxes can spoil the vine. This means that if there is a crack in our foundation, no matter how small, if it is in the right spot, it can cause the whole building to crumble. The issue that Solomon had, at first glance, seemed so insignificant, but it ultimately became the seed that cost him and the entire nation of Israel heartache and trouble. The Bible informs us of his problem in these words:

> *But king Solomon loved many strange women, together with the daughter of Pharaoh, women of the Moabites, the Ammonites, Edomites, Zidonians, and Hittites: of the nations concerning which the* Lord *said unto the children of Israel, Ye shall not go in unto them, neither shall they come in unto you; for surely they will turn away your heart after their gods. Solomon clave unto these in love. And he had seven hundred wives, princesses, and three hundred concubines: and his wives turned away his heart. For it came to pass, when Solomon was old, that his wives turned away his heart after other gods, and his heart was not perfect with the* Lord *his God, as was the heart of David his father. For Solomon went after Ashtoreth the goddess of the Zidonians, and after Milcom the abomination of the Ammonites. And Solomon did evil in the sight of the* Lord*, and went not fully after the* Lord *as did David his father. Then did Solomon built an high place for Chemosh, the abomination of Moab, in the hill that is before Jerusalem, and for Molech, the abomination of the children of Ammon. And likewise did he for all his strange wives, which burnt incense and sacrificed unto their gods.* 1 Kings 11:1-8

This is one of the most tragic descriptions in all of scriptural history concerning a great man brought down and reduced to pagan worship. The question is before us: how did this mighty fall take place? And, more specifically, what was Solomon's tragic flaw? As always, the answers are contained in the text: *"But king Solomon loved many strange women."* This was the root cause of Solomon's dilemma.

I want to explain the spiritual connotation of the text, but I want to begin by reemphasizing the point that every word is important. The Bible did not say that Solomon loved women. It did not need to say that; any man who has natural affections and passions has a God-given attraction to women. According to *Strong's Exhaustive Concordance of the Bible,* the word *love* in the context of this verse means "sexual or physical desire." For a man to have passions and affections is natural, as long as he does not allow lust to enter into his heart. The problem with Solomon was that he was attracted and fascinated to a type of woman the Bible calls a *strange* woman.

Now I want to define the word *strange* as it is used in the Bible. As I stated before, once you understand the terminology of the Scriptures, you have put yourself on the path to understanding them. In our modern society, when we hear the word *strange*, it is associated with "something that is odd or different." That can be a good thing or a bad thing, depending on what is being discussed. In the days of the Bible, anytime the term *strange* was used, it was meant to define one as "foreign or alien." The nature of their otherness had nothing to do with race or ethnicity, but, rather, with their spiritual condition and their world view. A person's spiritual condition and the values and beliefs which make up their world view stem directly from the God or gods they serve. According to both the *Strong's Exhaustive Concordance* and *Vine's Expository Dictionary of Old and New Testament Words*, every time the word *strange* is mentioned in both the Old and New Testaments, it is in relation to anyone or anything that is "foreign." The very first time this word is used in the Scriptures is in the book of Genesis:

> *And God said unto Jacob, Arise, go up to Bethel, and dwell there: and make them an altar unto God, that appeared unto them when thou fleddest from the face of Esau thy brother. Then Jacob said unto his household; and to all that were with him, Put away the strange gods that are among you, and be clean, and change your garments: and let us arise, and go up to Bethel; and I will make there an altar unto God, who answered me in the day of my distress, and was with me in the way which I went.* Genesis 35:1-3

There is a certain law that is applied to biblical studies known as the Law of First Mention. This law states that when you seek to understand a certain subject in the Word of God, you start by looking at the very first time that particular subject is mentioned in the Scriptures. Once you locate that passage, you then proceed to examine what the Bible is saying through that text. You then use the foundational doctrine gleaned from that passage as a pretext for every other reference of scripture that you find because it, too, will line up with the first time the subject is mentioned in the Bible.

In relation to the strange woman, the first time the word *strange* is used in the Scriptures was when Jacob commanded his family members to no longer worship false gods, which he referred to as "strange." These gods were *strange* because they were foreign, and they were foreign because they existed outside of the will and the ordinances of God Almighty. Therefore, every time the word *strange* is used in the Scriptures to describe a spirit, a person, or a thing it is in relation to the fact that what is being described is outside of the jurisdiction and the values of either God's laws or the laws of some other kingdom.

In Paul's letter to the church of Ephesus, he addressed Christians, reminding them of their spiritual condition before coming to salvation through Jesus Christ. In his descriptive language, he also used this term strange (here *strangers*). He told the Ephesian believers:

> *That at the time, ye were without Christ, being aliens from the commonwealth of Israel, and strangers from the covenant of promise, having no hope and without God in the world.* Ephesians 2:12

Here Paul was building on the Law of First Mention that I referred to and using descriptive words that his readers understood the context and meaning of. The Bible called the false gods in Genesis *"strange gods"* because they were in opposition and outside of God's Kingdom. From that first foundational use of the term, Paul, speaking to another generation of people, yet living in a day in which that term was still understood, called them *"strangers from the covenant"* before they came to know Jesus. The covenant he spoke of was the one that God made with Abraham, when He promised him that from his posterity would come a people who would have a relationship with the one true God. At one time, that promise could only apply to Abraham's natural descendants, but, thanks be unto God, after Jesus died on the cross and rose again, salvation was made available to all who wanted to receive it. So, when Paul was referring to the Ephesians as *"strangers,"* he was speaking of their spiritual condition. Therefore, a *strange* woman is any female who does not know Jesus as Lord and Savior, and, as a consequence of this lack of enlightenment, whether knowingly or unknowingly, she is under the influence of Satan and his realm of evil spirits.

This brings me back to Solomon. Here was a man whom the Bible says very clearly was attracted to this type of woman and only this type of woman. He was the king of all Israel, and he was the wisest and most outstanding monarch of his day. He could have charmed, pursued, and married any woman from his own nation who worshiped the God he served. And yet the text makes it plain when it declares that he only desired *strange* women.

Once again, I want to stress that this has nothing to do with race or ethnicity. The Word describes Solomon's wives as being from a variety of nations, and so they came in all shades and colors. Ethnicity was not the issue because God has made all peoples of one blood, and there is no prohibition from God regarding intermarriage. This is a matter of the spirit and the inner person behind the flesh. Solomon was looking for a woman with a certain personality type. As a result of his connection to these *strange* women, he ended up worshiping their *strange* gods. We know that it was not his original intention to do this because we are given the following information regarding Solomon's character:

> *And Solomon loved the LORD, walking in the statues of David his father; only he sacrificed and burnt incense in high places.* 1 Kings 3:3

The question that confronts us is this: How could a man who loved God and was so gifted with insight and understanding become a follower of false gods? What was it about these women that so attracted him, that he chose to look past the very fact that they were pagans or, we would say in our Christian vernacular, unsaved individuals? What was their appeal? In addressing these questions, we will be able to see the dominant characteristic of the strange woman. Once again, let us look to the Bible and see how Solomon himself describes this type of woman. His descriptions and observations offer keen insight, shining a light on this type of personality. I want to quote several passages from the book of Proverbs that, while lengthy and numerous, are necessary for our knowledge. The Bible speaks to us in these words:

> *My son, attend unto my wisdom, and bow down thine ears to my understanding: that thou mayest regard discretion, and that thy lips may keep knowledge. For the lips of a strange woman drop as an honeycomb, and her mouth is smoother than oil: but her end is bitter as wormwood, sharp as a two-edged sword. Her feet go down to death; her steps take hold on hell. Lest thou shouldest ponder the path of life, her ways are movable, that thou canst not know them. Hear me now therefore, O ye children, and depart not from the words of my mouth. Remove thy way far from her, and come not nigh the door of her house: lest thou give thine honor unto others, and thy years unto the cruel: lest strangers be filled with thy wealth; and thy labours be in the house of a stranger; and thou mourn at the last, when thy flesh and thy body are consumed, and say, How have I hated instruction, and my heart despised*

reproof; and have not obeyed the voice of my teachers, nor inclined mine ear to them that instructed me!
Drink waters out of thine own cistern, and running waters out of thine own well. Let thy fountains be dispersed abroad, and rivers of waters in the streets. Let them be only thine own, and not strangers with thee. Let thy fountain be blessed: and rejoice with the wife of thy youth. Let her be as the loving hind and pleasant roe; let her breast satisfy thee at all times; and be thou ravished always with her love. And why wilt thou, my son, be ravished with a strange woman, and embrace the bosom of a stranger? For the ways of man are before the eyes of the Lord*, and he pondereth all his goings. His own iniquities shall take the wicked himself, and he shall be holden with the cords of his sins. He shall die without instruction; and in the greatness of his folly he shall go astray.*

Proverbs 5:1-23

My son, keep my words, and lay up my commandments with thee. Keep my commandments, and live; and my law as the apple of thine eye. Bind them upon thy fingers, write them upon the table of thine heart. Say unto wisdom, Thou art my sister; and call understanding thy kinswoman. That they may keep thee from the strange woman, from the stranger which flattereth with her words.
For at the window of my house I looked through my casement, and beheld among the simple ones, I discerned among the youths, a young man void of understanding, passing through the street near her corner; and he went the way to her house, in the twilight, in the evening, in the black and dark night; and, behold, there met him a woman with the attire of an harlot, and subtil of heart. (She is loud and stubborn, her feet abide not in her house: now is she without, now in the streets, and lieth in wait at every corner.) So she caught him, and kissed him, and with an impudent face said unto him, I have peace offerings with me; this day have I paid my vows. Therefore came I forth to meet thee, diligently to seek thy face, and I have found thee. I have decked my bed with coverings of tapestry, with carved works, with fine linen of Egypt. I have perfumed my bed with myrrh, aloes, and cinnamon. Come, let us take our fill of love until the morning; let us solace ourselves with loves. For the goodman is not at home, he is gone a long journey: he hath taken a bag of money with him, and will come home at the day appointed. With her much fair speech she caused him to yield, with the flattering of her lips she forced him. She goeth after her straightway, as an ox goeth to the slaughter,

or as a fool to the correction of the stocks. Till a dart strike through his liver; as a bird hasteth to the snare, and knoweth not that it is for his life. Hearten unto me now therefore, O ye children, and attend to the words of my mouth. Let not thine heart decline to her ways, go not astray in her paths. For she hath cast down many wounded: yea, many strong men have been slain by her. Her house is the way to hell, going down to the chambers of death.

Proverbs 7:1-27

What powerful words! They are often overlooked by the casual Bible reader, but they contain great nuggets of truth, there for those with eyes to see. Solomon wrote these passages in Proverbs, describing the characteristics of the strange woman, and he used as a pretext for his analysis the approach of an elder writing to a younger man. Many biblical scholars believe that he wrote the sections of Proverbs ascribed to him in his later years. By then, he had certainly learned from his mistakes, and now he composed these sayings, to give counsel to a young man about the kind of woman he should avoid getting entangled with. Even though Solomon wrote these words from that perspective, it is still instructive for women to learn from this in order to help them to see if their character matches the character of the strange woman Solomon spoke of. I chose to share the entirety of both chapters for the purpose of showing the pattern that runs through the stream of verses contained within them.

Solomon described a woman who was extremely appealing, so much so that he instructed his reader to avoid even going to the door of her house. This speaks of abstaining from keeping company with her or allowing any attachment with her to develop, because *"evil communications corrupt good manners."* The command to refrain from keeping company with this type of woman is so emphatic because there is something within her that has the potential to bring this man down.

Remember that the woman has a God-given power of influence, a potential to move others. You, as a woman, have the potential to bring out the very best and noblest attributes in a man. On the opposite side of that equation, you also have the potential to bring out the most foolish and vile instincts in a man—depending on the spirit you yield yourself to.

Here was a woman who was very skillful in her choice of words, very cunning and brazen in her approach toward this young man, and completely devoid of any sense of godly propriety. All of this was a result of her being outside of the household of faith, because she did not have the revelation of the true and living God in her heart. At the center of all her characteristics, the predominate aspect of her inner makeup was her sexual, carnal appeal. If you read through these scriptures and see Solomon's description of the woman, you can see a pattern of physical seduction running through her words, gestures, and very appearance. At the core of her inner being was the presentation of all the aspects of the pleasures of sin. She presented physical intercourse without standards, rules, or any sense of there being consequences as a result of this transgression. The young man Solomon was addressing was admonished to avoid this type of woman because the spirit that was influencing her was so appealing to men Solomon knew that the allure of this personality type would ultimately destroy the young man's life if he allowed himself to be attached to her.

I want to state this truth again with the purpose of making it emphatically clear: the overall distinguishing character trait of the strange woman is that she projects a way about her that is primarily sexual in nature. Her words, her dress, and the way in which she carries herself is projecting that spirit. Some might take issue with this viewpoint, but the Bible is very clear in its description, and the evidence that confirms the accuracy of the Word of God is clear to see in every area of society. Consider the following points, and you may see yourself or someone you know. Why is it that, when going to work at an office, you feel the need to wear clothing that reveals certain body parts that should be covered? Why is it that you have no compunction about saying certain things to men you are interested in, things that seek to arouse their physical nature? Why is it that you have no sense of propriety in your interpersonal reactions with men so that you allow a man to touch you inappropriately or you touch him inappropriately, all under the pretext of innocent flirtation? Both you and he know that such body language is communicating thoughts and intentions that are contrary to the values of Almighty God. Ask yourself this question: why are there adultery and fornication running rampant in our society today? Why does nearly every television program and movie and even certain so-called children's programs have so much illicit sex saturating the stories? Advertisers use sex to sell health products, beauty products, electronic products, and practically everything in between in order to get you to buy what they are selling. On top of that, every aspect of the social culture physiologically seeks to program you into thinking that in order to be interesting and appealing, you must present yourself in a way that is sexual in nature.

These are not things that have come from God; they are, rather, the afflictions of the age, manifested by Satan himself. He understands that if sexual immorality becomes the dominant force in the cultural, spiritual, and moral life of a community, then the door will be open for every other wicked spirit to come in. This is why Solomon warned the young man to whom he wrote the Proverbs to avoid the strange woman. He knew that the sexual immorality that would result from entertaining her would not stop there. The ultimate plan of the devil was to destroy the young man's future, his family, and the work he was put on earth to do. The grand plan was to destroy his soul, by using the weapon of the false idea of sexual immorality without consequences. When you, as a woman, continue to present yourself in a manner that is unwholesome and immodest, you make yourself one of the unwitting stars in Satan's grand stage production, with the goal of bringing down the whole family of humankind.

If you are offended by my words, you might be wondering: what part does the man play in all of this? Everyone has their part to play in doing what is right, to be sure, but, in order to change the world, you have to start with yourself. You must come to know the ways of the Lord and why He is so strong in His prohibition against sexual immorality.

Very often, in certain segments of society, the Christian Church is ridiculed and accused of being too preoccupied with issues involving sex. Secularists and humanists attempt to tell the church to stay out of what happens in people's bedrooms and that we have no right to tell someone what they can and cannot do with their own body. Such attacks have gained so much ground that even some churches have shied away from addressing these matters. However, the Bible has much to say along the lines of sexual morality and immorality, and because the Bible is very emphatic when dealing with the subject, then the followers of the Bible should take the same mindset. Consider some of the scriptures that confront this topic very candidly and directly:

> *Now the works of the flesh are manifest, which are these; Adultery, fornication, uncleanness, lasciviousness, idolatry, witchcraft, hatred, variance, emulations, strife, sedition's, heresies, envyings, murders, drunkenness, reveling,*

and such like: of the which I tell you before, as I have also told you in times past, that they which do such things shall not inherit the kingdom of God.
Galatians 5:19-21

Paul was listing the characteristics of the human condition when it has not yielded itself to the obedience of Christ. It is key to our understanding of the importance of this subject to note that the top four things he mentioned involve sexual immorality. This shows us the depth of this problem. Paul chose to address these matters first.

For the sake of adhering to the principle of confirming something by two or more witnesses, I want to highlight another passage of scripture parallels with the previous text. There is a particular account in the gospel of Saint Mark where the Lord Jesus was instructing His disciples on the inherent nature of the human heart when it is not in line with God's Word, and He used the following words to make His point:

And he said, That which cometh out of the man, that defileth the man. For from within, out of the heart of men, proceed evil thoughts, adulteries, fornications, murders, thefts, covetousness, wickedness, deceit, lasciviousness, an evil eye, blasphemy, pride foolishness: all these evil things come from within and defile the man. Mark 7:20-23

In these passages, Paul and Jesus both place an emphasis on issue of sexual immorality. This was not because God was obsessed with the subject. Nor was it because He was trying to withhold pleasure from humanity. He was emphasizing it to confront a society consumed with sexual impropriety. Just as our culture is saturated with these sins today, Jesus and the early Church leaders also lived in a time where this issue was prevalent, so they took great care to confront it and place emphasis on abstaining from it. We must do the same.

In the days of the early Church, there was a dispute among the leadership as to what rules and practices should be instituted that would provide a foundation for what made a person a true Christian. After the deliberations were over, the Church elders came to an agreement, concluding that the following standards should apply to all converts to Christ:

For it seemed good to the Holy Ghost, and to us, to lay upon you no greater burden than these necessary things; that ye abstain from meats offered to idols, and from blood, and from things strangled, and from fornication: from which if ye keep yourselves, ye shall do well. Fare ye well. Acts 15:28-29

The council of elders that had authority over the early Christian churches came to this conclusion by the revelation they received from the Holy Ghost regarding what practices were necessary for all who wanted to live the Christian life. They emphasized avoiding any practice that related to idolatry, or the worship of false gods, and abstaining from fornication, any type of sexual practice outside of the covenant of marriage.

Here we are confronted once again with the Bible's emphasis on the necessity of refraining from sexual immorality. As a consequence of this discovery, we must ask the question: why does God place such emphasis on this issue? As I stated previously, one of the most obvious reasons for this is that it is so pervasive in our culture and results in our world being so corrupted. This then leads to a second question: why does Satan use this as one of his primary tactics to destroy people's souls? Why is the predominant characteristic of the strange woman the fact that she communicates—both verbally and non-verbally—thoughts of a sexual nature. What is going on behind the scenes, working in the realm of the spirit, seeking to deceive the populace into going against the command of God? Why is something that appears, on the surface at least, to be so exciting and pleasurable, a thing which God takes such strong issue with? Once we come to an understanding of these matters, having the eyes of our understanding opened, then we can make clear and sound judgments based on seeing the whole picture.

In order to deal with this matter in the fullest possible measure of revelation, I want to refer once again to the text in Genesis, where the word *strange* is first mentioned:

And God said unto Jacob, Arise, go up to Bethel, and dwell there: and make there an altar unto God, that appeared unto thee when thou fleddest from the face of Esau thy brother. Then Jacob said unto his household, and to all that were with him, Put away the strange gods that are among you, and be clean, and change your garments. Genesis 35:1-2

As we look at this passage of scripture, we are informed that, at this point in the life of Jacob, God had given him instructions concerning making a move for both him and his family. Concerning this relocation, he was then commanded to build an altar (an ancient meeting place where human beings came to fellowship with God). Based on these instructions, Jacob then commanded his family to throw away any statues of false gods they had in their possession and to discontinue their practice of idolatry. The Bible calls these "strange gods," because, as I established, the word *strange* in the Bible means "any person, spirit, or thing that is outside the boundaries of God's ways." Even though Jacob had the revelation of the one true God, several members of his household still practiced idol worship.

In order to understand the magnitude of this problem, you must first understand this truth: anywhere the Bible speaks of idol worship or the worship of other gods, it is not referring to some backwoods practice conducted by Neanderthals who believed in silly statues. The peoples of the ancient world understood that their false gods were real entities that could be seen and interacted with. In our modern society, it has come to be generally accepted that anytime the Bible (or any other ancient text) speaks about gods, the people who believed in such things were living in a delusional fantasy. Nothing could be further from the truth. If the Bible speaks about there having been one true God who was real, then it must also be acknowledged that there were other gods who were just as real. This is why ancient people kept statues of these beings. Such images were made based upon the fact that these entities manifested themselves to human beings. As a result of this, humans could make statues or likenesses of these gods, because they had seen them.

Anytime the Bible (or any other ancient document) speaks about other gods, whether it be in the form of a poetic narrative or historical treatise, it must clearly be understood that these were actual beings that lived then and still exist today. The question is: what were they and what were their origins? The beings that ancient societies called gods were actually fallen angels that had joined with Satan when he sought to rebel against God Almighty in the time before human history began. After that rebellion was put down, Satan and the angels that sided with him were cast out of Heaven and placed here on the earth, where they became demonic spirits. Sometimes the Bible refers to them by other names, but they are essentially fallen angels that became disembodied demonic spirits.

Once humanity was created and came on the scene, these spirits sought to interact with humans by posing as gods, seeking to deceive mankind into worshiping them instead of the one true God. These fallen angels, or we can call them spirits, were known by the different things they did and for certain differences in characteristics. This is why the Bible often distinguishes between the various types of spirits, by mentioning either their names or the particular trait they manifest. This is also why other ancient texts take great pains to highlight the various differences between false gods. Therefore, when I use the terms *gods* or *demon spirits*, I am using them interchangeably, because I'm speaking about the same thing.

One of the most wicked and active demon spirits that was at work in the time of the Bible and is still at work today is what is known as the "unclean spirit." This spirt's primary objective is to seek to turn humanity from the Lord by corrupting men and women through sexual immorality. I want to quote that scripture again from Genesis and focus your attention on a particular phrase used there:

> *Then Jacob said unto his household, and to all that were with him, Put away the strange gods that are among you, and be clean, and change your garments.*
> Genesis 35:2

Notice the phrase *"and be clean."* Then ask yourself the question: why did Jacob say that and what does it mean? To answer that question, I wish to quote another passage of scripture from the New Testament book of Hebrews:

> *Marriage is honourable in all, and the bed undefiled: but whoremongers and adulterers God will judge.* Hebrews 13:4

In this passage, the writer speaks of marriage, which the Bible clearly defines as a covenant union between a man and a woman, and shows that it is a thing which God honors. *"The bed,"* we are told, is *"undefiled."* This refers to the marriage bed shared by husband and wife where their sexual intercourse takes place. God said that it is *"undefiled,"* meaning that it is clean and pure. On the opposite side of the coin, the Bible says that whoremongers and those who practice adultery will be judged by God. These two terms, *whoremongers and adulterers,"* covers any and all sexual activity outside of the marriage union. Such practices *are* defiled.

This word *undefiled* means "to be free from contamination," and any sexual practice outside of marriage is a contamination of the body that will ultimately poison your spirit. The apostle Paul, writing to the Church at Corinth, said something very similar:

> *Flee fornication. Every sin that a man doeth is without the body; but he that committeth fornication sinneth against his own body.* 1 Corinthians 6:18

Here we have the answer to why there is an epidemic of sexually transmitted diseases sweeping the human populace. The Bible is very clear when it informs us that sexual immorality is an offense and a attack upon our own body. Not only does it harm us physically; it has negative consequences for our inner being as well, because such practices will keep us from eternal life with God.

This takes us back to the account of Jacob in Genesis. When he had instructed his family to put away their strange gods, he then told them to *"be clean."* He understood that the false gods they worshiped caused them to commit unlawful sexual practices, and, as a result of these ungodly acts, they were yielding their bodies to be influenced by the demonic realm. Such abominations corrupted their bodies in the manner Paul spoke about in his letter to the Corinthian church.

In the time in which the events of the Bible took place, the people of that day understood the concept of bodily sacrificial rituals to other gods. In our time, such ideas are either misunderstood or scoffed at as being the silly notions of unenlightened pagans. The people of ancient times understood things in a much greater way than we might think; in some areas, they had greater understanding than the modern cultures of today. It then behooves those of us who seek to grasp the full picture to draw from the well of biblical records, to gain wisdom that can be applied to our own time.

Throughout the Bible, particularly in certain books of the Old Testament, God gave His people ordinances regarding bodily purity. For example, after the children of Israel were delivered from the bondage of the Egyptians and were being prepared by God to enter into their Promised Land, He gave them such ordinances to ensure that they did not defile their bodies. The Lord understood that the people of Israel were coming from a land where their oppressors practiced many unholy and profane rituals. He also knew that they would continue to live in the midst of other nations that practiced ungodly rituals. Therefore, He wanted them to understand the importance of being a holy people, and He focused much time on bodily purity, because that was the primary transgression of the ancient pagan nations. And, because there is nothing new under the sun, just as sexual immorality was rampant in the ancient world, it is also true in our modern culture. Why? Because that is the primary weapon Satan uses to turn humanity away from the true and living God. If the devil can manipulate and pervert humanity's need for physical intimacy by promoting practices that are contrary to God's plan, then he can infiltrate people's hearts and minds and cause them to worship and serve him. When you engage in sexual immorality or present yourself as a sexual object, you are allowing Satan to have dominance over your life. This is why this subject of sexual purity is so vital, even though it seems to be taboo to discuss it in certain circles.

The Word of God is not silent on the great pressing problems of the human condition, and, therefore, I will not be silent on addressing this issue. I am compelled to bring to light certain truths that must be viewed for what they are. When God told Jacob to put away the strange gods *"and be clean,"* He wanted Jacob and his family to refrain from violating their own bodies by engaging in profane sexual practices that were connected with idol worship. This is still the reason God prohibits sexual intercourse outside of marriage today. Not only is it a sin and an offense against your own body; those unholy practices are also openings for demonic spirits to take hold of you. Those spirits are directly related to sexual impurity.

This may sound unusual and maybe even far-fetched to some. However, you have to go beyond the natural understanding of your mind and see the truth that is contained in the counsel of God found in His Word. Sexual immorality—whether it be fornication, adultery, homosexuality, lesbianism, or anything else outside of holy matrimony—is the yielding of your bodily members to participate with fallen spirits in the worship of that which is unlawful in the sight of God. I will use the Scriptures to verify this statement.

Throughout the Old Testament, there is a certain phrase that is used in connection with false gods. If the Bible is read in passing, this phrase can appear to be insignificant in meaning, but if you pierce the veil of revelation, God can open your eyes to something extremely powerful. One of the most prominent forms of idolatry that took place in biblical times was the worship of a being named Molech. Although Bible scholars do not all agree on everything regarding the origin and history of Molech and his worship, there are certain truths that have come to be accepted by most scholars. Molech was a deity that was worshiped by several different heathen nations, sometimes under the guise of different names. He was a deity associated with the occult and with sacrificial offerings involving children. In God's dealings with His chosen people, He gave strict orders for them not to participate in anything connected with this deity. Here are some passages that bear this out:

> *And thou shalt not let any of thy seed pass through the fire to Molech, neither shalt thou profane the name of thy God: I am the Lord.* Leviticus 18:21

> *Again, thou shalt say to the children of Israel, Whosoever he be of the children of Israel, or of the strangers that sojourn in Israel, that giveth any of his seed unto Molech; he shall surely be put to death: the people of the land shall stone him with stones.* Leviticus 20:2

These are strong words that may be jarring to the modern ear, but God was severe in His decree for a specific reason. He wanted to keep His people free from all worldly contamination, and Molech worship was one of the primary ways humanity had corrupted itself. The worship of Molech was dangerous, not only because it was connected with the cult of fertility and its practices, involving perverted sex acts, but also child sacrifice. Yes, parents offered up their children as temple prostitutes, to engage in carnal activity for the purpose of glorifying Molech. When the Bible speaks of the people causing their children "to pass through the fire" of Molech, it is referring to the fact that those parents offered their children as sexual commodities in service of an unholy temple. The Bible helps us to understand this by saying the same thing in another passage, this time making it even more plain for us:

> *And I will set my face against that man, and will cut him off from among his people; because he hath given of his seed unto Molech, to defile my sanctuary, and profane my holy name. And if the people of the land do in any ways hide their eyes from the man, when he giveth of his seed unto Molech, and kill him not: then I will set my face against that man, and against his family, and will cut him off, and all that go a whoring after him, to commit whoredom with Molech, from among their people.* Leviticus 20:3-5

Notice the phrases *"go a whoring after him,"* and *"to commit whoredom."* These phrases, of course, deal with sexual immorality, which is unlawful in the sight of God. Take heed to the fact that the *"whoredoms"* were committed *"with Molech."* And, let me remind you of this truth: when the Bible speaks about gods other than the Almighty God, it is referring to demonic spirits that were cast out of Heaven after they rebelled against God. These demonic forces sought to pervert humanity by posing as gods, for the purpose of making themselves objects of worship. So, as we seek to understand the full truth of what God is wanting to say to us, we must understand that fact.

That being once again established, take heed now to the wording of the verse, particularly when it says, *"to commit whoredom with Molech."* The Bible is telling us that God did not want His people to participate in Molech worship because, when they allowed themselves to commit acts of sexual immorality, they were sinning against their own bodies and opening themselves up to be dominated by a demonic spirit, whose chief *modus operandi* was to corrupt humanity through the avenue of carnal desire. Once we put all these pieces together, we can then step back and see the message God wishes to speak to us in our own time.

You must come to an awareness of how your decisions affect you, both in the natural realm, as well as the spiritual realm. Physical impurity is prohibited by God, not to withhold pleasure from you, but to keep you from danger. Just as the ancient Israelites were instructed by God that to engage in ungodly sexual practices was to offer their bodily members to demonic influences, the same principle applies to our time. Illicit sex is not just a matter of a physical act, but how that act will be used to corrupt you. Take your mind back to Solomon and consider again how God was displeased with him for entangling himself with strange women. Those women turned his heart away from worshiping the Lord. Notice that the Bible gives details regarding the extent of Solomon's idolatry:

> *Then did Solomon build an high place for Chemosh, the abomination of Moab, in the hill that is before Jerusalem, and for Molech, the abomination of the children of Ammon. And likewise he did for all his strange wives, which burnt incense and sacrificed unto their gods.* 1 Kings 11:7-8

Solomon not only built a place of worship for Molech; he did the same for Chemosh. Chemosh was another demonic spirit, one that was worshiped by the people of Moab. Like Molech, Chemosh reigned over a cult that was known for its deviant sexual practices. The text clearly states that these spirits were *"the abomination"* of those nations.

When the Bible speaks of something being an abomination in the sight of God, it is referring to things He considers to be defiled or despicable. We have many scriptural references for things that were abominations, and they were mainly connected with bodily impurity through unlawful sexual practices. This is what God wants us to see. It is contained within the text but must be understood with perceiving eyes.

Solomon, so wise in other ways, was attracted to women who exuded an aura that communicated unbridled sexual lust. These women had a look, a personality and a way of presenting themselves that—subconsciously and/or consciously—said to the man that he could do anything he wanted to with their bodies. There was nothing pure about these women; they did not present themselves in such a way as to convey to Solomon that he must court their favor in a wholesome manner in order to be with them. Instead, they would allow him to use their bodies for whatever sexual act he wanted, no matter how profane or unrighteous it was. The result was that in spite of all Solomon's great strengths, he was brought down because he pursued this type of women. The greatest tragedy of all was this: because these women worshiped and served idols of sexual immorality, they took on the nature of these spirits, and Solomon, following his lust for cheap love and sinful pleasure, became so corrupted by his sexual sins that he joined himself to serve and honor these demon spirits.

Does any of this have something to do with us? Yes, what was in the past is a prologue for the present. You have, no doubt, seen certain women who carry themselves in a similar manner. When simply walking into a room, they exude a certain unwholesome sensuality. They approach men in a brazen manner. They dress in provocative clothing and give the impression, with their body language that a man can have their body without any pretext of standards. Does this perhaps describe you? If that is the case, then this self-examination is not meant to condemn you, but to help you see the truth behind your actions. You act and comport yourself this way because you are under the influence of demon spirits. The same forces that were at work in the days of the Bible are still at work today. This is why unrighteousness pervades our culture. This is why young girls become pregnant at a time in their lives when they have not yet stepped into womanhood. What causes it? The television shows, the social media platforms, the movies, and everything else under the sun that seek to indoctrinate children at a young age to the false notion that they need to engage in indiscriminate sex to be happy and fulfilled.

This is also what the Bible means when it speaks of parents making their children "pass through the fire" of Molech. Far too often parents allow their children to engage in certain forms of entertainment, even something as simple as watching certain programs that are destructive. And when a woman takes pride in presenting herself in a way which our culture considers "sexy," and she takes that as a badge of honor, she is on dangerous ground. She is being influenced by what the Bible calls the unclean spirit.

As time marched on in the history of the world, nations rose and fell, and empires came and went. The demonic spirits that once dominated the old empires ultimately took hold of the new ones that entered the scene. Even though they were known by other names, they were still the same forces that deceived those of old. Then, when Jesus Christ came on the scene and the events of the New Testament began to take place, the deities of the previous empires now influenced humanity to erect new temples in which the sacrifices of evil would be offered up to the heavens. The Greeks, the Romans, and other people of that time constructed edifices in which sexual fornication rituals were practiced as occultist worship to demon forces. Prostitution, child sacrifice, and other forms of perversion were common in these places. Even though the names of the deities were changed, behind the name was still the same unclean spirit.

The Bible informs us that there are many different types of demonic forces that have been at work in the world in the past and are also active in our own time. These spirits manifest in different ways and affect mankind in different ways. In the area of sexual perversion, which is the most prevalent problem that plagues our society, the spirit that brings about this problem is the unclean spirit. The reason the Bible refers to this spirit as being *"unclean"* is that it influences people to engage in sexual activity outside of the covenant of marriage. And, because the Bible says that only the marriage bed is undefiled, this means that every form of sexual activity that happens outside of marriage, in contradiction with the biblical definition of marriage, is defiled in the sight of God. Hence it is unclean.

This is why it is important to understand the truth behind what we experience with our natural senses. What appears to be so enticing by appearance and so stimulating by experience is a force that is corroding and decaying our inner being and contaminating our outer being as well. This is why our society runs rampant with sexually transmitted diseases. Humanity has taken something that God instituted for marriage and opened it up as a free-for-all, not truly realizing that the impurity of these acts leads to the decay of the human body. Just as ancient people had their temples, in which sexual sacrificial rites were offered up to the unclean spirt, modern mankind has also constructed new houses of worship in glorification of the unclean spirit.

The temples of today are not built like the Temple of Aphrodite, nor are they fashioned like the high places of Molech. Today's temples are movie theaters, where illicit sex is prominently and casually displayed in the great majority of films. Today's temples are the casinos and resorts where women are instructed by their employers to wear provocative clothing to promote what they consider to be an atmosphere of fun and relaxation. The altars of the past, where children were sacrificed as temple prostitutes before wicked priest, have now been replaced with schools that teach unrighteousness in the guise of sex education. They are the cartoons and the marketing campaigns that seek to subtly introduce illicit sex into impressionable young minds, and too many parents fail to realize that it is the modern-day equivalent of what the Bible said when the parents of old made their children pass through the fires of Molech. This is all motivated and directed by Satan's faithful worker—the unclean spirit.

In the New Testament, when the term *unclean* or *uncleanness* is used, it is, again, often in connection with sexual perversion. Here are a few passages that bear this out:

Who being past feeling have given themselves over unto lasciviousness, to work all uncleanness with greediness. Ephesians 4:19

But fornication, and all uncleanness, or covetousness, let it not be once named among you, as become the saints. Ephesians 5:3

Mortify therefore your members which are upon the earth; fornication, uncleanness, inordinate affections, evil concupiscence, and covetousness, which is idolatry. Colossians 3:5

The Bible, in each of these references, connects uncleanness with sexual immorality. This lets us know that God is trying to get something across to us. In these portions of scripture, God is telling us that uncleanness (the contamination of our bodies) is directly related to sexual activity outside of marriage. These practices are influenced by the demonic force that took on many names in the ancient world but is ultimately known as *"the unclean spirit."* This unclean spirit is behind it all. In the last verse I quoted, the Bible says that all of these practices are forms of *"idolatry,"* which is, by definition, the worship of false gods. This is why adherence to God's laws are so vital to a society, and this is also why Jesus Christ came to earth, so that we could be set free from the powers of darkness.

Throughout the life and ministry of Jesus, He confronted every force of evil in this world. There are several instances in which the Bible records the times in which Jesus Himself set people free who were bound and influenced by unclean spirits. One of the most famous accounts is recorded in the gospel of Saint Mark:

And they came over unto the other side of the sea, into the country of the Gadarenes. And when he was come out of the ship, immediately there met him out of the tombs, a man with an unclean spirit, who had his dwelling among the tombs, and no man could bind him, no, not with chains: because that he hath been often bound with fetters and chains, and the chains had been plucked asunder by him, and the fetters broken in pieces: neither could any man tame him. And always, night and day, he was in the mountains, and in the tombs, crying, and cutting himself with stones.

But when he saw Jesus afar off, he ran and worshiped him, and cried with a loud voice, and said, What have I to do with thee, Jesus, thou Son of the most high God? I abjure thee by God, that thou torment me not. For he said unto him, Come out of the man, thou unclean spirit.

And he asked him, What is thy name? And he answered saying, My name is Legion: for we are many. And he besought him much that he would not send them away, out of the country.

Now there was nigh unto the mountains a great herd of swine feeding. And all the devils besought him, saying, Send us into the swine, that we may enter into them. And forthwith Jesus gave them leave. And the unclean spirits went out, and entered into the swine: and the herd ran violently down a steep place into the sea, (they were about two thousand;) and were choked in the sea. And they that fed the swine fled, and told it in the city, and in the country. And they went out to see what it was that was done. And they come to Jesus, and see him that was possessed with the devil, and had the legion, sitting, and clothed, and in his right mind: and they were afraid. And they saw it told them how it befell to him that was possessed with the devil, and also concerning the swine. And they began to pray him to depart out of their coasts.

And when he was come into the ship, he that had been possessed with the devil prayed him that be might be with him. Howbeit Jesus suffered him not, but saith unto him, Go home to thy friends, and tell them how great things the Lord hath done for thee, and hath had compassion on thee. And he departed, and began to publish in Decapolis how great things Jesus had done for him: and all men did marvel. Mark 5:1-20

This is one of the greatest testimonials of supernatural deliverance from satanic forces recorded in the Scriptures. Here was a man (which shows us, from the onset, that the unclean spirit can dominate men as well as women), who was totally bound by this demon force. As a result of his participation with sins of lust and perversion, he had become consumed with madness, to the point that he now made his abode among the dead. He was completely without sense of self-control and was so set on edge that no other person could restrain him. He had become totally and completely possessed by the unclean spirit ... to the point that he had now become a plague on society.

Did that only happen in ancient times? No, today we see similar cases of people committing acts of violence and murder motivated by jealousy and crimes of passion that result from sexual delinquency. In spite of the depravity of this man's condition, hope was coming his way. Suddenly, Jesus Christ came on the scene, and He delivered this man from every tormenting entity that had possessed him. The unclean spirits within the man asked Jesus to cast them into a herd of swine in a nearby field, and Jesus did so. When the demons entered into the swine, those animals then became so violent and so frantic that they threw themselves into the sea and were drowned.

Even that detail was recorded for our learning. Satan wants to consume humanity with lust to the point that we destroy ourselves because of passion gone out of control. It was the grace of God that saved this man, and we are given a description of his condition after he was delivered. The Bible tells us that the people who knew him were astonished to see him. He was seated, fully covered, and had regained his mental faculties. Just as we see the ultimate result of living a perverted lifestyle, we are also presented with the truth that Jesus has the power to set people free. The Lord wants us to come to an awareness of the power that comes when we live a life of purity and holiness. He desires to transform our inner being to such a supernatural degree that it influences how we carry ourselves in our physical appearance, even down to the type of clothing we wear.

Chapter 4

The Attire of An Harlot

Costume, hair, and makeup can tell you instantly, or at least give you a larger perception of, who a character is. It's the first impression that you have of the character before they open their mouth, so it really does establish who they are.

– Colleen Atwood, Costume Designer

It has often been noticed, by social scientists and keen observers of human behavior, that the majority of communications between people is primarily non-verbal rather than verbal. As a society in general, what a person *does not* say can be just as powerful as what a person *does* say. The reason is that we are always communicating and sending off messages to other people, even when we say nothing at all with our lips. This non-verbal communication is expressed in our body language, our demeanor, and in the clothing a person wears. The old adage that clothes make the person does contain a grain of truth within it, because other people are making judgements about us every single day. Before you have the opportunity to verbally present yourself to a potential employer, client, or suitor, they have already made a preconceived judgement about you based on the way you dress.

In this day and age in which individuality and freedom of self-expression has thrown generally acceptable standards of good taste out the window, some would reject such notions of presenting oneself in a sober and serious way as stifling who they are. However, if you wish to be treated a certain way, and you would like those around you to see you as person who deserves respect and honor, then you must present yourself in a way that non-verbally communicates to others that you should be taken seriously.

This point is particularly necessary to embrace in our current culture. Society as a whole is being challenged on how women are treated in our culture and our institutions. Women are rising up and demanding that they no longer be viewed simply as objects or some sexual commodity. But in order for real change to take place, every aspect of the equation must be examined. Although it is not always popular to speak, truth must be declared, no matter how hard it may seem. You, as an individual, have a part to play in how you are treated by other people, particularly those of the male gender. This requires that you examine yourself to see if the way you non-verbally communicate is one which says to the other person, "I am a person and not an object." Do you, by the way you dress, say on a sub-conscious level, "I want to be treated as a object, and I can be approached and talked to in any way, no matter how disrespectful or vulgar it may seem?"

While it is never correct to blame a person who is attacked on the street and robbed of their goods and say it was their own fault, there is something to be said for projecting an image of power and security when you walk the mean streets of rough neighborhoods. A predator will attack anyone if they are desperate and hungry enough, but they will first try to find someone who projects an air of insecurity and weakness in the way they carry themselves. Such behavior says to the predator that this person is an easy target. On the other hand, when a person walks with confidence and carry's themself in a way that suggests that, if trouble does arise, they can defend their person and goods with absolute force, a predator will think twice before attempting to attack them. The same principle holds true in every area of life. If you, as a woman, want to be treated in a way that communicates to others that you are a serious individual who expects others to take you seriously, you have to present yourself in that way. This includes the way you dress. To put it rather succinctly, if you do not wish to be treated as a physical object, one area that can help dispel that notion about you is to stop wearing clothing that sends off signals of "anything goes" sexuality.

I opened this chapter with a quote from one of the most celebrated costume designers in the history of motion pictures, and I did it to highlight the fact that, even in an industry that promotes such negativity in our culture, the motion picture people understand this principle. What I have stated is not the rattling off of a dogma stuck in a kind of Puritanical time warp; it is simply a fact of life. When a great artist, whether in front of or behind the camera, seeks to create a certain type of character, they understand that the wardrobe of that character is vitally important. How that character is dressed speaks to the other actors, as well as the audience, a great deal about who that person is intended to be. If they are supposed to be heroic, they will be dressed in a heroic fashion. If they are supposed to be the comic relief, they will be dressed in a costume befitting a clownish figure. If they are supposed to be the *femme-fatale*, they will wear clothes that send the message of free love sensuality. This is part of what is known as archetypical characters. An actor is put in wardrobe that reinforces their desired character type, because we, as human beings, are naturally inclined to make judgements about people based on their outward appearance.

The Bible, as with every other issue of life, addresses this principle and shows to us, once again, that God is the ultimate authority on all facets of the human condition. There is an account in the Old Testament in which the prophet Samuel was told by God to go to a certain man's house and anoint one of his son's to be the next king over Israel. When the prophet arrived and spoke to the father about his intentions, he asked to have all the sons brought before him so that God could speak to him as to who among them was chosen to be king. When the prophet Samuel laid his eyes on the eldest son, he immediately assumed that this man was God's choice to be king. He based his assumption on appearance alone. In his eyes, the eldest son fit the image of what a king should look like. He was straight out of central casting. However, the Lord spoke to Samuel and told him that this young man was *not* the chosen vessel:

> *But the LORD said unto Samuel, Look not on his countenance, or on the height of his stature; because I have refused him: for the LORD seeth not as man seeth; for man looketh on the outward appearance, but the LORD looketh on the heart.*
>
> 1 Samuel 16:7

Here we see two great truths laid out before us in this simple verse. The most important truth that we are to grasp from this passage is this: the Lord loves each person enough to not base their worth and their value on their outward appearance, because He judges each one of us by examining our hearts. What is also shown to us from the text is that while God looks from within, human beings make judgements and observations based on the outward appearance of another person. This is just a reality of life, and it is confirmed to us by what we just saw from the Bible. Therefore, if you wished to be perceived a certain way and expect to be treated with a certain level of respect, then you must present yourself in a manner that will earn the respect of others. Some may reject such a statement and take the position: "I don't care what other people may think of me. I will dress in whatever manner suits me." While this position is within your right, it may rob you of your future. In order to realize your full potential in God's plan for your life, you must present yourself in a way that brings honor to Him. The ultimate purpose for you to read this book is to help you become the person God has called you to be. That person is a representative of Jesus Christ, and because you are one of His representatives, your outward appearance is important. Why? Because other people will judge you based on how you appear on the outside. Your way of dressing should communicate a level of holiness that will show others that you are God's child, and being God's child, you expect to be treated like God's child.

This brings us once again to the strange woman, the female who does not know Jesus as her Lord and Savior. In consequence of this lack of knowledge, she lives her life according to the dictates and attitudes of this corrupt world. She practices sin as a way of life, and that includes acts of sexual immorality because that is the dominant problem in our culture. In living a lifestyle of free love, she reflects this mentality, even in the type of clothing she wears and the way she adorns her body.

The Word of God addresses this issue, and we looked at the key verses that do so in the previous chapter. Here I want to highlight some of those verses again in greater detail, but first I must again emphasize this point: King Solomon, the author of most of the book of Proverbs, was writing about the strange woman from the perspective of counseling a young man regarding the type of woman he should avoid. He constructed a character type in great detail for the purpose of enlightening this young man, so that he could pick up on the traits she uses to get what she wants. When the young man noticed these things, he could discern that he was in the presence of a *"strange"* woman.

This exhortation of Solomon is so strong that he leaves the distinct impression: if the young man were to see this type of woman walking down the street, he should avoid contact with her. The question then arises: could the young man detect that a female was a strange woman by eyesight alone? Let us review once again the words of the wise king:

> *My son, keep my words, and lay up my commandments with thee. Keep my commandments, and live; and my law as the apple of thine eye. Bind them upon thy fingers, write them upon the table of thine heart. Say unto wisdom, Thou art my sister; and call understanding thy kinswoman: that they may keep thee from the strange woman, from the stranger which flattereth with her words. For at the window of my house I looked through my casement, and beheld among the simple ones, I discerned among the youths, a young man void of understanding, passing through the street near her corner; and he went the way to her house, in the twilight, in the evening, in the black and dark night: and, behold, there met him a woman with the attire of an harlot, and subtil of heart.*
>
> Proverbs 7:1-10

Here we have Solomon laying out in great detail to this young man to be careful how he lived his life. He told the young man that if he would retain the commandments of the Lord in his head and allow them to consecrate his body, he would be safe from evil influences. Solomon did not just generalize this evil; he spoke very specifically, with details, of what he was talking about, and he named the strange woman. This wise king understood that the power of seduction this woman possessed was strong because of the spirit that influenced her, so that the young man could be swayed by her charms. To emphasize his point, Solomon described an incident in which he once observed another young man, one who lacked discernment and perception. This simpleton just casually strolled through life, taking no thought of the dangers around him. He walked the dark streets where nocturnal creatures lay in wait to catch their prey. As we look at the specificity of Solomon's words, we see that this young man encountered a strange woman, and she was immediately recognizable, but not by her speech or her conduct. What immediately identified her was the way she was dressed.

Notice again the words of the last verse.

> *And, behold, there met him a woman with the attire of an harlot, and subtil of heart.*
>
> Proverbs 7:10

Again, what made this woman instantly identifiable as the type of woman to avoid was the way she was dressed. Notice the careful wording of the sentence. It does *not* say that she was a harlot, but that she was dressed like one. A harlot is another word for a prostitute, and a prostitute, by definition, is "a woman who engages in sexual activity for the purpose of receiving payment." In order for a prostitute to be successful at her trade, she must first present herself in a manner that appeals to men's sexual appetites. She does this by wearing revealing clothing that exposes areas of her body that should be covered. This sends a signal to a prospective client that she is open for business.

What is of great importance to understand from this text is the impression, given by Solomon, that the woman was of a certain social status in the community. Further down in the text, we are told that she was married and that her husband was a man of financial means. In her attempt to seduce the young man, she told him that her husband had gone out of town, and that he took a bag of money with him for his journey. For all intents and purposes, we could say that this woman would be considered an upper-class citizen of the community. Just as it is now, wealth and status did not equal class and sophistication back then. This woman crept about town in the late hours of night, looking to satisfy her lusts, and she was dressed the same way a woman who sold herself would dress. This is one of the marks of the strange woman.

The Bible tells us that there is nothing new under the sun. So what we witness in our time is nothing new, but, instead, a repeat of mankind going around the wilderness, seemingly always learning, but never attaining to the knowledge of the truth. Today this has become so pervasive and commonplace in our culture that we think nothing of the fact that women in every profession and social sector of society dress in a way that if they were to stand beside a prostitute, the casual observer could not tell the difference. Thankfully, not every woman adorns herself in such a fashion, but too many do, and it is an epidemic that must be corrected, if complete social change is to take place.

This should not be the case today. We have modern conveniences that provide us clothing that can cover body parts that should not be exposed. We should not be seeing scantily clad women in our everyday life. And yet our doctors' offices, banks, corporate law firms and everything in between are full of women who present an inappropriate dress code to their colleagues and clients. Such adornment (or lack thereof) only adds to the causes of unwanted sexual advances and inappropriate conduct. While the women are certainly not solely to blame (for every person must take responsibility for his or her personal actions), women could help themselves so much by presenting themselves in a manner that communicates to others that inappropriate behavior will not be tolerated.

Even on a subconscious level, human beings with any sort of depth and perception understand that clothes communicate a message to those around us. The woman Solomon described went out in the heat of the night looking for pleasure, knowing that if she dressed in a seductive manner, she would attract a man who also wanted sexual pleasure. Such a mentality is not in line with the character of God. Once again, looking back to the Law of First Mention, the first time the Bible speaks of strange gods, it also says:

> *Then Jacob said unto his household, and to all that were with him, Put away the strange gods that are among you, and be clean, and change your garments.*
> Genesis 35:2

Line upon line, precept upon precept and revelation upon revelation, all form a progression of knowledge that allows us to see the full diamond of truth that is laid out before us. In the previous chapters, we examined what the Bible meant when it said we should put away strange gods. We also examined the meaning of the statement, *"Be clean."* Now we see how the Lord is using Jacob to further instruct his family. As a result of the unclean spirits that dominated his household, Jacob's family also dressed in ways that were unbecoming and unholy in the sight of God. As a result of ceasing to practice idolatry by participating with those demonic spirits, the change that took place on the inside was ultimately to manifest on the outside. The message behind this account and the ultimate principle which the entire Bible builds upon from the foundation point of this scripture is this: holiness and purity are to be manifested in every area of our lives, including how we dress.

You, as a woman, should not present yourself in such a way as to send a signal that you are just a sexual commodity to be lusted after by men. No matter how intelligent, educated, or advanced in the hierarchy of society you may be, if the way you clothe yourself is indistinguishable from any streetwalker, then this is a problem. Wearing tight clothing, showing cleavage, and carrying yourself in a brazen manner only diminish your worth as a woman and bring dishonor to the Lord. This type of presentation is what the Bible calls "playing the harlot." This simply means that, even though you are not a prostitute, you present yourself in a way that communicates that you are willing to behave like one. The only difference is that there will be no money exchanged in the process. God wants you to be a person who is taken seriously and seen as a person deserving of respect. You, too, should want to be viewed as a woman who wishes to be pursued and wooed in a loving, romantic, and respectful way. However, if you dress in a way that says "anything goes with no effort involved," then you will be treated that way.

The Word of God tells a fascinating account of a woman named Tamar, the wife of one of the sons of Judah (a great-grandson of Abraham). Tamar's husband died before she could bear a child by him, and she was given in marriage to another man in the hope that she could become pregnant. This was one of the common social customs of that day, because, in that culture, it was considered shameful for a woman not to have a child. Unfortunately for Tamar, her new husband refused to impregnate her, and he ultimately died too. Refusing to be denied, Tamar concocted a terrible plan. She would trick her father-in-law into impregnating her. The Bible gives us the following details of the account:

> *Then said Judah to Tamar his daughter in law, Remain a widow at thy father's household till Shelah my son be grown: for he said, Lest per adventure he die also, as his brethren did. And Tamar went and dwelt in her father's house.*
> *And in process of time the daughter of Shuah Judah's wife died; and Judah was comforted, and went up unto his sheepshearers to Timnath, he and his friend Hiram the Adullamite.*
> *And it was told Tamar, saying, Behold thy father in law goeth up to Timnath to shear his sheep. And she put her widow's garment off from her, and covered her with a vail, and wrapped herself, and sat in an open place, which is by the way to Timnath; for she saw that Shelah was grown, and she was not given unto him to wife.*
> *When Judah saw her, he thought her to be an harlot; because she had covered her face. And he turned unto her by the way, and said, Go to, I pray thee, let me come in unto thee; (for he knew not that she was his daughter in law).*
> *And she said; What wilt thou give me; that thou mayest come in unto me?*
> *And he said, I will send thee a kid from the flock.*
> *And she said, Wilt thou give me a pledge, till thou send it?*

And he said, what pledge shall I give thee?
And she said, Thy signet, and thy bracelet, and thy staff that is in thine hand. And he gave it her, and came in unto her, and she conceived by him. And she arose, and went her way, and laid by her vail from her, and put on the garments of her widowhood.
And Judah sent the kid by the hand of his friend the Adullamite, to receive his pledge from the woman's hand: but he found her not. Then he asked the men of that place saying, Where is the harlot, that was openly by the way side?
And they said, There was no harlot in this place.
And he returned to Judah, and said, I cannot find her; and also the men of the place said, that there was no harlot in this place.
And Judah said, Let her take it to her, lest we be shamed: behold, I sent this kid, and thou hast not found her.
And it came to pass about three months after, that it was told Judah, saying, Tamar thy daughter in law hath played the harlot; and also, behold, she is with child by whoredom.
And Judah said, Bring her forth, and let her be burnt. Genesis 38:11-24

In this rather insightful chronicle, we are given quite a glimpse into the customs of the people of that day and are invited to draw a spiritual principle from the well of knowledge presented to us. As the scene opened, a man named Judah was seeking to comfort his daughter-in-law after the death of her husband. As time passed, Judah's wife also died, and he went among those who were shepherds for fellowship in an attempt to forget his misery. Tamar, in her desire to have a child and secure a posterity for herself, decided to trick Judah into impregnating her. What is fascinating is the way she went about doing this. Being a widow, she wore the garments of widowhood, and now the first things she did was to change her garments, removing the clothes of widowhood and, instead, dressing like a prostitute of the day. She even wore a veil over her face as prostitutes commonly did, to conceal their identity.

There was another important element at work here. Women who practiced prostitution to earn an income understood that they were selling a fantasy, not genuine love and affection. They wanted their clients to be able to project onto them any image that person desired and simply use their body as the channel by which their lust could be satisfied. It was not about being with that particular woman for the person she was, but projecting onto that woman whatever idea the client wanted to have. This is one of the great tragedies of sexual immorality, and it is a problem that still exists today. Because Satan has so skillfully saturated the culture with all manner of impurities, many go into relationships, being with someone, not for who they really are, but for how that person's body can be used to play out the ungodly fantasies of their partner. They are not focused on pleasing their mate and not losing them but simply pleasing themselves.

This is often the case with married men who secretly view pornographic videos. They watch as the women on those videos perform acts of indecency and lewdness, all designed to stimulate an appetite of unwholesome sexual practices. As a result of these men feeding their minds and their spirits with such filth, they then take those wicked thoughts into the sanctity of their marriage bed, expecting their wife to play out those acts of unrighteousness with them. The poison of that sin is so great that some men even picture in their minds the women they have seen on pornographic videos while they are engaged in intercourse with their wife. This forces her to play the harlot in her own bed. Tamar understood this concept, so she veiled her face and changed her clothes, so that when Judah saw her he would automatically assume that she was a woman who sold herself for profit.

You may not be a woman who engages in such practices, but you still need to examine yourself and ask yourself if you dress in a way that sends a signal to men that you are a woman who, even though she does not sell herself, can be viewed as a cheap thrill and a good time. Then, after the deed is done, you are left with nothing but soured expectations. This is even worse than a prostitute. At least she is paid for demeaning her body, while you get nothing for demeaning yours.

The Lord's desire for your life is that you come to a place of awareness and see yourself in the way He wants you to be seen. He is calling you to take heed to every aspect of your life, even regarding things that may seem to be insignificant. Again, the Bible tells us that it is the little foxes that spoil the vine, meaning that the areas of our lives we consider to be unimportant are actually of great relevance to presenting yourself as someone who will be pleasing and acceptable before God. This brings me to how you adorn yourself with regard to makeup, body piercings, and tattoos. The way you paint the canvas of your body, how you choose to mark your body, and the places on your body you chose to mark all speak of the type of woman you are. I want to draw your attention, once again, to the phrase, *"playing the harlot,"* for this does not mean that the woman who does this is a prostitute, but she is acting in a way that one cannot distinguish her from a woman who engages in that act.

God is not opposed to makeup or body piercings. As a matter of fact, while some try to make this an area of theological contention, God Himself is not bothered one way or the other by makeup or body piercings. However, because He knows that we live in this world and that how a person presents themselves is a non-verbal form of communication to other people regarding the type of person they are, He does give us advice on how we should approach these issues. Here is a passage of scripture that, while brief, contains a powerful truth:

> *Let your moderation be known unto all men. The Lord is at hand.*
>
> Philippians 4:5

This simple verse is telling us that what we do in life should be done in balance and moderation. Why? Because other people are watching, and because the Lord is soon to come, and we want to make sure we do not open ourselves up to the possibility of falling back into sin. This means that just because you *can* do something doesn't necessarily mean you *should* do it. You can wear makeup, but you should be mindful of the fact that your makeup must be done in good taste and in moderation, so that you don't give the appearance to others that you are the type of woman who is of questionable morals.

God has no issue with body piercings as a general rule. However, you should not pierce you body in sensitive areas that should be covered and then expose those areas for everyone to see.

With regards to tattoos, some believe that God prohibits them under all circumstances, while others believe it is perfectly acceptable to have them. There is only one scant reference in the Scriptures that can be applied to tattoos. Other than that, the Bible gives no clear prohibition against the practice or a clear teaching one way or the other. That is not a license to put tattoos on the parts of your body that no one but your spouse should see and then go out into society dressed in revealing clothing, showing those tattoos and drawing attention to parts of your body that have no business being exposed in public. While some may scoff or even mock at this, it is a serious problem. Once again, it is nothing more than the modern-day equivalent of playing the harlot.

The Bible informs us (if we read it with perceptive eyes) that the prostitutes of old not only dressed in a sexual manner; they also arrayed their bodies with objects and markings that drew attention to the body parts that men find appealing. Hosea, an Old Testament prophet, brought forth a message of repentance to the people of his day. In one of his exhortations, he made a fascinating statement that has come down to us through history:

> *Say ye unto your brethren, Ammi; and to your sisters, Ruhamah. Plead with your mother, plead: for she is not my wife, neither am I her husband: lest ye therefore put away her whoredom out of her sight, and her adulteries from between her breasts.* Hosea 2:1-2

The man of God was speaking a prophetic word to the people of Israel, and he used the names *Ammi* (meaning "my people") and *Ruhamah* (meaning "pity"). God, speaking through this man, referred to the nation of Israel by those names in order to represent their spiritual condition. The nation, as a whole, had given themselves over to idol worship, and God compared their behavior to a spouse who had gone outside of marriage and joined themselves to a prostitute. Because of their sin, God went further in the analysis of their moral condition, by talking about how a harlot would put her adulteries between her breast, symbolizing how the nation had branded themselves with the mark of sin in their hearts. This language was used because the harlots of that day would put markings between their breasts to draw the attention of perspective clients.

As I have stated before, what once was is what we are seeing today. How many young women tattoo the upper part of their breast, and then go out into society and expose that area, drawing attention to a spot that should not be visible for all to see. God is trying to tell you something. This will help you to see the origins of these things. It was an ancient custom connected to prostitution and idolatry. It should also help you to see that you cannot complain about men looking at you a certain way if that is what you parade in public for all to see.

God has put all of these things in His holy Word, not to condemn you or pass judgement on you, but, rather, to change you for the better. If you desire to be treated with honor and respect, you can empower yourself to be seen that way by clothing, not only your inner being, but also your outward appearance with the attire of grace and sophistication. Edith Head, an award-winning costume designer, once said, "A woman's clothes should be tight enough to know that she is a woman and loose enough to know that she is a lady." If this is to be the era of the woman, it must begin with being the glorification and the uplifting of the lady—first and foremost. Let this be the hour when you cast off the robes of unrighteousness and put on the armor of light.

Chapter 5

Subtle of Heart

In studying the character type of the strange woman, we have looked at the dominant spirt that influences her life. We have also examined how this spirit affects her to influence how she dresses and presents herself to society. In this chapter I want to shine the light on the way in which this type of woman communicates and expresses herself and her intentions. All of these are the result of the inner workings of her heart, and there is a passage of scripture that gives us insight into this principle:

> *O generation of vipers, how can ye, being evil, speak good things? For out of the abundance of the heart the mouth speaketh.* Matthew 12:34

Jesus, in speaking these words to a corrupt and hypocritical leadership council, gave us a spiritual principle: whatever is on the inside of you will come out through the words you speak. When the word *abundance* is used in this text, it implies "a storehouse, or a place in which supplies or goods are kept." When you go about your daily life and attempt to interact with other people, whatever spiritual and emotional equipment is in your inner storehouse will ultimately come forth in how you communicate. Jesus also placed strong emphasis on a wholesome inner life, when He taught the religious leaders of his day the importance of inner purity being the basis from which outer purity springs forth.

After Jesus addressed the religious hierarchy, one of His disciples asked Him to explain His words in a simpler fashion. He answered in this way:

And Jesus said, Are ye also without understanding? Do not ye understand, that whatsoever entereth in at the mouth goeth into the belly, and is cast out into the draught? But those things which proceed out of the mouth come forth from the heart; and they defile the man. For out of the heart proceed evil thoughts, murders, adulteries, fornications, thefts, false witness, blasphemies: these are the things which defile a man: but to eat with unwashed hands defileth not a man.

Matthew 15:16-20

In speaking to His disciples, Jesus once again shows us the foundation on which so much of our lives rests. He says that it is those things which come forth out of our mouth that have the potential to bring destruction to our lives. If a person does not know Jesus as their Lord and Savior, or if they do know Him but are not walking in fellowship with Him, their heart will be a cesspool of contaminated and perverted thinking. This corrosion will ultimately affect the way they seek to get what they want out of life. You must stay on guard as to what you allow yourself to be consumed with in your inner being, for the Bible also tells us:

Keep thy heart with all diligence; for out of it are the issues of life.

Proverbs 4:23

This command is stating that if you seek to master life, you must make sure your heart is pure and your motives are in right standing with the ordinances of God. Why? Because whatever is on the inside of you will determine how you deal with the issues of your life.

Perhaps the greatest issue a person deals with is interpersonal relationships. This covers every part of your life, from your relationship with those in your career, your relationship with your friends, and, most especially, your relationship with the person with whom you seek companionship. I stress this relationship in particular because it is the primary need of all humanity, and how you go about seeking to satisfy that need says a great deal about the content of your character.

This brings me back, specifically, to the strange woman and exploring her personality type. Because the strange woman is an individual who does not have the knowledge of God within, her heart is not purified to the wonders of the principles of the Kingdom of Heaven. Therefore, as a result of this lack of awareness, she seeks to fulfill her needs through devices and tactics antithetical to those ascribed and endorsed by the Word of God. I want to quote once again from Proverbs 7, this time going deeper into the specific way in which the writer described her personality traits and the degree to which she would go to satisfy her need for companionship, the way in which she seduced the young man:

> *And, behold, there met him a woman with the attire of an harlot, and subtil of heart. (She is loud and stubborn: her feet abide not in her house: now is she without, now in the streets, and lieth in wait at every corner.) So she caught him, and kissed him, and with an impudent face said unto him, I have peace offerings with me; this day I have paid my vows. Therefore came I forth to meet thee, diligently to seek thy face, and I have found thee. I have decked my bed with coverings o tapestry, with carved works, with fine linen of Egypt. I have perfumed my bed with myrrh, aloes, and cinnamon. Come, let us take our fill of love until the morning: let us solace ourselves with loves. For the goodman is not at home, he is gone a long journey: he hath taken a bag of money with him, and will come home at the day appointed. With her much fair speech she caused him to yield, with the flattering of her lips she forced him.*
>
> Proverbs 7:10-21

As we proceed, I want to draw your attention once again to the fact that this was written to a young man for the purpose of instructing him on the type of woman he should avoid. I make this point once more, first, because repetition is good for the soul, and the more you are reminded of an important truth the better it will be for your personal enrichment. Second, I highlight this point because it brings more context to the detailed language of the text. It is within these details that we see how instructive it is to help men avoid the wrong type of woman, but also for women to ensure they do not match the character traits of this type of woman.

I have already written in detail regarding what the scripture means by the phrase, "*the attire of an harlot.*" Now I want to proceed with the next clause of that verse and use the proceeding verses in constructing the further spiritual and psychological profile of the strange woman. Once again, I want to focus your attention on these verses:

And, behold, there met him a woman with the attire of an harlot, and subtil of heart. (She is loud and stubborn; her feet abide not in her house.)

Proverbs 7:10-11

This phrase, *"subtil of heart,"* refers to the inner intentions of the woman. According to the original language from which the King James Version was translated, the word *subtil* can be defined as "that which is concealed or hidden for the purpose of besieging a prey." The word also denotes "the connotation of a subtil watcher." This is letting us know that this woman has been watching and waiting to see who she can ensnare, who she can lure in, so that she can fulfill her carnal desires. Her motives are not pure, and neither are they unselfish, for it is all about fulfilling her needs, no matter how immoral and unethical her actions may be in furthering that goal.

If physical immorality is the primary sin that affects the world today, then the second would certainly be selfish pride. The glorification and the self-preservation of the individual regardless of the needs of any other person is a spiritual cancer that is sweeping our time and, unfortunately, has been throughout most of history. This woman was approaching a young man, getting ready to make him an offer, which many in his position would find very difficult to refuse. But because her motivation was to fulfill her desire to commit an immoral act, she was willing to destroy, not only her own life, but the future of the young man as well—regardless of who got hurt in the process.

This can help you to examine yourself, particularly in the area of needs and desires. To have a need or a desire to obtain something is, in and of itself, not a negative thing. What you must be mindful of is the principle of ensuring that your needs and your desires are in accordance with the will of God. This woman mentioned in the book of Proverbs was seeking companionship and sexual fulfillment outside of her marriage, and the Bible calls this an *"inordinate affection"* (Colossians 3:5). Simply defined, it is "a desire for something that is not right to have." Because she was motivated by an unwholesome desire, her intentions were not honorable toward the young man. She was willing to manipulate the situation to get what she wanted.

This brings me back to the point I made early on of the area of influence in the life of the woman. As a woman, because God has equipped you to be able to have such an impact, you cannot allow yourself to be overtaken by wrong desires that will lead you into manipulating others to get what you want. Instead, you must submit your emotions and affections to the Lord, and He will cause you to pursue the right things and to go about that pursuit in the right way.

The next thing the Bible tells us about this woman is that she was both loud and stubborn, and her feet did not abide, or remain, in her house. It is important, in this analysis, to remember that the Bible does not waste words and that every descriptive detail has been recorded for our learning. A great philosopher once quipped, "Empty vessels make the loudest sounds," and so is it with the strange woman. This type of woman may put on a charming demeanor, but if she feels that she may not get her way in the situation, she will reveal an aspect of her true nature which is to be uncouth and theatrically abrasive. This passage allows us to see beyond the veil of her facade and shows us a person who is rude, coarse, and insists that her way is the only way.

The fact that the woman was described as being loud has nothing to do with showing strength, for this type of behavior is not speaking of assertiveness or emotional strength. This word *loud* refers to the fact that she communicates, both verbally and non-verbally, that she is going to have her way, no matter how low she has to sink. There is no meekness or comeliness in her approach, for she equates bombast and braggadocio with strength. This is not in keeping with the character of God. He resists the proud, but gives grace to the humble (see James 4:6).

The text also refers to the woman's stubbornness. This tells us that she did not have a teachable spirit. Not only did she live her life always seeking to push her point of view onto others, not only did she go about being coarse and abrasive, always thinking that she had to give everyone a piece of her mind, not caring if she was being rude or unladylike in doing so, but this woman was also determined never to change, never to grow spiritually or emotionally. She was determined that no one would correct her, instruct her, or attempt to change her mind in any of her wrongheaded thinking.

Perhaps the most dangerous type of person walking the earth today is the person who always thinks they are right, despite every evidence to the contrary. This type of behavior can manifest in something as simple as an employer seeking to correct you about your conduct, but because you are so determined to win the argument and do things your way, you are willing to risk losing your job over a simple request to change. It could manifest in losing a relationship with a loved one as a result of being unwilling to change and take steps to ensure that productive communication exists between the two parties.

This goes directly to the point of her feet not abiding in her house. When the Scriptures speak about our feet, they do so as a metaphor to deal with the decisions we make and the steps we take along the journey of life. God has a plan for your life, but that plan is dependent upon the supposition that you seek Him to help you know the places you need to be, in order for the promises of God to materialize in your life. This woman should have been in her home waiting for her husband rather than walking the streets at night, seeking the company of others to commit fornication. The danger of being in the wrong place is that you can open yourself up to being influenced by satanic thoughts that you might not otherwise have if you stayed in the place of protection and blessing God prepared for you. Provision and security result from consistently remaining in fellowship with the Lord and allowing Him to lead and guide you in the paths He has ordained you to walk in.

As we read more of this text, we are given further insight into the way in which the strange woman communicates and seeks to draw attention to herself:

> *(Now is she without, now in the streets, and lieth in wait at every corner.) So she caught him, and kissed him, and with an impudent face said unto him, I have peace offerings with me; this day I have paid my vows. Therefore came I forth to meet thee, diligently to seek thy face, and I have found thee. I have decked my bed with coverings of tapestry, with carved works, with fine linen of Egypt. I have perfumed my bed with myrrh, aloes, and cinnamon. Come, let us take our fill of love until the morning: let us solace ourselves with loves.*
>
> Proverbs 7:12-18

This is a very seductive and persuasive sales pitch. The woman gets this man's attention and then proceeds to beguile him into throwing his life away. Let us examine her approach more closely, because these same tactics are being used in our time by the strange women of today. First, we read that she positioned herself in the marketplace of social interaction, like an animal on the prowl, she waited for her prey. Once she spotted a man who looked like he could satisfy her needs, she caught him, using her body to communicate the fact that she was willing and ready to do all manner of wickedness. I raise this point because the Bible does, and because the need for companionship is the most common human desire. Therefore, how you go about attracting men to you says a great deal about yourself and how far you are willing to go to find companionship.

This woman built the foundation of her appeal on her physical prowess, and she used inappropriate body language to get the man's attention. She was much more obvious than some, but the principle by which she was operating is very much at work in the earth today. How many times have you sought to attract a man by using touching in a flirtatious manner, for example, for the purpose of expressing your interest? Why is there a need to slide your hand across a man's shoulder or enter his personal space while having a simple conversation with him? Whether you understand it or not, you are seeking to build a romantic relationship on the foundation of physical attraction, rather than a spiritual connection. While physical attraction has its place, it is not the fountainhead upon which a quality relationship is built. You should not be using your body as a way of communicating interest simply because you are opening yourself up to committing fornication. See how this woman looks and speaks to the man, and then ask yourself if you, perhaps, conduct yourself in a similar manner.

The scripture declares that after the woman had grabbed the young man and kissed him, she then looked at him *"with an impudent face."* That phrase simply means "without any shame or sense of decorum." She looked at him and let him know, through her facial expressions, that she was not ashamed of what she has just done, and it was only a taste of what was to come. This type of behavior has been forced upon some women by Satan, in order to make them believe they are being strong and sexually independent through such displays of forwardness. Satan has deceived these women into thinking that this is the way you get a man or show equality with a man—by being unabashedly free with your sensuality. But Jesus said that Satan was a liar, the father of lies, and that he still lies today. If you conduct yourself in such a way, all you are doing is allowing yourself to be seen as a object, to be used for nothing more than satisfying a man's fantasy.

Next we see how the woman began to make her case to the young man. She appealed to his ego by stating that she had sought for him diligently, when, in reality, she would have been satisfied with any man who fit her criteria. He just happened to have come along first. She then proceeded to tell him how she had decorated her bedroom to be a palace of lust and defilement, enticing him with images of the possibilities of a night of passion.

In order for us to understand the seriousness of this exchange, the Holy Spirit caused Solomon to write very descriptively, even describing the tools the woman planned to use at her home to enhance their pleasure. Again, there is nothing new under the sun. Just as our society has stores that sell perverted sex objects and paraphernalia designed for acts of fornication, so, it was as well in the days of the Bible. The fine linen and the carved works of Egypt the woman had placed on her bed were ancient sex objects that came from pagan cultures and were used in fertility cults for perverted sexual practices for idol worship. This woman was filling the young man's mind with such demonic depravity, hoping to lure him into her bed. Maybe you have used such devilish objects for sexual intercourse or ton engage in different types of perversion and called it *normal*. If so, God has allowed you to read these words so that the truth of His Word can open your eyes to see that such things are wrong and are not in keeping with the purity of God's design for physical intercourse.

Finally, the woman summed up her proposal by coming right out and saying that she would stimulate his body the entire night. She said her husband was gone and would not be coming home anytime soon. All of this was used purposefully to let the young man know that because she was married, she had no vested interest in their relationship going any further than mutual fun. In a sense, she was saying that the man could have his cake and eat it too, without fear of any long-term commitment or concern for consequences of any kind.

This is always the strategy of the devil. He will only show you the short-term pleasure of sin, without revealing the long-term pain that will come as a result of your fleeting fun. How many people have had unwanted pregnancies? How many marriages have been torn apart? Or how many lives have been ruined as a result of paying for the wages of sin? You may be reading this, seeing yourself and your condition clearly for the first time in a long time. If so, this is the hour for change. The behavioral practices that the Bible speaks of have consequences that will affect both you and the men you seek to connect yourself with. In the next chapter, we will delve into the final act of how these things ultimately played out.

Chapter 6

Hunting for the Precious Life

Beauty is power, a smile is its sword. – John Ray

An astute minister of the Gospel once told his parishioners that within every man there is a king and a fool. He went on to address the men in the congregation directly, saying, "You need to find the woman who brings out the king in you instead of the fool in you." This statement, while being very witty and charming, not only had a great deal of profundity to it, but was also completely grounded in biblical truth. The Word of God tells us that, for those who are believers in the Lord Jesus Christ, there will be a conflict engaged within us. This conflict will be based upon the desire to want to live a life that is pleasing and acceptable before God and a human nature that wishes to fulfill the lusts and desires of the flesh.

When a person comes to God and receives forgiveness for their sins, they become born again. The born-again experience means that your spirit, the real you on the inside, becomes alive unto God, and you have the nature of wanting to live your life holy unto Him. However, although you have been changed from within, your body has not been recreated, and, at times, it will want to do those things that are contrary to the Word of God. The apostle Paul described this conflict in his letter to the churches of Galatia:

> *This I say then, Walk in the Spirit, and ye shall not fulfill the lust of the flesh. For the flesh lusteth against the Spirit, and the Spirit against the flesh: and these are contrary the one to the other: so that ye cannot do the things that ye would.* Galatians 5:16-17

The meaning behind these words is an exhortation to understand that the child of God has the nature of God within him or her, embodied in the Person of the Holy Spirit. The Holy Spirit will communicate to your spirit those things that you should do that will please your heavenly Father. While this operation is taking place, your body will, at times, want to react in the opposite way, because your body is still in need of consecration. When you learn to live you life in a continual process of fellowship with the Lord, then you will not be so inclined to fulfill the carnal desires of your unsaved body. A part of the process Paul referred to as *"walking in the Spirit"* is not only fellowshipping with the Lord, but also surrounding yourself with the kind of people who will build you up and not tear you down.

Your relationships say a great deal about you, and who you choose to connect yourself with can either help propel you to reaching your divine destination or plunge you into the abyss of failure and destruction. The Bible admonishes us along these lines with this sound advice:

Be not deceived: evil communications corrupt good manners.

1 Corinthians 15:33

This concise verse affirms to us the great truth that our associations can corrupt our thinking and cause us to behave in ways that will lead to our ruin.

This brings me back to the words of the minister and his advice to the men in his congregation. What this pastor was saying to his male parishioners was this: there are seeds of greatness that God has placed within the hearts of every man. This is what he meant when he said there was a king inside of them. Within them was the potential to be a dynamic man of faith and destiny.

When speaking about the aspect of the fool, the interpretation of the saying is directly related to the verse I quoted from the book of Galatians, when Paul spoke about the flesh warring against the human spirit. Within the man also dwells the potential to be a male who is weak and has no self-control over his life or his purpose. If he walks through his existence only satisfying his basest instincts, he is always falling short of achieving the high quality of life that God intended for him to have. This pattern can become so prevalent that he could end up destroying himself as a result of his foolish choices.

Between these two dynamics of potential for both good and evil is a woman who has the ability to bring out the best in a man or the very worst in him. The question you need to ask yourself is: which woman are you?

If you hope to meet and marry a man of great potential and a strong sense of purpose, you first have to ask yourself: are you the kind of woman who is capable of helping to bring out that potential within him? Or, are you the type of woman who always seems to bring out the foolish aspect in a man? Are you a woman who pursues married men and influences them to leave their wives and their children, thus making the disastrous choice of breaking up their home? Are you the type of woman who prides herself on being able to incite thoughts of lust in a man, so that he behaves so irrationally and unwisely that he throws his future away by attaching himself to you? Or, to put it in a more direct fashion, are you the type of woman who could help groom a man and prepare him for the White House? Or are you simply the party girl who, while being fun and a good time, is ultimately someone who would cause a man to lose his status and position because he is so caught up having a good time with you?

Genesis records the account of Abraham sending one of his servants to find a wife for his son Isaac. Abraham gave the man very detailed instructions with regard to where he should go to find the right woman, and where he should not go to find her. What is even more interesting is that while the servant was yet on his journey, he prayed and asked God to lead him to the woman who was appointed, or, we might say, chosen by God for Isaac. This man understood that Isaac was destined to carry forth the promise that God had given to his father Abraham. In order to fulfill his destiny, Isaac needed the right woman, one who could help him achieve all that God had intended. Therefore, I propose the question to you again: are you a woman who can bring out the best in the man in your life? Or are you good for bodily pleasure but corrupt in spirit, so that you have the potential to corrupt and abort the plan of God for your own life and also for the life of your man?

It all goes back to the power of influence and deciding that you are going to be an agent of positive influence or of negative influence. Are you a vessel that can pour life into a man? Or are you a hunter seeking to destroy a precious life, because you are influenced by the god of this world who seeks to corrupt and destroy all of humanity?

I want to return once more to the passage in Proverbs which has been my foundational text in examining the personality type of the strange woman. In the previous chapter, we examined how she went about getting what she wanted. Now I want to focus on the final result, what happens to a man who connects himself with this type of woman. The young man Solomon described in the passage was so enticed by this woman's words, her body language and her unabashed forwardness, that he gave in to her charms. One of the great blessings in studying the Word of God is that the Lord gives us the full picture and shows us the consequences of wrong choices. Therefore, Solomon did not end his narrative with the yielding of the temptation. He went on to describe what happened as a result of the yielding:

> *With her much fair speech she caused him to yield, with the flattering of her lips she forced him. He goeth after her straightway, as an ox goeth to the slaughter, or as a fool to the correction of the stocks; till a dart strike through his liver; as a bird hasteth to the snare, and knoweth not that it is for his life.*
> *Hearten unto me now therefore, O ye children, and attend to the words of my mouth. Let not thine heart decline to her ways, go not astray in her paths. For she hath cast down many wounded: yea, many strong men have been slain by her. Her house is the way to hell, going down to the chambers of death.*
>
> Proverbs 7:21-27

In this way, the greatest of all tragedies unfolds right before our very eyes. A life that is just beginning to step into the flower of manhood is destroyed by lust and a desire to attain something that he never should have had in the first place. For our learning, the Bible expounds further regarding the force that operates in this woman's life, the force that makes her so dangerous. We are told in no uncertain terms that this woman should be avoided at all costs because she has brought down many others. The Scriptures tell us that even some of the strongest of men have been seduced by her powers.

That kind of power is not natural; it is spiritual. There are many beautiful women in the world today, just as there were back in biblical days, and not every attractive woman has this type of sway over men Also, because beauty is so often in the eye of the beholder, no one can define with certainty what type of woman is attractive. That is based on the preference of the individual admirer.

What is being revealed to us is the fact that, because this type of woman is influenced by the unclean spirit, which promotes sexual immorality and acts of perversion, that spirit is very enticing to men and is not something that is easily resisted.

Consider the statement once again that many strong men had been slain by her. Strength can be measured in a variety of ways. A man can be strong physically, intellectually, materially, or spiritually. What makes the unclean spirit so destructive is that it can pierce beyond that strength and appeal to a man's bodily desires, thereby weakening him and causing him to cast aside all logic and reason and pursue this woman without being mindful of the consequences.

How many times in history has the story been told of some famous man—whether he was a preacher, a politician, an athlete, or some promising young student—throwing away everything for an indiscretion with a woman? No matter how often it happens, people always wonder: how is it that a man who is so gifted and wise in so many other areas can behave so foolishly when it comes to the women he involves himself with? Some might even look at the woman and say to themselves, "She is not attractive to me." The issue is not whether or not the person is attractive; the issue is what is she offering that made the man disregard his better judgement and enter into a relationship with her? Whether the man was married and had an affair or was single but gave himself over to fornication, the end result of the sordid connection was a loss in some area. This is all the result of the unclean spirit, which is also a seducing spirit that seeks to appeal to the flesh and promises all manner of enjoyment.

Once sin has finished its course, the consequences are more bitter than a man could ever have imagined. That spirit has sought (and, too often, succeeded) to wipe out his strongest points. Whether the strength was financial, physical, or spiritual, once the spirit finished with the man, his strength was gone. And not only would there be loss; that dishonor would remain with the man and become a permanent part of his legacy. All we have to do is read about famous world leaders who became embroiled in sexual scandals. No matter how much they apologized and sought restitution by doing good things with their remaining days, history has always held that as a major chapter in their life story. Because the devil caught them, he was still flaunting that victory.

Today, we come to a perfect understanding of these matters, and you must decide if you will be the woman who seeks to hunt and destroy a precious life, or will you be the woman who has the power to speak life and help someone achieve their highest potential in the areas that God has called them to? If you want some great man to come into your life, you must first allow God to make you into the great woman that can help that man achieve his greatness. Otherwise, you will be the woman who, while being able to offer physical pleasure, ultimately contributes to his downfall because you do not help him keep his eyes on Jesus. If your heart is not toward the Lord, this may well be the result.

God has given you, as a woman, such an awesome ability to influence a man and help him go forward in the plan of God. You must not allow Satan to distort that power and use it to make you the kind of woman who destroys a man's call and destiny. One of the sobering examples of this truth is found in the account of the lives of Samson and Delilah.

The name Samson has echoed out of the mystic chords of historical memory and has become synonymous with strength and physical prowess. Even for those who may have never picked up a copy of the Holy Bible, this name and the fame of the man who bore it have become a part of humanity's collective consciousness. Samson was truly an extraordinary man, and yet for all of his greatness, his story is always fatefully linked with the woman, Delilah. No matter what Samson accomplished and in spite of all his miraculous achievements, when a person hears his name, the next name that follows is Delilah. This was never intended to be the case, but as so often happens with humanity, we fall short of the glory of the Most High. For those of us who are alive now and have the Scriptures recorded for our learning, we need to examine the Word and learn from the mistakes of those who went before us, so that we do not repeat them in our generation.

Often, when we endeavor to understand the downfall of a person, it is helpful to trace their path by starting at the beginning. The origins of a person and the foundational elements of their life are enlightening when we seek to grasp the full picture as to why certain people succeeded and why others failed. We are very fortunate in terms of studying the life of Samson because the Bible tells us a great deal about his background and also reveals certain things relating to his character. The fact that God made sure these points of information were recorded tells us that everything written is of value for our learning. I want to shine the light on certain main points of Samson's life in order to show how the appetites of this man led to his ruin. I also want to use the Scriptures to see how Delilah was used by the enemies of Samson to manipulate his sexual appetites for the purpose of taking away his source of strength and making a mockery of a once-great man. All of this is for the ultimate goal of helping you to decide what kind of woman you wish to be. Will you use your power and influence as a catalyst for good or as a weapon of destruction? The choice is entirely up to you.

The story of Samson and Delilah is found in the book of the Bible known as Judges. This book is a record of the times in which the Israelites were led by certain men whom God raised up to protect His people from their enemies, and to counsel them as to how they should live their lives. These individuals were known as judges, hence the title of the book. The pattern of the history of the time would unfold in this fashion: the people of Israel would turn away from the Lord and worship idols. As a result of their sin, God would allow a foreign power to invade and subdue them, forcing them to turn back to Him and seek Him for deliverance. In the process of time, God would raise up a new judge to deliver them and help put them back on the right spiritual course. The record of Samson opens with this same pattern. God was preparing to raise up Samson to deliver His people from bondage.

The circumstances of Samson's birth are rather supernatural, because his life was meant to be supernatural. His story began in this way:

> *And the children of Israel did evil in the sight of the Lord; and the Lord delivered them into the hand of the Philistines forty years. And there was a certain man of Zorah, of the family of the Danites, whose name was Manoah; and his wife was barren, and bare not. And the angel of the Lord appeared unto the woman, and said unto her, Behold now, thou art barren, and bearest not: but thou shalt conceive, and bear a son.*
>
> *Now therefore beware, I pray thee, and drink not wine nor any strong drink; and eat not any unclean thing: for, lo, thou shalt conceive, and bear a son; and no razor shall come on his head: for the child shall be a Nazarite unto God from the womb: and he shall begin to deliver Israel out of the hand of the Philistines.* Judges 13:1-5

In these few verses, we are given a great picture of the sovereignty of God at work in a person's life. This woman, the wife of Manoah, was visited by the angel of the Lord and told that, not only would she have a child, but that the child would be a male. This male child would grow to be a mighty deliverer on behalf of his people. Because of the extraordinary call upon this child's life, the mother was instructed that the child would be a Nazarite all the days of his life. The Nazarites were a special group of individuals who were set apart by God for fulfilling divine purposes. As a consequence of the mandate upon their lives, Nazarite were instructed to abstain from certain things as a sign of their consecration to God. This level of consecration enabled them to be empowered by the Holy Ghost to do extraordinary things.

The mark of consecration was so strong that even Samson's mother was restricted from partaking of certain things during the period of her pregnancy. All of this was to show us that Samson was a man of purpose and destiny who had a great call to fulfill in his life. He was a man anointed by the power of the Holy Spirit, to achieve great victories for God.

This is something that one must understand regarding the anointing. When this term was used in the Scriptures relating to a person, it meant that the person was empowered by the Holy Spirit to be able to complete the assignment given to them. Often the anointing was connected with something outward, as a mark of that person's covenant with the Lord. In the case of Samson, his anointing was connected with his hair. His parents were instructed not to allow any razor to touch his head. As a result of the mighty anointing upon Samson's life, he was endowed with supernatural strength. One example of this power is given to us in the following verses:

> *And when he came unto Lehi, the Philistines shouted against him: and the Spirit of the Lord came mightily upon him, and the chords that were upon his arms became as flax that was burnt with fire, and his bands loosed from off his hands. And he found a new jawbone of an ass, and put forth his hand, and took it, and slew a thousand men therewith. And Samson said, With the jawbone of an ass, heaps upon heaps, with the jaw of an ass have I slain a thousand men. And it came to pass, when he had made an end of speaking, that he cast away the jawbone out of his hand, and called that place Ramathlehi.* Judges 15:14-17

This supernatural endowment of strength caused Samson to be able to subdue the Philistines, who, at the time, were the nation that sought to oppress the Israelites. But for all of Samson's great power and ability, he was a man with an Achilles heel. This weakness proved to be fatal and, ultimately, led to his brokenness and humiliation before his enemies. Like Solomon who came after him (and so many other men), he was attracted to strange women. Even though Samson was born to deliver God's people from the grip of the enemies known as the Philistines, this did not stop him from lusting after their women. The Bible makes this point clear to us:

> *And Samson went down to Timnath, and saw a woman of Timnath of the daughters of the Philistines. And he came up, and told his father and mother, and said, I have seen a woman in Timnath of the daughters of the Philistines: now therefore get her for me to wife. Then his father and his mother said unto him, Is there never a woman among the daughters of thy brethren, or among all my people, that thou goest to take a wife of the uncircumcised Philistines? And Samson said unto his father, Get her for me; for she pleaseth me well.*
>
> Judges 14:1-3

In another passage of scripture, we are told:

> *Then went Samson to Gaza, and saw there an harlot, and went in unto her.*
>
> Judges 16:1

In the first passage I referenced, we see the initial character flaw in this man's life. He had been chosen by God to live a consecrated life, one of purity and integrity, and that level of purity was to give him great strength. This was for the purpose of being able to fulfill his divine destiny with longevity and honor. As a man of God and a judge over Israel, Samson was expected to marry a woman who worshiped the God he served and to live a righteous life. Sadly, he did not want that type of woman. His personal tastes gravitated toward women who were not holy and pure in their daily lives, and that is who the strange woman is. She is loose in her morals, loose in the way she dresses, vulgar in speech, and easily willing to give her body to a man for sexual pleasure. In spite of the great anointing upon Samson's life, he only wanted loose women.

Samson's parents tried to admonish him to marry a woman who was of the household of faith and worshiped the true and living God, but Samson was determined to marry the loose woman who pleased his body. Therefore, he did not heed the words of his parents when they tried to counsel him against this action. They understood that the strange woman was motivated and inspired by the demonic forces that govern this world system, and that she would cause him to take his eyes off of the things of God. But Samson, in his desire to have his way, insisted, and he married the woman.

In the process of time, Samson was given another chance to make a wiser choice regarding the kind of woman he chose to be in a relationship with. Sadly, instead of rising up, he now sunk even lower into depravity and joined himself to a prostitute. This continued his pattern of lusting after and pursuing unsaved women, whom the Old Testament refers to as "the strange woman."

As so often is the case with men in power who behave inappropriately, Samson believed that he could continue with his behavior and still maintain the power of God that was upon his life. But, as I read in a medieval novel, "Sin will always pluck out sin," and the day will come when a penance must be enacted to pay the wages of the sinful life. Samson came to just such a moment when he met the woman called Delilah. After all the games he had played with evil (flirting with disaster and coming so close to the edge and yet, by God's grace, never falling off the precipice), the day came when he finally met his match. Delilah was a woman of such cunning and deception that her powers of seduction were channeled wholly and completely into bringing Samson down. For all of his mighty strength and incredible anointing, he could not resist the charms of this woman. This point is of such great importance in understanding the spirit world and how it affects the natural world in which we can see and perceive with our physical senses.

Delilah's ability to ensnare this man was not simply because she was beautiful. If that were the case, then no man would be able to resist the charms of any woman he found physically attractive. No, her power came from the fact that she was a woman who was part of a nation that served a demonic spirit. As a result of her association with and practice of worshiping demon powers, those powers bequeathed to her the ability to present an appealing facade, capitalizing on her beauty and using it to ensnare Samson. She had such power in her words, in her femininity, and in her ability to excite Samson to lustful passions that he was willing to give her what she wanted.

This phenomenon is often seen in celebrities or people of a certain notoriety in popular society. There is something about them that draws others to them, almost like a magnet, so much so that those who feel this pull toward the famous person do not fully understand what is happening. Why do certain rock stars have female fans who are willing to give their bodies over to these personalities in any way possible just to be with them? How can certain female entertainers stand on a stage and move their bodies in such a fashion that male admirers become consumed with passion, almost as if they were intoxicated with desire? Some define this type of fan adulation as being "charismatic," or they say the person has a "winning personality." But there is a much deeper component to this, and it is spiritual in nature. Just as Samson was gifted by the power of the Holy Spirit to perform mighty acts of physicality and had the presence and stature to lead a nation, so, too, was Delilah empowered by a force that made her seem so totally appealing to Samson.

Yes, this is charisma, but in the most ancient meaning of the term. The ancients defined *charisma* as "a gift that draws people to you in a supernatural way." On the side of righteousness, which is motivated by God, charisma is a gift that helps a person draw people in fulfilling a just cause. On the negative side of the equation, however, charisma is a gift perverted by the devil that draws people into committing acts of immorality and indecency.

This appeal is, more often than not, sexual in nature because it pulls one into lust and emotions that stir a lack of self-control. This is why entertainers have groupies who will do anything to sleep with them, because the spirit attached with that entertainer draws the masses in. This is why politicians and certain world leaders have legions of fans who are swept up, sometimes in lust, willing to do anything to follow that person. And this is how Delilah was able to ensnare the mighty man of God, Samson. Oh, that he had heeded the warning of his parents. The leaders of the Philistine nation understood this demonic influence, and, therefore, sought to enlist Delilah and use her to trap their enemy.

Before I proceed further, I want the Bible to speak for itself, so that you can grasp the full context of the message I am sharing with you:

> *And it came to pass afterward, that he loved a woman in the valley of Sorek, whose name was Delilah. And the lords of the Philistines came up unto her, and said unto her, Entice him, and see wherein his great strength lieth, and by what means we may prevail against him, that we may bind him, to afflict him; and we will give thee every one of us eleven hundred pieces of silver.*

And Delilah said to Samson, Tell me, I pray thee, wherein thy great strength lieth, and wherewith thou mightiest be bound to afflict thee.

And Samson said unto her, If they bind me with seven green withs that were never dried, then shall I be weak, and be as another man.

Then the lords of the Philistines brought up to her seven green withs which had not been dried, and she bound him with them. Now there were men lying in wait, abiding with her in the chamber. And she said unto him, The Philistines be upon thee, Samson. And he brake the withs, as a thread of tow is broken when it toucheth the fire. So his strength was not known.

And Delilah said unto Samson, Behold, thou hast mocked me, and told me lies: now tell me, I pray thee, wherewith thou mightest be bound.

And he said unto her, If they bind me fast with new ropes that never were occupied, then shall I be weak, and be as another man.

Delilah therefore took new ropes, and bound him therewith, and said unto him, The Philistines be upon thee, Samson. And there were liers in wait abiding in the chamber. And he brake them from off his arms like a thread.

And Delilah said unto Samson, Hitherto thou hast mocked me, and told me lies: tell me wherewith thou mightest be bound. And he said unto her, If thou weavest the seven locks of my head with the web.

And she fastened it with the pin, and said unto him, The Philistines be upon thee, Samson. And he awaked out of his sleep, and went away with the pin of the beam, and with the web.

And she said unto him, How canst thou say, I love thee, when thine heart is not with me? thou hast mocked me these three times, and hast not told me wherein thy great strength lieth. And it came to pass, when she pressed him daily with her words, and urged him, so that his soul was vexed unto death; that he told her all his heart, and said unto her, There hath not come a razor upon mine head; for I have been a Nazarite unto God from my mother's womb: if I be shaven, then my strength will go from me, and I shall become weak, and be like any other man.

And when Delilah saw that he had told her all his heart, she sent and called for the lords of the Philistines, saying, Come up this once, for he hath shewed me all his heart. Then the lords of the Philistines came upon her, and brought money in their hand. And she made him sleep upon her knees; and she called for a man, and she caused him to shave off the seven locks of his head; and

> *she began to afflict him, and his strength went from him. And she said, The Philistines be upon thee, Samson. And he awoke out of his sleep, and said, I will go out as at other times before, and shake myself. And he wist not that the* LORD *was departed from him.* Judges 16:4-20

It is a very dangerous thing to play with sin. To think that you can dance with the devil by the pale moonlight and then sashay into the presence of the Almighty is a fool's game and one that has no winners, only losers. The Bible tells us that Samson saw this woman and was so overcome with desire that he immediately fell in love with her. However, because she was a member of a group of people who were the enemies of God's people, that made her Samson's enemy. He clearly did not realize it at the time, but she was, indeed, his enemy. She did not worship the God he served, and because of her loyalty to her god and her fellow countrymen who also followed that god, she joined in a conspiracy to destroy Samson's life.

Those who were in charge of doing away with Samson had consistently failed in all of their previous attempts, but they didn't give up. Now, they realized that they had found his weak spot, and that weak spot was his affinity for this loose woman, Delilah. She was the perfect bait to catch the wanted prey. When the agreement was reached with these conspirators, the game was set. Together they would destroy this man and bring disgrace to the work of God.

It is fascinating to see just how much detail is given in this story. We can account for these lengthy details by understanding that they have been placed there for our learning. Delilah understood that to get to the man, she first had to take away his strength. This is one of the marks of the strange woman, and the spirit which seeks to work through her. Many men throughout history have been lured into a false sense of security by their lust for a woman. Sometimes they lost their families as a result of such associations. At other times, it might have been their careers. But, whatever the loss was, it was the source of their strength. Then, once their strength was gone—whether family, profession, or anointing—they were brought low and became like any other man, without purpose or destiny.

This is what the unclean spirit seeks to get at, the source of strength that saturates a man with the ability to accomplish great things. Because the devil knows that men are so swayed by sexual stimuli, he uses that unclean seducing spirit to influence the woman to bring the man down.

When Delilah began to ask Samson about the source of his strength, he toyed with her, giving her several untruthful answers. Each time, she took the bait and did what he said, and each time the Philistines came to attack him, but he just shook them off and went on his way. The most tragic part in all of this is that Samson should have realized, after these several attempts, that this woman cared nothing for him. She only craved power and money. Why didn't he realize it until it was too late? Such is the stronghold of lust. Many men get caught up with a woman when logic and reason present clear evidence that she is not there to help them. Because the woman has the ability to bring out the fool in that man, he continues to follow his baser instincts and proceeds with his poor choices.

Consider it from this perspective: why do certain men frequent strip clubs and restaurants that feature scantily clad women, throwing their money away on females who care nothing for them? It is because the spirit at work in that woman is drawing these men into a web, and the plan is to consume and destroy their soul, along with the women's.

After all of Samson's lies and manipulation, Delilah grew impatient and wanted to get to the heart of the matter. The Bible says that she began to question him so vociferously about his secret that he became tormented in his mind. In time, his vexation grew to the boiling point. Still, because his body was being satisfied by the physical pleasure of Delilah's company, he did not regard the condition of his tormented soul. He refused to see that, as good as this woman was to him physically, she was poison to his destiny. She was now hunting for the precious source of life that sustained him. When Samson finally relented and communicated with her everything about him that was worth knowing, she somehow knew it. She realized that he had finally told her all that was in his heart and that she had him right where she wanted him.

All of the *femme fatales* of modern cinema or the video vixens of the music industry could not compete with the combination of sensuality and deviousness this woman displayed in her next act. We are told in the text that Delilah caused Samson to fall asleep in her lap. Once again, she was using her body as a tool of evil. While Samson lay in his bed of sensual roses, Delilah called for a man to come and cut his hair—the point of contact by which God anointed him with supernatural strength. After this deed was done, to make sure that Samson had not told her another lie, Delilah began to subtly attack his body. To her great delight, she discovered weaknesses she had not seen before, and she knew that the champion was now just an ordinary man.

Even when all of this had taken place, Samson was still unaware of the state he had placed himself in. Just as before, Delilah sounded the alarm, saying that his enemies had come to destroy him. Just as before, Samson woke up and shook himself, ready to go forth into battle. He was supremely confident that he could do what he had always done, shaking off the wine of desire and sobering himself enough to meet and defeat his foes. But, unlike before, to his shock and horror (and his great shame), he suddenly realized that he was no longer the mighty man of power he had been. He had joined the sad ranks of men who throughout history had been brought down by the seductive charms of the strange woman.

Once Samson had his great strength stripped from him, the sun began to set on what had been a life of great achievement. Next, we read these sad words:

> *But the Philistines took him, and put out his eyes, and brought him down to Gaza, and bound him with fetters of brass; and he did grind in the prison house. Then the lords of the Philistines gathered them together for to offer a great sacrifice unto Dagon their god, and to rejoice: for they said, Our god hath delivered Samson our enemy into our hand. And when the people saw him, they praised their god: for they said, Our god hath delivered into our hands our enemy, and the destroyer of our country, which slew many of us. And it came to pass, when their hearts were merry, that they said, Call for Samson, that he may make us sport. And they called for Samson out of the prison house; and he made them sport: and they set him between the pillars.* Judges 16:21 and 23-25

Here was a man who, at one time in his life, could kill a thousand men with nothing more than a bone and his own strength, but now he found himself blinded and forced to perform for his enemies as if he were some sideshow attraction.

By the mercy and the providence of God, Samson was able to redeem himself and cause a final blow to the enemies of his people, but the way in which his life unfolded was not the best that God wanted him to have. Samson paid a great price for his final triumph, and the price he paid could have been avoided had he taken heed to his parents' warning by refusing to join himself to a strange women.

The Word declares that the adulterous woman will hunt for the precious life, and, by wiping out a man's vision—the source of his strength for the future—will bring him low. The question that you need to decide for yourself is this: what type of woman will you choose to be? Will you be a woman who allows her God-given ability of influence others, to bring out the best in them? Or will you be a woman Satan uses to bring out the darker aspects of those around you? Are you hoping to meet a man who will fulfill all your dreams and desires of meaningful and passionate companionship? Then, you must ensure that you have within you the qualities that can help bring out the God-implanted potential in that man rather than simply being, for him, an object of physical enjoyment while bringing him spiritual damnation. Do you desire to advance further in your goals for your career, your vision, and your future? If that is the case, you must allow the Lord to perfect you and lead you on the path He has called you to tread. Only then can you become a vessel of honor fit for the Master's use.

The young man in the book of Proverbs was instructed not to even go near the house of a strange woman. Why? Because the pull to surrender to her enticing presence would lead him on the path to destruction. Do not allow yourself to be this type of woman. Allow God to save you and shine His marvelous light upon your countenance. As you surrender yourself to this process, you will begin to come into an expansion of your consciousness that will take you into a greater plane of self-discovery, walking with the One Who truly does make all things new.

Part Two

The Silly Woman

Chapter 7

The Parable of the Ten Virgins

All things being equal, if a human being is living life as they should, then that life should always be characterized by progression. We progress from childhood into adulthood. We attend school and progress from one level to a higher grade level, until we are able to receive a diploma of completion. A person starts out their adult life single, and then, in the process of time, progresses into marriage and, ultimately, into raising a family. As the cycle of time continues, the children that this person raises grow into their adulthood, becoming parents themselves, and then the original parent progresses into the role of grandparent.

All of life is about progressing, going from one stage to another, hopefully learning something along the way, and refusing to grow despondent during those stages of life that pose challenges and trials that demand of us to stretch ourselves and be an overcomer. In the midst of changes and transitions, we must constantly be vigilant not to grow complacent or take on the mindset that would keep us in a certain stage, when we are being urged to go on to a higher way of thinking and living. If we grow complacent in a stage in which we are called to go deeper, we will never fully come to the place of living the abundant life of purpose and destiny God intended for each of us to have.

This principal is, most importantly, connected with our spiritual life and soul development, as it relates to our relationship with God and becoming the individual He has preordained us to be. Becoming aware of the knowledge that Jesus Christ is the Savior and Lord and embracing that great truth by receiving Him into your life is only the first step to living on a plane of existence that will take you on a journey of continually progressing from one level of faith to another. If you were to become stagnant at a stage of spiritual babyhood in your relationship with Christ, not only would you fail to develop into spiritual maturity as you should, but you might also open the door for Satan to cause you to miss divine opportunities that God has arranged for you. Such opportunities will help you to see all of your dreams and desires come to pass. Refusing to develop to Christian maturity will also cause you to take steps that will ensnare you into living your life in the same manner as you did before you came to a saving knowledge of Jesus Christ. Most importantly, a life of spiritual complacency could cost you to ultimately travel down a road that could even cost you your eternal soul. Then you would be found in a place of everlasting torment, without hope, without peace and without God.

These are the issues that I will be addressing in this section of the book, as I construct a spiritual and psychological profile of the second type of woman the Bible speaks of—the Silly Woman. This is the woman who has taken the first step into greatness by accepting Jesus as her personal Lord and Savior, thus progressing from a life of spiritual darkness into a life of spiritual enlightenment. However, this woman who, even though she has taken the first step, does not continue growing in the knowledge of conforming herself to be in alignment with the character of Jesus. Whether this is due to a lack of knowledge regarding how to grow spiritually or a refusal to do so, this woman lives her life with only a form of godliness; she is not walking in the power of the resurrected life Jesus has made provision for her to have.

Because of this state of complacency and stagnation, the silly woman lives in a carnal way, with her life being dominated primarily by the corruption of this world's system. Although she is not the strange woman, who does not know Jesus as Lord and Savior, she lives like the strange woman in most respects, the only difference being that one is uninformed about Christianity, while the other only wears her faith like some name tag that is easy to put on and take off. The silly woman is the Christian female who lives in the same mindset as the strange woman. Even though she has been made a new creation in Christ Jesus, she has not allowed the Lord to renew her mind to think in the way that conforms to the principles of the Kingdom of Heaven.

This lack of complete spiritual awareness causes this type of woman to behave in ways that are very similar to that of the strange woman. As this pattern continues in her life, it causes her to miss her divine appointments and initiates within her a desire to live in the same way as the strange woman, and if she does not work at perfecting her spiritual life with a reverential and earnest state of mind, it will ultimately take her down the path of losing her salvation. The Bible speaks very emphatically about men and women being in the middle of the road as it relates to living a godly lifestyle, and such a passive posturing is strongly prohibited by God. In the very last book of the Bible, the Lord Jesus spoke through His beloved disciple John and giving him a message to one of the churches that existed at the time. The words of that message echo down through the ages:

> *I know thy works, that thou art neither cold nor hot: I would thou wert cold or hot. So then because thou art lukewarm, and neither cold nor hot, I will spue thee out of my mouth.* Revelation 3:15-16

This is the overriding characteristic of the silly woman, a person who is indifferent to her spiritual condition and is passive in developing her personal relationship with the Master. Jesus made it clear that such a person has no place within the divine plan. It is not that God is seeking to show malcontent to this type of individual, but that their own carnality hinders them from perceiving people and situations as God would have them to. As a result of this, they are hindered from moving and cooperating with the Holy Spirit, as He seeks to lead them and guide them into all truth.

The cry from the heart of God is that you become all that He has called you to be. Otherwise you will fall short of achieving His high call in your life, and this can come with a price you are not ready to pay. It is my hope that, as you read these next chapters, you will come to an understanding that allowing Jesus to come into the door of your heart is only the first step in reaching wholeness of spirit, soul, and body. After Jesus enters into your life, you must allow Him to make of it what He wants it to be. Anything contrary to that is a waste of time and eternity. With that as the fountainhead of our quest for enlightenment, let us now open further the treasure that is the full counsel of the wisdom and revelation knowledge of the Almighty.

I want to begin the study of the silly woman by looking first at the words of Jesus Christ Himself. He was (and is) the Master Teacher and the greatest

Expositor of the Word of God that history has ever known. When He came into this world and walked as a man anointed by the power of the Holy Spirit, He preached a message of a new and glorious Kingdom that would be the hope of all the world and a joy that would enlighten the universe. This Kingdom would be the restoration of the order and the harmony that once existed between humanity and God before the Fall in the Garden of Eden, and this utopia would also bring about the fulfillment of all the wondrous promises God had in store for those who were hungry and thirsty for His glory.

As Jesus proclaimed this great message of the coming Kingdom age, He also taught the people of His day about the way in which they were to live their life on this side of eternity, in preparation for the other side. In His teachings, He explained that the life we now live is a rehearsal for that which is to come in the ages yet unknown to us. How we live today will affect where we spend tomorrow's eternity and what role we will play in that future.

To help His followers prepare for the world to come, Jesus spoke to them in the form of parables, using stories as comparisons to show how the inner workings of the Kingdom of God function. Of all of the parables Jesus spoke, perhaps His most comprehensive and most fascinating is the Parable of the Ten Virgins. In this particular parable, Jesus gave a full panoramic description of the Christian experience in this world, in preparation for the world to come. He set about this by painting a portrait of two distinctive categories of women and, based on the way in which the story of each type unfolds, allows us to see how God views His people. Also, as a result of this parable, we gain revelation as to how one lives their life and seeks to grow in their Christian walk or, to the contrary, chooses not to grow, and how this affects the manner and the quality of their eternal destiny.

Before I proceed further in the explanation and address how it directly ties into the understanding of the silly woman, I want Jesus to speak for Himself, as we read His words that have been preserved for our benefit. As we sit at the feet of the Master, He invites us into His thoughts, and He says to each of us these words:

> *Then shall the kingdom of heaven be likened unto ten virgins, which took their lamps, and went forth to meet the bridegroom. And five of them were wise, and five were foolish. They that were foolish took their lamps, and took no oil*

with them. But the wise took oil in their vessel with their lamps. While the bridegroom tarried, they all slumbered and slept.
And at midnight there was a cry made, Behold, the bridegroom cometh; go ye out to meet him.
Then all those virgins arose, and trimmed their lamps. And the foolish said unto the wise, Give us of your oil; for our lamps our gone out.
But the wise answered, saying, Not so; lest there be not enough for us and you: but go ye rather to them that sell, and buy for yourselves.
And while they went to buy, the bridegroom came; and they that were ready went in with him to the marriage: and the door was shut.
Afterward came also the other virgins, saying, Lord, Lord, open to us.
But he answered and said, Verily, I say unto you, I know you not.
Watch therefore, for ye know neither the day nor the hour wherein the Son of man cometh. Matthew 25:1-13

This is a portrait of how things will be in the last days, before the second coming of the Lord Jesus. The parable gives us insight into the condition of the Church of the Lord Jesus and how some will be ready for His appearing, while others will not. While this teaching highlights those things that are yet to be, it still manages to shine a light on the present and speak to the here and now regarding the spiritual state of the Body of Christ. The fact that this life we now live is merely preparation for the age to come shows us that the parable not only applies to the future, but also directly addresses that which is present. To understand the players in this drama and what each person and object Jesus described symbolizes is to see yourself and identify where you are in your personal development with the Lord. Let us now permit the Holy Spirit to enlighten our understanding as we look at this passage with fresh eyes, to see what the Spirit would say to the churches.

Jesus started this teaching by mentioning how the Kingdom of Heaven (which represents the Body of Christ both in the present and the future just before His coming) can be compared to ten virgins. The fact that Jesus used women is there to serve a dual purpose. The first reason for this usage is that Jesus was showing the value and the important role that women have in His Kingdom. Even though He walked the earth as a man, He was speaking under the inspiration of the Holy Ghost, and God knew that throughout history, women would be considered to be inferior and of little importance by many of the male gender. Jesus was using this illustration to help set women free, so that they could see that in the eyes of God males and females are of equal importance and that there is no inequality with Him. Second, Jesus was using virgins in this text because throughout the entirety of the Word of God, the Bible has compared God's relationship with His Church to that of a bridegroom and his bride. This is to symbolize that the collective Church that exists all over the world will one day join the Lord Jesus in a spiritual union that will bring about divine perfection and perfect order for all of creation.

I chose to use this parable as a pretext for my analysis because, since I am addressing the woman question from a biblical world view, this story is useful for that purpose as it is speaking about women. Even though the virgins represent the entire Body of Christ in a larger sense, I am breaking down the deeper facet of the diamond of revelation in order to emphasize the point the Lord would have me to get across to you.

In my analysis of the text, I want to focus once more on the phrase, *"the Kingdom of Heaven."* As I stated previously, the Kingdom that Jesus is referring to is the entire Body of Christ, which consists of the Church of the living God. I emphasize this point once again because, as we shall see, as we continue to dissect the text, each person and object in this parable is a representation of someone or something that speaks of a spiritual principle that we need to draw upon. Bearing that in mind, Jesus was presenting a message about His people, those we call, in our modern society, Christians. The Kingdom of Heaven is that spiritual institution that is made up of people who have accepted Jesus Christ as their Lord and Savior and have submitted to His authority as the King of Kings. We know this to be true because the apostle Paul corroborated this interpretation of the Kingdom of Heaven, when he wrote these words that have been preserved for us:

> *For the kingdom of God is not meat and drink; but righteousness, peace, and joy in the Holy Ghost.* Romans 14:17

Here Paul was stating that the Kingdom of God, which is simply another name for the Kingdom of Heaven, is not made up of natural objects, but rather spiritual principles that have been give by the Holy Ghost. These truths were bequeathed to those who call upon the name of the Lord. So, for all intents and purposes, we can surmise that Jesus was speaking about Christians.

Another fact that attests to this point is the method by which Jesus made His comparison. He stated that within this Kingdom there were virgins who were going forth to meet their bridegroom. Throughout the Bible, the Holy Spirit has compared the relationship of Jesus and His Church to that of a husband and wife, or as bride and her bridegroom. This is to symbolize the unity that exist between Jesus and the Church and that we are to be united with Him in a relationship of divine harmony. This spiritual union will be manifested in its ultimate perfection after the Second Coming of Christ. Until that day, we live in constant preparation for His glorious coming, and everything that God does for us is to ultimately prepare us for that blessed event.

We understand that the virgins in this story symbolize Christians, more specifically, Christian women. This point is not stated to exclude men from the ultimate application of the text, but because I am dealing specifically with women, I will make that specific application.

The Bridegroom in the story is Jesus speaking directly about Himself. And, as the final piece of the equation found in this verse, we have the lamps that each virgin possessed. These lamps symbolize the Word of God. Another name for it would be the Bible. I make this statement because, in the Old Testament, the Word of God is compared to a lamp:

Thy word is a lamp unto my feet, and a light unto my path. Psalm 119:105

Because the Word of God contains all the wisdom one needs to live a victorious life, it is compared to a lamp, because it can shine the light of truth to help guide us in the midst of this dark and crooked world. So, from this one verse, Jesus has given us an amazing cast of characters that will each play their part in the drama that is about to unfold. In this *dramatis personae,* we have the Kingdom of Heaven, which is the institution of the Christian Church. Within this Kingdom, we have ten virgins who symbolize women who have been made saints of God through their acknowledgement of Jesus as their Savior. Hence, they are now Christians. On the other side is the Bridegroom, Who is a picture of the Lord Jesus Himself, the Lover of the souls of His people. And at the center, we have the lamps that each virgin holds that are symbolic representation of the Word of the Almighty God that is contained in His Holy Bible. Now that the stage has been set, the cast has been introduced, and the parts been made known, let the action of the drama unfold before your eyes and hear what the Spirit would say to His people.

These women are starting a journey; they have an appointment with the Bridegroom. All of life is a series of steps in preparing and keeping your divine appointments. At each stage of your life, God has prepared moments in which you will meet the right set of friends who will provide you with godly companionship that will strengthen and enhance your faith. God has also set up appointments for you to be in the place where you get the exact job you need, a job that will not only meet your financial obligations, but also bring you a sense of purpose and fulfillment, because you find yourself doing something you were born to do.

The Lord has set the specific moment in eternity when you are to be at the right location at the right time to meet the man of your dreams, who will love you and care for you, just as Christ loves and cares for His Church. In between these big appointments, there are also small appointments that God has for you to keep, and if you are there, it will save you time and energy and could even save your life. All of these divine appointments are stepping stones to help prepare you for the greatest Appointment, which will be when Jesus comes to this earth again to take His church with Him into Glory. Within the framework of this parable, the women going to meet their appointment with the Groom is the picture of your entire Christian experience, making sure that you are receptive enough to recognize when God has arranged a divine appointment for your life. The key to obtaining this level of awareness is found within the words of Jesus, as He provided more information concerning these virgins.

As Jesus constructed the narrative about these women, He told us that while all ten were virgins and each of them had an appointment with the Bridegroom, five of them were wise, and five of them were foolish. As a consequence of the condition of the foolish ones, they missed their appointment. But before I begin to explain the how and why of one group getting it right while the other got it so terribly wrong, I want to define the words *wise* and *foolish.* Often we hear things and define terms based upon our cultural world view or personal biases. While such practices are not sinful, they can be counterproductive. In order to truly receive all the knowledge that a biblical text has to offer, you must first know what the words mean and, more specifically, what they meant to the person who spoke them. Understanding this helps you to understand the text, and understanding the text causes you to receive the blessing that the text brings. In defining these terms, I would like to refer to *Vine's Complete Expository Dictionary of Old and New Testament Words.*[1] W.E. Vine was a Bible scholar of the first order, and his writings contain a storehouse of revelation. The word *wise* speaks of "wisdom," and, according to *Vine's*, the word *wisdom* comes from two Greek words, *sophia* and *phronesis. Sophia* refers to "spiritual wisdom," while *phronesis* deals with "understanding and prudence." For more clarification along these lines, I would like to quote *Vine's* directly: "While *sophia* is the insight into the true nature of things, *phronesis* is the ability to discern modes of action with a view to their results; while *sophia* is theoretical, *phronesis* is practical." [2]

In defining the word *foolish, Vine's* again gives much clarification to a word that is often thrown around without the true understanding of the nature of it. The original Greek word for *foolish* is *aphron*, and it means "one who is without reason." I want to use the complete definition given in the text, so I will once again quote *Vine's* directly: "*Foolish. Aphron* signifies 'without reason, want of mental sanity and sobriety, a reckless and inconsiderate habit of mind, or a lack of common sense perception of the reality of things natural and spiritual, or the imprudent ordering of one's life in regard to salvation.' " [3]

Based on these definitions, we can look at the text again and draw from it a greater clarity than we had through a casual reading. Jesus described ten women who were virgins, and their virginity symbolized the fact that they were all believers in the Lord; they were all Christians. This comparison can be made unequivocally due to the fact that when we come to Jesus and repent of our sins and acknowledge Him as Savior and Lord, we are cleansed from all unrighteousness and made pure by the blood of the Lamb of God. So, in a spiritual sense, we have been born again, hence we are untouched and undefiled by the things of this world, just as a virgin's body is untouched and undefiled because she has not engaged in sexual intercourse.

---

1. *Vine's Complete Expository Dictionary of Old and New Testament Words* (Nashville, TN: Thomas Nelson Publishers: 1996)
2. Vines, page 1233
3. Vines, page 443

However, even though each of these women was a Christian, I draw your attention to the point once more that there was a great distinction between them. Jesus said that five of them were wise, which, based upon the definitions provided for us by Vine's expository, meant that these women possessed a spiritual depth and perception that allowed them to see the true nature of a situation, whether it was in the spiritual dimension or the natural. As a result of this spiritual maturity, they also had the ability to discern right from wrong and to know what they needed to do in order to prepare themselves to receive all the blessings God had afforded.

In the context of the parable, the blessings of God are represented by the marriage supper, because the ultimate blessing that will come to every child of God will be to spend eternity in fellowship with Jesus. The spiritual maturity and understanding these women had was combined with practical insight on how to govern the affairs of their lives and how their lives should be ordered and structured. All of these graces are contained within the state of having wisdom.

On the opposite side of the coin, Jesus mentioned the five women who were foolish, which we have seen defined as being dull of spiritual understanding and lacking in the ability to discern right choices from wrong choices. The foolish individual does not possess common sense, which hinders them from making sound judgements. And, most damaging of all, this person does not properly order their spiritual life in a way that God can lead and guide them. This results in every other area of their life not coming into proper focus.

All of these points come together to speak a powerful truth: even though every woman in this parable was a Christian, and they were all waiting for the Lord to come and bless them, there were five who missed their destiny because they were fools. One of the follies of human beings is that we equate intellect and education with wisdom. Even though these areas are often connected to each other, they are not necessarily intertwined. There are many people who have several degrees in front of their name, and yet they lack plain common sense, when it comes to making wise choices.

There are multitudes of individuals who have applied themselves and acquired certain skill sets that have afforded them the opportunity to obtain a high level job, which they can do extremely well. However, when it comes to their personal lives, they are so dense in understanding that they live in a perpetual state of disorder and chaos. There are even persons who are trained psychiatrists whose jobs it is to counsel people for the purpose of helping them solve their problems. In spite of their training, however, because of their lack of spiritual perception, their minds might be just as confused as the patients they are treating. The eternal principle behind these realities is that education does not make a person wise. The accumulation of facts does not automatically grant someone knowledge. And an understanding of the afflictions of the mind does not always mean that one has the ability to cure them. These are ultimately spiritual matters, which must be addressed by acknowledging the supremacy of the greatest source of wisdom and knowledge—the holy Word of God. The Bible is the only true source for every problem that afflicts humanity. With that understanding, let us go deeper.

Just because you believe and respect the Bible does not mean that you know it or adhere to its teachings. Just because you believe in God does not necessarily mean that you know God. Just because you go to church from time to time does not mean that the church is in you and that you have consecrated your body to be the temple of the Holy Spirit. Because terms such as *saved* and *born again* are thrown around so casually, most people do not know what they truly mean. And, because they do not know what these terms mean, they might not truly be saved.

On the other side of the coin, even though a person is truly born again they can still live a meaningless life—if they have not applied themselves to building their faith. Because faith has not been developed, they fail to grow spiritually, and ever seem to reach the place in their life where the Spirit of God is leading and guiding them into all truth. Someone can be a regular church attendee and leave the sanctuary just as bound and defeated as when they walked in. All of these conditions, while tragic in nature, unfortunately occur in multitudes of peoples.

I want to go deeper, speaking directly to you as a woman and asking you some questions, to see if they apply to you. Have you devoted yourself to training and development, gaining a successful career in your desired vocation, while, at the same time, still being unable to master your emotions and overcome phobias and tendencies that hinder the quality of your life? Are you someone who has acknowledged Jesus as your Savior and asked Him to be the Lord of your life, and yet you still find yourself living the same way you lived before you came to Jesus? Are you one of the many women who go to church, sing in the choir, work on the usher board, and do all the other church duties, while, at the same time, sleeping with men who are not their husband, using coarse language in their speech, and generally behaving in a manner unbecoming of godly conduct? Do you constantly find yourself in abusive relationships? Do you struggle with thoughts of insecurity and inferiority? Are you a religious individual who goes through the motions, but, because of a lack of true spirituality, you never receive victory over the world, your flesh, and the devil? If so, this is the same condition the silly women were in. They were to be a part of this great occasion, this great marriage supper, and yet they missed it. The key to understanding the dilemma they faced and the dilemma you might be facing is understanding the words of Jesus:

> *They that were foolish took their lamps, and took no oil with them: but the wise took oil in their vessels with their lamps.* Matthew 25:3-4

The key issue was the lack of oil. As I stated before, every element in this parable is symbolic and contains a spiritual application. In the Bible, God uses different things – whether they be objects, animals, or places – to serve a type that gives a comparison to describe what He is actually like. In both the Old and the New Testaments, oil is an object that is a symbolic representation of the Holy Spirit. The Holy Spirit is the third Person of the Trinity who is the manifestation of heavenly power in the earthly realm.

Before Jesus died on the cross, He walked among humanity for thirty-three years and lived a life that was of such exemplary excellence in character and power that His life serves as a model for every Christian to follow. Jesus was able to achieve this quality of life because He was empowered by the Holy Spirit, not just to perform great deeds, but also to live a great life. Jesus was not just a *hearer* of the Word; He was also a *doer* of the Word. Jesus did not just talk the talk; He walked the walk. He walked in the light of the lamp of God's Word and had His bodily vessel consecrated to the leading of the Holy Spirit.

After Jesus rose again and ascended into Heaven, He sent the Holy Spirit to indwell believers so that we could live as He had lived. The believer who consistently falls short of achieving this position is the one who does not allow the Holy Spirit to anoint and equip them to live as the Bible says we should.

These women, whom Jesus referred to as being *foolish,* are the exact portrait of what I term the silly woman. The silly woman is that female who, although she has a form of godliness and piety, does not walk in the power of that godliness. She denies it either willfully or as a result of lacking the knowledge of how to access that power.

In the Scriptures, the concept of silliness speaks of someone who is weak-minded. This condition has nothing to do with intellect, education, or breeding, but rather being unable to properly discern good from evil. People with high levels of intelligence sometime still make extremely poor choices. A person can have numerous degrees in higher education and yet still lack the wisdom that is required to properly discern a good decision from a bad one. This ultimately leads to a life that is out of order and counter-productive. And, most alarming of all, a person can sit in church and perform religious rituals, and yet, because they do not practice what they profess in their daily lives, they find themselves producing no everlasting fruit of good results.

Unless you allow the Holy Spirit to be the dominating force in your life, leading and guiding you in the choices you make, there will never be enough oil in your lamp when you need it. Without the anointing of the Holy Spirit functioning within, you will lack the spiritual perception that is required to know when God has set a path in place for you which you are to follow. Life is all about making choices, and a person makes choices based upon the conditioning of their mind. If a person is weak-minded (because they have not allowed the Lord to renew their mind by conditioning and training it to think in accordance with the Word), when a choice is set before them, they will choose the wrong course of action. If you are a person influenced by the wrong spirit, when life choices are put before you, you will be influenced to choose that which is detrimental to your eternal well-being.

After God used the prophet Moses to deliver His people from the bondage of Egypt, He presented them commands and ordinances by which they were to govern their life. In addition to presenting them with all of the blessings that would come as a result of them submitting their lives to Him, He also gave them the knowledge of what would happen if they chose to reject His program for living. After He had laid everything out, He spoke through His servant Moses and said:

I call heaven and earth to record this day against you, that I have set before you life and death, blessing and cursing: therefore choose life, that both thou and thy seed may live: that thou mayest love the Lord thy God, and that thou majesty obey his voice, and that thou majesty cleave unto him: for he is thy life, and the length of thy days: that thou majesty dwell in the land which the Lord sware unto thy fathers, to Abraham, to Isaac, and to Jacob, to give them.

Deuteronomy 30:19-20

God was making His people aware that His laws and statues, taken as a complete whole, encompassed a way of life, one in which a person would be led by Him in how they governed their affairs. The opposite factor would be a rejection of those laws, by which a person would be choosing a pathway that leads to death and destruction. God's plan of life would produce blessings, while the devil's plan of life would produce curses. The choice of what they would and could choose would be entirely up to the people.

This spiritual principle connects directly to the Parable of the Ten Virgins. Just as all of the women were within the household of faith and able to access all the blessings God had laid up for them, so, too, were all of the children of Israel under one banner and all had the opportunity to take full advantage of what God had for them to obtain. But they had to choose to obey God's Word, train their minds to submit to His leading, and allow Him to show them how to prepare to be ready for every divine appointment in their lives. That was (and is) the key issue.

God's plan for every Christian is to take them on a path of life with many divine appointments. These are situations and circumstances in life in which you find yourself at the right place at the right moment in time to receive your blessing from the Lord. That blessing could be the right job, the perfect spouse, or a place of safety from harm or danger. If you are not careful to have oil in your lamp, you could miss your divine appointments, just as the foolish virgins did. It is not enough just to confess that Jesus is Lord; you must live like He is Lord and allow Him to *be* Lord of every aspect of your life. If you don't, you could miss you moment of destiny, and it could cost you pain, trouble, and maybe even your eternal future.

Ultimately, you greatest divine appointment will occur at the end of your life or the end of this present age—whichever comes first. There will come a day when Jesus will return to take His Church into Heaven with Him. If you are not ready, you could miss that moment. The divine appointments leading up to that time are days of preparation and stepping stones that will take you higher and higher in life, ushering you into your ultimate destination—Heaven. However, if you are like the foolish virgins, who were the silly women of their day, not only will you miss your ultimate goal, but in every other chapter of your life, you will fall short of seeing the glory of God manifest in and through you.

This is the hour to put away childish things and mature into the strong woman of God He has called you to be. In order to achieve that goal, you must place yourself on the Potter's wheel and allow Him to mold and shape you into a vessel of honor ready for His use. That will require you to examine yourself and go deeper, to ensure that no one but the Lord is in control and influencing your life. The steps and ways by which that process takes place will be revealed as you read on.

Chapter 8

The Deaf and Dumb Spirit

Within the vastness of this Universe that God has created, He often reveals His wisdom and majesty in threes. For example, He reveals His nature in the Person of God the Father, God the Son, and God the Holy Spirit. God made the substance known as H_2O to exist as a solid, a liquid, and a gas. The concept of a day is divided into morning, noon, and evening. A story has a beginning, a middle, and an ending. And the list of the three-fold divisions of life could go on and on. One of the most important ways in which God has used the concept of three in revealing His wisdom is in creating humanity and the forces in this world that humans must contend with.

Every human being is a three-part creation, which consist of a spirit, a soul, and a body. Within the framework of the life a person lives, they must contend with three forces, which consist of this world, a person's human flesh with its carnal desires, and the devil. Although a person must contend with these forces and is subject to being affected by them, these are not the most powerful entities that influence an individual life. The three most powerful forces that have a direct influence on your life are God's Spirit, your own spirit, and the spirit of this world, otherwise known as the devil.

You must always be aware of the truth that you are a spirit being, you have a soul, and you live in a body. The outer shell that is your human body is not the real you; it is just the suit you live in that allows you to exist in this natural world. At the core of your being is a spirit. Your soul consists of your mind, your emotions, and your intellect. Your goal, as a spirit being who confesses Jesus as Lord and Savior and identifies as a Christian, is to train your mind, emotions, and intellect to yield to the leading of God's Spirit—the Holy Ghost. If you do not train yourself along these lines, then your soul will come under the domination of Satan and all the demonic spirits that are a part of his kingdom.

As a mature believer, you must understand the ways in which God has chosen to work in our lives. When a person gives their life to Jesus, they go through a process in which they become born again. In this process, the natural body is not reborn, but the real person on the inside is recreated. I am referring to your spirit. The apostle Paul explained this work within us when he wrote to the Corinthian church these words:

> *Therefore, if any man be in Christ, he is a new creature: old things are passed away; behold, all things are become new.* 2 Corinthians 5:17

Any person who has given their heart to Jesus is made into a new creation. The part of you that is renewed is not the outer shell of your body, but rather, the inner being we sometimes refer to as your *heart*. You are a recreated spiritual being, but with the same mind and body you had before you were saved. Because your spirit has been made new, Satan does not have access to you in that arena. However, because you still live in this world, and because your mind is not born again, Satan will seek to plant within your mind thoughts that are contrary to the Word of God. If you allow those thoughts to become ingrained within you, they will penetrate your spirit and take hold of you, causing you to live a lifestyle that is not the one God has intended for you to live. You must train yourself to think about yourself and your circumstances the way God thinks about you. The thoughts that come to you that are contrary to the images of faith and victory come from the devil and his forces. As long as you exist in this world, you will have to contend with these forces.

Paul also explained this point very clearly in his letter to the Christians of Ephesus, when he said:

> *Put on the whole armor of God, that ye may be able to stand against the wiles of the devil. For we wrestle not against flesh and blood, but against principalities, against powers, against the rulers of the darkness of this world, against spiritual wickedness in high places. Wherefore take unto you the whole armor of God, that ye may be able to withstand in the evil day, and having done all, to stand.* Ephesians 6:11-13

Notice the precision in which Paul spoke about the demon forces. He did not mention just one type of spirit, but made clear the distinctive nature of the forces that are arrayed against God's people. It is our job, as Christians, to understand these forces and the ways in which each of them operates. Not understanding your opponent opens you to being overcome by that opponent.

When a person gives their heart to Jesus and becomes a born-again recreated spirit, the demonic forces that once tormented them are forced to leave their spirit, soul, and body. After that initial experience, the process of surrendering your total being to the Lord must continue. If there is no progression, you open yourself up for other wicked spirits to come and influence you.

In one of the teachings of Jesus, He shared with the people a message that gives greater clarification of this principle. He said:

> *When the unclean spirit is gone out of a man, he walketh through dry places, seeking rest, and findeth none. Then he saith, I will return unto my house from which I came out; and when he is come, he findeth the it empty, swept, and garnished. Then goeth he, and taketh with himself seven other spirits more wicked than himself, and they enter in and dwell there: and the last state of that man is worse than the first. Even so shall it be also unto this wicked generation.*
>
> Matthew 12:43-45

In this short teaching, Jesus presented a great lesson on how the spirit world functions. He said that when a person (the use of the word *man* does not exclude women; He was speaking here of any human being) is delivered from an unclean spirit, that spirit will return to the dry places of the demonic realm from whence it came. After a time in that place of despair, the demon spirit will desire to return to the vessel which it once inhabited and will attempt to do so. This is why there are times in the life of a Christian when they feel compelled to fall back into the sinful behavior from which they were once delivered. If Christians have not trained themselves to fill their mind with the Word of God, that unclean spirit will plant wrong thoughts into their mind, and those negative seeds will grow within the person until they are once again controlled and influenced by that spirit.

What makes this even more tragic is the fact that the unclean spirit will bring with them other demon forces more wicked than themselves, ultimately making the latter condition of the person worse than their former spiritual state. This is why so many Christians fail to receive victory over the world, their flesh, or the devil. This is also why Jesus, after healing the man at the pool of Bethesda, admonished him to take heed to himself. The Scriptures record the Master's words:

> *Afterward, Jesus findeth him in the temple, and said unto him, Behold, thou art made whole: sin no more, lest a worse thing come unto thee.* John 5:14

What was the *"worse"* thing that Jesus was alluding to in this passage? In order to answer that question, we must understand that this individual Jesus spoke to had been healed of a physical infirmity brought on by a demonic spirit. After the man was made whole by Jesus, the spirit no longer had access to him. However, if he returned to a life of sin, then, not only could the infirmity return, but Jesus said that a far more deadly thing could come upon him. Since the first problem was caused by an evil spirit, then the other problem that would occur had he not obeyed would also be brought on by an evil spirit. You must understand that the spirit world is very real, and, whether you realize it or not, that world affects this world—both you personally and also the situations you consistently find yourself in. How you cooperate with this world and depending on the spirit you yield yourself to will determine the course of your life.

I want to turn your thoughts again to the passage in Matthew that I referenced earlier. It is important to note that Jesus spoke about the unclean spirit being cast out of a person. He specifically mentioned this spirit because it was the spirit Satan dispatched to be the dominating force at work in the earth today. As I stated before, the unclean spirit is manifested in society through sexual perversion and immorality, and because these are the most prevalent issues that affect our culture, we see the results of the unclean spirit at work in the world today. This spirit is the dominating force that influences the strange woman, and this is why Jesus spoke about how, when a person is delivered, or, to put it more succinctly, when they come to a saving knowledge of Jesus Christ, they are set free from a lifestyle of sexual immorality. However, once the strange woman has given her life to the Lord and been made a new creature in Christ, she must then develop her relationship with the Lord and fill her inner life with the presence of Almighty God. If she does not do so, not only does she leave herself open to the unclean spirit returning to influence her again, but other spirits will accompany that spirit, and she will be in even greater danger of spiritual destruction. This process can occur even if this woman goes to church and professes Jesus as Lord. If she does not have a lifestyle of being in God's presence and surrendering her will to Him, she will be governed and motivated by the forces of this present evil world.

Just because a person is a churchgoer does not automatically make them an overcoming Christian. A person can perform religious rites and participate in religious ceremonies and be no more spiritual than the worst heathen. There were several instances in the gospels in which Jesus had to confront some of the most wicked people, and they just happened to be those who frequented the houses of worship. Christianity is a way of life, and if a woman does not practice the faith she professes, her mind will continue to think like this world, and she will become the silly woman.

When the apostle Paul sought to counsel his protégée, Timothy, on how to be an effective pastor, he shared with him great wisdom on understanding different types of people. In one of Paul's exhortations to Timothy, he spoke about a particular type of woman, and he made this insightful observation as to how these women lived their life:

> *Having a form of godliness, but denying the power thereof: from such turn away. For of this sort are they which creep into houses, and lead captive silly women laden with sins, led away with divers lusts, ever learning, and never able to come to the knowledge of the truth.* 2 Timothy 3:5-7

Clearly Paul was writing to Timothy about religious people. He was not dealing with those who were unbelievers and did not know the Lord. He was giving spiritual counsel to Timothy regarding his pastoral work, as it related specifically to dealing with people who professed to know Jesus but did not follow His teachings. When Paul referred to these individuals as *"having a form of godliness, but denying the power thereof,"* this was what he meant. The deeper reality within this text is that Paul was speaking about the spirits that are often at work in these days. He went on to say that these spirts of false piety creep into houses and find silly women, burdening them with sin and leading them astray with wrong desires. In his explanation of this condition, he brought further power to his narrative, when he said that even though these individuals were learning and growing in natural head knowledge and religious creeds, they were never able to come to the truth of their spiritual condition. They never grew into Christian maturity. Considering this silly woman, in order to understand her, you must know what spirits are at work, seeking to dominate her life.

Before I deal with that aspect, I want to first emphasize this point: in the case of demon spirits, there are degrees to which a person can be affected by them. Usually, when this subject is mentioned, people automatically think of someone being possessed by a demon, meaning that the evil spirit has taken up residence within that person and gained control over their mind. That phenomenon is the final result of a process that begins with the demon spirit first influencing them. If given space, they then possess them.

A person who has given their life to Jesus and has been given a recreated spirit cannot be possessed by a demon spirit because the Spirit of God is living within them. However, a believer can be influenced by the devil with negative thoughts or attacked in their bodies by sickness or disease. This is why we are told in the Scriptures to resist the devil, because he will come with his forces and seek to gain a hold over the child of God. If a believer does not resist these attacks, the wicked spirts will begin to accompany that person, just as a another human will keep company with you if you allow them to. Once this happens, the spirit or spirits will have access to possibly possess the believer (because they have opened themselves to the attack and caused the Holy Spirit to remove His presence from them, putting them into the state of being a prodigal).

God wants us to be made aware of these great truths, and this is why Jesus spoke these words to His disciples regarding the Holy Spirit:

> *If ye love me, keep my commandments. And I will pray the Father, and he shall give you another Comforter, that he may abide with you forever; even the Spirit of truth; whom the world cannot receive, because it seeth him not, neither knoweth him: but ye know him; for he dwelleth with you, and shall be in you.* John 14:15-17

Jesus was referring to the Person of the Holy Spirit and was promising His followers that the Spirit would come after He, Jesus, left them and returned to

Heaven. Because the Spirit of truth is a spirit being, Jesus said that He would be both *with* them and *within* them. This speaks of His companionship being a very present help in life and His indwelling of the heart of the believer. This principle also applies to demonic spirits. They can be present, seeking to accompany and influence a person, and if they can gain access to that person, they can take hold of them and poses them. This may be why you have thoughts that try to make you fearful, insecure, or unworthy. These are from the powers of darkness that seek to attach themselves to you and torment you, hoping that, ultimately, you will be consumed by them. This is what Paul meant when he said that the silly women was *"laden with sins."* When you are laden with something, you are burdened down by it. This burden seeks to pile on you and weigh down the healthy self-image that God wants you to have about yourself.

The spirit that most affects the silly women is what the Bible refers to as the *"deaf and dumb spirit."* When I use those terms, *deaf and dumb,* the first thought that comes to our minds is of an inability to hear and a lack of intelligence. While these concepts are, by no means, foreign to the definition of the terms I used, they are limiting due to the fact that the words are only seen through the prism of our modern vernacular. My intention is to go deeper, to discover the greater truths, and, because I have described this spirit in the exact way the Scriptures describe it, it becomes important to clarify these words by thinking about them the way the Bible does. By approaching the subject from a biblical point of view, the revelation that comes from those words will be made clear to us.

In the original Greek from which the New Testament was translated, the word *deaf* comes from the word *kophos,* while the word *dumb* was translated from the word *alalos.* According to *Vine's Expository Dictionary of Old and New Testament Words, kophos* is defined as "to beat or make one tired." It also signifies "the act of making something dull or blunted, as a weapon." *Alalos* is defined as "speechless." The two words are connected in meaning and signify "the act of making one's resources or weapons ineffective against the powers of darkness." One of the greatest assets and tools God has given you is the power to think about yourself from the lens of how He sees you and the ability to call those things into existence through your words. As we know, *"death and life are in the power of the tongue"* (Proverbs 18:21). If the deaf and dumb spirit is influencing your life, you will be hindered in walking in victory, because the weapons that God has given to you have been made ineffective, causing you to have a negative self-image of yourself.

The other part of this ungodly force is how it makes one dumb. Once again, you cannot look at that word solely from the prism of a modern understanding of the term. You must understand the word as the Scriptures teach you to understand it. Once again I want to go back to the original Greek to define the word, in order to draw greater understanding. According to the original Greek, the word *dumb* comes from two words, *alalos* and *aphonos*. Both of these words are used to define "the state of being voiceless or an inability to speak." It is also connected with the word *deaf*, and that is why when the Scriptures speak about this demonic force, they refer to it as *"the deaf and dumb spirit."* The terms and the symptoms of the terms are related. This spirit seeks to work in the lives of any person in an attempt to diminish their value and self-worth, which causes them to speak and think negatively about themselves, thereby robbing them of the ability to create a positive point of view for their life. Ultimately, this can cause them to make continual poor choices that bring harm and destruction to their lives.

What I am doing is addressing a spiritual problem and an affliction of the soul. This has nothing to do with how intelligent or educated a person may be. You can be highly trained and taught in a natural discipline, but at the very same time, be so weighed down by the devil that your soul is handicapped, and you see yourself so negatively that you make poor choices. You must always understand that the battles you are fighting are spiritual conflicts. Although they will have natural outcomes and affect the natural areas of your life, the source of the force at work is spiritual in nature. If you are ignorant of the devices and the devil's army of allies, you will go down in defeat because you are not allowing the Word of God to be the dominating factor in your life. This is the reason Satan primarily uses the deaf and dumb spirit to attack the silly woman, because she has not allowed the Lord to renew her mind according to the principles of the Bible. Therefore, she lives in a constant state of defeat, even though she may have a form of godliness.

In order to break this down even further, I want to highlight specific areas in which this spirit operates in the life of the silly woman. As always, I want to reference the Scriptures, because the Bible is our Guidepost for all things, and we must judge every matter according to the Word. During the life and the ministry of Jesus, He confronted this deaf and dumb spirit, and while it is encouraging to see that His power prevailed over this demonic force, it is also instructive to see how this spirit affected the individuals it had possessed. We are given a full account in the Gospel according to Saint Mark:

> *And one of the multitude answered and said, Master, I have brought unto thee my son, which hath a dumb spirit; and wheresoever he taketh him, he teareth him: and he foameth, and gnasheth with his teeth, and pineth away: and I spake to thy disciples that they should cast him out; and they could not.*
> *He answereth him, and saith, O faithless generation, how long shall I be with you? how long shall I suffer you? bring him unto me.*
> *And they brought him unto him: and when he saw him, straightway the spirit tare him; and he fell on the ground, and wallowed foaming. And he asked his father, How long is it ago since this came unto him?*
> *And he said, Of a child. And ofttimes it hath cast him into the fire, and into the waters, to destroy him: but if thou canst do any thing, have compassion on us, and help us.*
> *Jesus said unto him, If thou canst believe, all things are possible to him that believeth.*
> *And straightway the father of the child cried out, and said with tears, Lord, I believe; help thou mine unbelief.*
> *When Jesus saw that the people came running together, he rebuked the foul spirit, saying unto him, Thou dumb and deaf spirit, I charge thee, come out of him, and enter no more into him. And the spirit cried, and rent him sore, and came out of him: and he was as one dead; insomuch that many said, He is dead.*
> *But Jesus took him by the hand, and lifted him up; and he arose.*
>
> Mark 9:17-27

There is much insight and revelation contained within this testimony. We see the power and the compassion of Jesus to heal and deliver. We witness the deep anguish in the soul of a parent, crying out on behalf of his child. And we are also afforded a great object lesson on the strategies of the devil to destroy a human life. While much could be said in relation to all of these facets of this account, I want to draw your attention to the final point that I emphasized that deals with the demonic activity in the life of a person. By breaking those aspects down and extracting the spiritual and natural applications from those portions of the text, the Bible will speak directly to the heart of many of the problems that plague the silly woman. Remember, the deaf and dumb spirit, which Jesus Himself identified as being the source of trouble in this circumstance, is the spirit that primarily seeks to attach itself to the silly woman. By understanding how this happens, deliverance and wholeness came come.

I want to first make this point: even though this particular event concerned the demonic possession of a young boy, that is not a pretext for seeking to impose limitations on how demon forces seek to influence people. Wicked spirits do not discriminate concerning who they seek to influence and possess. They will take hold of any vessel who will give them a door of opportunity. The fact that, in this particular story, a boy was involved, the principle of how demon forces influence people is the same—whether it is male or female, man or woman, boy or girl. From the standpoint that the story deals with a youth, the principle that needs to be extracted from this part of the equation is not the gender of the youth, but the fact that the spirit attached itself to a person at that tender age. All too often, the areas of our self-image that are negative and contain a defeatist mentality are the result of the demonic spirits that attach themselves to us when we are still children, and we can carry those forces with us into adulthood—if we do not know how to break free from their chains.

In this particular event in the life of Jesus, we are presented with a very extreme case because the deaf and dumb spirit had fully possessed the individual. However, the ways in which the Bible describes how this spirit had affected the person gives us spiritual principles that have natural consequences. We must understand the pattern laid out before us so that knowledge and liberty can come forth in our lives.

This deaf and dumb spirit was a demonic force that affected the mind of a person by distorting their self-image and causing them to put themselves in harmful and dangerous circumstances. This spirit, while willing to attach itself to any vessel that will yield to it, is very much attracted to women, because they are more prone to think negatively about themselves. The spirit seeks out this kind of woman, desiring to influence and manipulate her mind, to take the negative self-image she already has and raise it to a new extreme, thereby initiating within her the desire to make choices that will lead her into emotional and spiritual ruin.

The fact that a woman is a Christian and performs religious activities makes no difference to this spirit. Unless that woman has renewed her mind according to the Word of God and chosen to see herself as God sees her, that spirit will sense her weak self-image and seek to capitalize on it ... until she becomes the silly woman who is led astray by deceitful lusts.

The Holy Spirit took great care in having Mark record specific details about this miracle so that one can observe the full portrait of how the devil operates. It is important to note that when the father of the child came to Jesus and described the situation to Him, he related how, when the deaf and dumb spirit would take full possession of the child, it would cause him to behave in certain self-destructive ways. The spirit would take control of his mouth, his gestures, and his mannerisms. This behavior would continue escalating until the child would just "pine away," meaning that the spirit would place the child in a state of numbness, to the point that he would just sit and waste away. These are the extreme manifestations of an extreme case of demon possession, but remember that we are looking at the principle, which is universal to all cases.

If a spirit is influencing you, even if it may not yet have fully possessed you, the influence of that spirit can cause you a great deal of harm. In the case of this child, the deaf and dumb spirit caused him to behave in an inhuman manner. The principle is this: if that spirit is influencing the silly woman, she will behave in unseemly ways and by communicate in an ungodly manner. She will behave in a way unbecoming to a Christian lady by displaying characteristics that are contrary to the fruits of the Spirit. This type of behavior is displayed in a woman who professes to know the Lord but still curses, backbites, gossips, and throws away her life by not allowing the Lord to govern her choices. This is what the deaf and dumb spirit does. It takes all the gifts and graces God has given to you and weakens them by infecting your mind with low self-esteem. As a result, you waste away your life, throwing away your potential and allowing Satan to pervert your talents and personality into something unbecoming of God's divine nature.

Perhaps the most tragic aspect of this account from the Scriptures was when Jesus asked the father how long this had been going on, and the father answered, *"From childhood."* He also provided another great piece of information, telling Jesus that when the spirit would take hold of his son, it would cause the boy to throw himself into fire or into water, all for the purpose of trying to kill him. Consider the severity of this situation, that a mind can become so depraved and tormented that it would seek to destroy itself.

Many would read this and only consider the extreme aspect of this particular manifestation. However, when one sees the principle of the story, the realization that such things take place quite frequently becomes clear. As a general occurrence, people put themselves in unnecessary danger every single day, and while some realize it, others do not. People smoke, consume alcoholic beverages, and ingest things into their bodies that are detrimental to any person's health. This is all the strategy of Satan. If he can use the deaf and dumb spirit to twist a person's mind into thinking that something that is obviously bad for them is actually good for them, that person will soon be destroyed.

In the case of the silly woman, the plight of this specific personality type is even more tragic than the generic ways in which Satan seeks to destroy people. In a broader context, people make unwise choices every day that cause them harm. With regard to the silly woman, she puts herself into harmful situations, most directly in the area of relationships. How many times does the news tell the story of some young woman who was killed by her psychotic boyfriend? How many sad tales are told of woman who are married to husbands who consistently abuse them, both verbally and physically, and yet the woman continues to stay in that relationship? I myself remember hearing of an incident in which a woman had discovered that her husband was having an affair with another woman. When she confronted her him with it, he beat her to a bloody pulp and left her half dead. In spite of all of that terrible abuse, she refused to press charges against him, and, after she recovered from her injuries, she returned to him, as if nothing had happened, only to suffer more and more abuse.

When we read in the Scriptures about how the spirit caused this young person to throw himself into the fire and into the water, this is the spiritual principle God is trying to get across to us. We may only see people throwing themselves in fire and water in extreme cases, but we see women putting themselves in danger in bad relationships every single day. Women with degrees, women with successful careers, and even women who go to church every time the doors are open, somehow continue to attach themselves to men who care nothing for them, men Satan uses for their destruction. This is a spiritual problem, and it is the result of the deaf and dumb spirit twisting hearts and minds to think less of themselves and cause them to connect their life to men who put them in constant danger. No longer does the Lord want Satan to continue to cause you to cast yourself into the fire. Jesus has come to set you free and to enlighten you, to see the true nature of the root of your troubles. If you are in this type of situation, begin to take authority over that spirit and rebuke it in the name of Jesus. Begin to get a positive image of yourself based upon what God's Word says about you, and walk in the liberty and freedom Jesus paid the price for you to have.

Chapter 9

Laden with Deceitful Lusts

All that glistens is not gold. – William Shakespeare

Now that I have laid the foundation for the spiritual plight of the silly woman, I want to build upon that foundation and probe deeper, to reveal the inner workings of this type of woman. Just as there must be a coming together of chromosomes to make up the genetic structure of a human being, so, too, are there combining factors that are joined together to make up the spiritual and moral fabric of a person's character. Not every aspect of a problem or a condition is the direct result of demonic activity. While the devil and his forces, ultimately, are the root source of the issue, there are still the components of a person's will and their choices that are also involved. These, combined with the spirit world, produce the results, whether they be for good or for ill.

As I established in previous chapters, there are varying degrees of demonic influence. Not every individual is possessed by a false spirit. However, every human being will be influenced by the spirit world, whether it be the Holy Spirit or a demonic one, and if you do not do your part in training your will to live in accordance with God's will, then the influence of the unrighteous forces will control you. While the silly woman may not necessarily have gone so far as to be possessed by a deaf and dumb spirit, her desires and her attractions are so attached to the things of this world that she allows herself to be influenced by that spirit, and, as a result, she puts herself into the danger zone because she does not live according to God's Word. The key is that the silly woman is that female who, even though she has the veneer of righteousness, still desires the ways of this world.

The Bible has much to say regarding our desires and passions. There is a passage in the New Testament that encourages all believers to follow this principle:

> *Set your affection on things above, not on things on the earth.*
>
> Colossians 3:2

The apostle Paul wrote this commandment to Christians because he understood that, even though a person professes to be a follower of Jesus, he or she can still desire to do things that are totally antithetical to the character of Christ. In our modern vernacular, this word *affection* implies merely "wants or attraction." However, you must be mindful of the translation and think in terms of the original thinking, of the original language, of the people for whom the Scriptures were first written. In the Greek, the word *affection* had to do with what a person experienced in their mind as a result of a passionate desire. That deep desire produced strong mental images within the person, so strong that they ultimately acted out what they had rehearsed in their mind.

In the ancient world, the word *affections* also had to do with the bowels of an individual, which contained their intestinal organs. The ancient Greeks believed that this part of the human being was the area that contained their most violent passions. The Jews also considered that this area of the body contained their most heartfelt desires. So, when Paul told his readers to set their affection on things above, what he was saying was to channel their deepest desires and their most intense passions toward the things that were pleasing to God.

This is also what is meant by the phrase, *"things above"* and *"not on things of the earth."* Paul was not referring to natural substances, but, rather, a way of life that wants what God wants and not to live according to the pattern of this corrupted society.

In John's first letter to the Christian disciples, the beloved apostle wrote some words to his readers that also convey this powerful message. He said:

> *Love not the world, neither the things that are in the world. If any man love the world, the love of the Father is not in him. For all that is in the world, the lust of the flesh, and the lust of the eyes, and the pride of life, is not of the Father, but is of the world.* 1 John 2:15-16

Here John expressed a sentiment similar to that of the apostle Paul. He just stated it in a more detailed way. Just as there were various understandings of the word *affection* in the ancient world, so, too, the word *love* was defined in numerous ways. In this particular passage of scripture, the word *love* is used to mean a deep emotional attachment that implies an inner passion of the soul. Clearly the Bible is speaking about one's deepest desires. God, speaking through His servant John, admonished Christians not to have a passion for the things of this world.

That phrase, *the things of this world* or *the world*, is thrown around a lot in religious circles, so much so that many do not truly comprehend what the Bible is saying by it. The Scriptures declare that the earth belongs to the Lord, which simply means that this planet called Earth is under the dominion of God's authority over all creation. But the Bible also declares that Satan is *"the god of this world,"* (2 Corinthians 4:4). Although in modern usage, the terms *earth* and *world* are used interchangeably, the Word of God makes a distinction between the two. When the Bible speaks about "the world," it is referring, not to the physical dimensions of planet Earth, but, rather, to a way of life and a mentality and culture that is saturated with evil and perversion.

When John declared that Christian should not love this world, what he was saying was that we should not desire to live according to the thinking and the way of life with which Satan has polluted this culture. The sad truth of the matter is that far too many Christians are infatuated with and desire the way of life this world's system offers. And this is the dilemma of the silly woman. She is constantly in the valley of decision, torn between two schools of thought, God's and the devil's.

Notice what John said in this passage, as he went into detail to explain what is in the cultural system of this present world. He said that it contains *"the lust of the flesh," "the lust of the eyes,"* and *"the pride of life."* The first two speak of things that are desirable to the carnal part of your nature, which has not been redeemed by the blood of Jesus. Even though a person is born again in their spirit, they still have a mind and a body that must be renewed and consecrated to the ways of God. If a Christian does not do these things, then they open themselves to be led astray by the lusts of the eye and of the flesh. These lusts present things to you that appear pleasing on the outside and have the ability to provide a short-term form of pleasure. But, once the moment has run its course, the reaping of the consequences will be far more bitter than one can imagine.

Another aspect of these two forces is that they have the ability to make something that is even dangerous seem so tempting and desirable that you run toward it, in spite of the negative consequences that will result in such entanglements. In the previous chapter, I touched on the aspect of casting oneself into the fire and how the demonic spirit caused the person to put himself in a dangerous situation. This is possible because a person is deceived into believing that the harmful scenario will be exciting for them to participate in. This is how many women end up in terribly abusive relationships; they are deceived into thinking that the man before them, although it is clear that he is dangerous and of no worth, is still so exciting and appealing that the woman will throw away all logic and common sense and enter into an abusive and destructive relationship with him. Even though her minister, family, and friends try to scream the truth into her ear, warning her that this is all wrong, she still rushes into a place where even angels would fear to tread. This mentality is the result of what John spoke of when he wrote about avoiding *"the pride of life."*

There is something about this life that we live. If you're not careful, you can start to believe that you are your own master, and not the Lord Jesus. A person can achieve great fame and status or they can amass a great sum of wealth. They can climb so high and go so far in life that life can start to play tricks on them. They can come to the place that they no longer feel a need for God or His ways. Too often pride is thought to be a vice that is exclusive to men, but virtue and vice do not discriminate, and a woman can also be susceptible to the pride of life.

When the Bible uses this term, *the pride of life,* it is dealing with the thought process that says that God is unnecessary, and it is no longer in one's best interest to follow His program. The pride of life says that I can live my life in the way I choose to live it, doing what I want to do, and attaching myself to whomever I wish to connect myself with, even though such decisions may run contrary to God's best plan for my life. Once these prideful thoughts become engrafted into a person's soul, they have no interest in hearing correction, nor are they perceptive in discerning that what they are doing is wrong. This then opens the door for the deaf and dumb spirit to come and influence a person to consistently put themselves in harmful situations. This is why some women keep connecting themselves with abusers, liars, and cheaters. The silly woman has a form of godliness but has not allowed the power of God to change her desires and bring them into sync with the thoughts and plans of our heavenly Father.

This device of Satan is as old as the days of Adam and Eve; the origins of this tactic began in the garden of Eden. The book of Genesis informs us that God made Adam and Eve and put them in the garden to have dominion over that territory. He informed His children that they could partake of all the trees that were in the garden (except for the one that contained the knowledge of good and evil). The Lord desired that His people walk in absolute purity and holiness, undefiled by the temptation to mix good with evil. He understood that to bring evil into that which is good would result in spiritual death, separation from God for eternity. The orders He gave were clear, and the consequences He laid out were even more clear. BUT then the tempter came, and he sought to bring division between God and mankind in a most curious way.

We read in the Scriptures that when Satan came to bring corruption, he approached Eve and asked her a question regarding God's commandment. Eve spoke to the tempter and told him that God had commanded that both she and Adam refrain from partaking of the tree of the knowledge of good and evil. She further explained that if they disobeyed God's command, they would die as a result of their transgression. Satan then began to seduce and deceive Eve by promising her that if she would partake of the tree, she would become *"like a god"* herself, enlightened with knowledge about light and darkness. The Word goes on to describe what happened within Eve as she pondered Satan's words:

> *And when the woman saw that the tree was good for food, and that it was pleasant to the eyes, and a tree to be desired to make one wise, she took of the fruit thereof, and did eat.* Genesis 3:6

This is a supreme example of just how the enemy operates. He caused Eve's desires to be fixed on that which she had no business seeking after. Then, once her desire was set toward it, she began to consider the pleasures the experience would bring. Images and thoughts flooded her mind ... until she forgot all about God's ordinance and the truth that behind all that pleasure was sorrow, the likes of which she could not conceive. Sadly, she partook of that which was unholy, and Satan has used that strategy ever since to draw God's people away, deceiving them with the burden of lusts that provide short-term pleasure but yield eternal consequences. Today, in the twenty-first century, Satan is still dangling in front of the silly woman the bait of a man who is not serving God, but promises the Christian woman he ardently pursues that he will be good and kind to her. Satan still dangles in front of the woman the idea that being unequally yoked together is not nearly as bad as God has said. The man then dehumanizes her and fails to see her true value. Maybe it's because she doesn't know her own value.

The tempter is still laying the trap of wrong career choices, ungodly friends, and a sinful lifestyle that will rob the woman of the life that Jesus paid the price for her to have. Right now, the Lord is saying, "Come out, come out, into the glorious Gospel of My Son. Do not allow the snares of the wicked one to take hold of you. But grow in grace and in the knowledge of My ways."

I believe that, as you have read these words, this growth process has started, and it will continue as you read more, as we progress deeper into this journey of self-discovery and spiritual awakening.

Chapter 10

Be Not Conformed to This World

A few years ago I had a little free time one afternoon and decided to sit down and watch television. I turned on one of the Christian channels, and, as it turned out, the program that was being aired at that moment was of a women's conference hosted by one of the most prominent Charismatic ministers of the day. This particular program was showing highlights of a panel discussion that included the minister's wife and several other prominent women who worked in business, entertainment, and ministry. They were discussing issues they felt were relevant to women, and I listened rather casually to their commentary.

What I found to be the most interesting that day, and, sad to say, the most disturbing was the way in which the minister's wife was dressed. She was wearing a dress that was low cut and revealed her cleavage. To me, it was unsettling to see a woman who was such a prominent person, highly respected within the Christian community, dressed in this way, giving the appearance of a woman trying to be overtly seductive.

On another occasion, more recently, I happened upon a YouTube showing of a well-known female Gospel artist perform on a certain variety program. Her appearance on the show drew some controversy, not for the fact that she was on the program, but, again, the way in which she was dressed. She was standing before an audience, wearing a very tight-fitting shirt, which was, again, low cut and revealed her cleavage. There was quite a stir about this on social media, and while the criticism that the singer drew from her appearance on the program was valid, it, along with the other story I related to you, speaks to a larger and deeper issue.

In the first instance I mentioned, what is tragic and shameful about it is this: here you have a Christian program, broadcast on Christian television, and featuring Christian leaders who have a platform to influence a large segment of the Body of Christ, and the woman who was hosting the forum was presenting herself like a woman you would see on a secular program. It is bad enough that our culture is so saturated with television programs that promote inappropriate attire, but to have to be exposed to it on Christian television and to have it influence other women to falsely believe that such attire is proper is wrong and not in line with the character of Christ.

In the second instance, here we have a prominent Christian woman, who has been blessed by God to have the opportunity to be an ambassador for Jesus Christ and present an image of holiness and purity to the world, and yet, instead of during this, she presents herself in a highly sexualized manner, thus making herself into a object and not a person, and presenting a perverted view of Christianity to the world. That view says it is acceptable to dress scantily clad. Again, this is not in line with the biblical view.

I do not write this with any gleeful intent to malign the individuals I mentioned in any way, and I purposely avoided mentioning their names. I have no desire to point the finger of blame at anyone. What I am dealing with is a symptom, and I simply used these examples to bring forth a point. The Bible states very emphatically how Christians should behave in this world:

> *Abstain from all appearance of evil.* 1 Thessalonians 5:22

When a woman puts on clothes that reveal parts of her body that appeal to sexual appetites and leaves her home to go out into society, she is sending a message. Through her actions, she is saying that she wishes to be viewed in a seductive way and that she desires attention to be given to her because of her body. These choices are one of the seeds that bring forth lust and that yield forbidden fruits, sins of sexual immorality.

Even though it is not fashionable to say such things in this post-modern society, sin is wrong. And, as a Christian woman, you have a responsibility to carry yourself and present yourself in a certain way, a way that is not only above reproach, but also does not even give the impression of impropriety. That is what the Bible means when it says to *abstain from* the *appearance of evil.* If it looks like sin, then you are commanded to avoid it. If it gives the appearance of indecency, then you should not do it. There should be nothing about you that says, "Open for business" or "I am available for anything and everything." I want to emphasize, again, that it is not my intention to be crass or condemning. These issues, however, are not being addressed in the church as they should be, and as a result, people have been fooled into thinking that it is acceptable to look and behave like the children of disobedience, those who walk outside of God's light of revelation. Although it may be unpleasant and perhaps even controversial to bring up the subject, such problems must be dealt with, and it must be done in accordance with what the Bible says about these issues.

The particular instances that I mentioned are just the fruit of the roots that have been planted into the soil of people's hearts and within the structural fabric of the church. It is my intention to pull up the roots, just as God called the prophet Jeremiah to do in the time he lived. Once the roots are pulled out, then a proper foundation can be laid, and that can be built upon, to achieve a life of walking in agreement with the full counsel of God.

In one of the most famous passages in the book of Romans, the apostle Paul admonished the believers who lived in his time to live their life in a way that allowed them to remain uncorrupted by the wickedness of this world. Because the Bible is a living book, one that contains ever-present revelation, his words still speak to us today:

> *I beseech you therefore, brethren, by the mercies of God, that ye present your bodies a living sacrifice, holy, acceptable unto God, which is your reasonable service. And be not conformed to this world: but be ye transformed by the renewing of your mind, that ye may prove what is that good, and acceptable, and perfect, will of God.* Romans 12:1-2

Because of the specific nature of how Paul constructed his words, it is worth examining the key points of this text, in order to gather the fruits of revelation that come from them. He began by saying, *"I beseech you."* This word *beseech* means "to call, to pray, or to desire in a longing fashion." So we see that the man of God was giving a strong summons to the people, a summons based upon his intense desire and affection toward them and his desire to see each one of them fulfill their high call in God. His desire and prayer for them was that they present a sacrifice unto the Lord.

A sacrifice is an offering of some kind or what we, in our modern vernacular, might refer to as a gift or a present. When most church people hear the term *offering*, they usually equate it with money or the animal sacrifices that existed during the era of the Old Testament. While both thoughts are correct and applicable in a larger context, Paul was specifically saying in this passage that the offering to be given to God in this context is your body. This refers to your flesh, the outward suit which houses your inner person. You are to present your body as a living sacrifice, meaning that it is not a one-time event, but a continual process that will go on for the duration of the time you have left on this side of eternity.

For even greater clarification, Paul laid out how your body should be presented. It should be done in a way that is *holy* and *acceptable unto God*. Some, in an attempt to circumvent this issue, would pose the question: Well, what does God consider to be "acceptable"? It is good for us that Paul answers that very question, first stating that the presentation of your body should be *holy*. The holiness of your body is what is acceptable to God. This means you should dress holy and present yourself in a manner that signals a godly life. You are not to live as the world lives.

Paul went on to say that this is considered by God to be *"your reasonable service."* This phrase, *reasonable service*, implies that it is an obligation that you have toward the Lord. It is reasonable because it is beneficial to you to consecrate your vessel to God, so that you do not open yourself up to going down forbidden paths. To put it more directly, it is expected of you that you do not dress in inappropriate attire, clothing that shows parts of your body that should be covered. It is expected of you that you consecrate your body to not engage in ungodly acts that are displeasing to your heavenly Father. It is also expected of you that you understand these expectations and govern yourself accordingly. The reason too many women who profess to be saints engage in activities contrary to these God-ordained expectations is that they are caught in the cycle of being the silly woman.

The greatest problem of the silly woman is that she moves back and forth between two worlds. In the previous chapter, I explained how Christians are commanded not to love the world, and that what is referred to in that verse is the system and the standards by which this world operates. There is the natural planet Earth, and there is the world system that is rooted in this planet, and it is controlled by the deceptive spirits of the age. On the other side of that spirit world is the realm of glory that God dwells in. The silly woman goes back and forth between these two aspects of the spirit world. She claims to love Jesus, but she lives in accordance with Satan's desires. The true Christian woman will live as the Bible says. She will live holy on this planet, as she goes about her daily roles and responsibilities, and will not behave as someone who is directed by the prince of darkness. This is what the Bible means when it says that we are *in* the world, but not *of* the world. Too many believe that they can live any way they please and still be considered acceptable to God. They say, "God knows my heart," justifying their outward actions by professing an inward piety. This mindset is so pervasive in the modern church that it stinks in the nostrils of God. This problem only grows worse as more and more Christians conform to the world.

In verse 2 of Romans 12, Paul exhorted us not to be conformed to this world, but, rather, to be transformed by renewing our minds to think like God thinks. When someone conforms to someone or something, they mold themselves into the image of whatever it is they are conforming to. This is what the silly woman does time and time again, always molding the fabric of her life to look like the clay of this wicked and perverted society. As believers, we are commanded to be transformed. This means that there is a complete metamorphosis that takes place within our spirit, and it causes us to have a holiness that radiates in our outward appearance. Too many women allow themselves to be influenced by what the culture considers to be acceptable and pleasing to God, rather than basing their lifestyle on what the Word of God clearly teaches. The silly woman continues to profess a belief and a respect for God, but she acts as if He either does not exist or that He will accept any type of behavior. She clearly believes that such conduct will be tolerated.

One of the ways Satan uses this world's system to deceive the silly woman to conform to his ways is through modern media and entertainment. Whether it be film, television, or social media platforms, there are all sorts of images that are put before the public consciousness that present a false view of what Christianity is meant to be. How many times do we see reality television programs that showcase women who call on Jesus, praise Jesus, and pray to Jesus, and then turn right around and behave in the vilest and most profane ways! They speak the Christian lingo, and then, moments later, they speak coarse language, engage in illicit sex, consume alcohol, and behave in vulgarity to such a magnitude that it would make a sailor blush. The saddest part of all this is that so many of these personalities call on the Lord and profess to know Jesus as Savior and Lord. How many "Christian" actresses perform roles that promote ungodliness and then are given platforms in Christian circles. Meanwhile the women who sit in these forums are hoodwinked into believing that God is pleased with such behavior. All the while, Satan is in the background laughing at the expense of the masses who are consuming this trash, and this is how the silly woman is conformed to this world.

The evil factors that exist in society are to be expected because the world system is controlled and dominated by the god of this world, who is the devil himself. People who do not know the Lord as their Savior will naturally act like sinners, because that is what they are if they are not saved. But when the people who profess to be in right standing with God live a sinful lifestyle, it is a reproach against the Gospel and a crime against God. The root cause of this spiritual blindness is a consequence of the Word of God not being proclaimed in the power and degree that it should be. There has not been such biblical illiteracy since the times of the Dark Ages before the Protestant Reformation. In that day, spiritual famine existed because people had no access to the Bible. In our day, people do have access to the Scriptures, but they fail to read them.

The books of the New Testament known as the epistles were letters written by the apostles to Christians, to instruct them how to live the Christian life and to explain to them what it meant to be born again. Contained within these letters are strong exhortations that were given for the purpose of letting the people who professed Jesus as their Savior know that ungodly conduct would not be tolerated. When a person lives an ungodly lifestyle, they will suffer the consequences.

The apostle Paul explained this principle when he wrote to the believers in Galatia:

> *Be not deceived; God is not mocked: for whatsoever a man soweth, that shall he also reap. For he that soweth to his flesh shall of the flesh reap corruption; but he that soweth to the Spirit shall of the Spirit reap life everlasting.*
>
> Galatians 6:7-8

The Bible is very clear. God is not a joke, nor is He to be treated like just any person on the street. His commands are to be taken very seriously. When someone disobeys those laws, they will reap consequences they do not want. This culture is shot through with the illness of lukewarm Christianity, where people think they can do anything they want to do, commit any type of sin they want to commit, and still come before the Lord and think they are going to be blessed.

This is particularly the case when it comes to fornication. Although it is taboo and uncomfortable to deal with, this problem must be addressed because it is running rampant in the modern church. Too many so-called Christian woman party and fornicate on Saturday and then walk into the church and praise Jesus on Sunday. This lifestyle is justified by slogans that pervert the Bible, such as, "We fall down, but we get back up." Or it is tolerated because of compromising principles, like establishing ninety-day rules for waiting to have sex (as if waiting a few weeks to commit sin, as opposed to a few days, makes it any more pleasing to God). Once again, we must look to the Word and see what God says about this issue. Here is God's position on the issue:

> *This I say then, Walk in the Spirit, and ye shall not fulfill the lust of the flesh. For the flesh lusteth against the Spirit, and the Spirit against the flesh: and these are contrary the one to the other; so that ye cannot do the things that ye would. But if ye be led of the Spirit, ye are not under the law.*
> *Now the works of the flesh are manifest, which are these; Adultery, formication, uncleanness, lasciviousness, idolatry, witchcraft, hatred, variance, emulations, wrath, strife, seditions, heresies, envyings, murders, drunkenness, revellings, and such like: of the which I tell you before, as I have told you in time past, that they which do such things shall not inherit the kingdom of God.*
>
> Galatians 5:16-21

Notice how Paul explained God's position on what it means to be a Christian. He first said that you must walk in the Spirit. This implies that Christianity is a way of life, and being led by the Holy Spirit is an essential part of that life. Once you make the decision to do this and begin to practice what you profess, you will not accommodate the appetites of your body. Because your body is not saved, there is a conflict between what your flesh may want and what God wants for you. In order for God to win the battle, you must let Him arise and discipline your mind to think according to the ordinances established in His Word. This will then help you to consecrate your body not to engage in those things that are called *"the works of the flesh."* These acts of depravity include fornication, alcoholic consumption, and unbecoming attitudes that run contrary to the standards of the Lord Jesus.

After Paul ran through the list of sins, he then reminded the Galatian believers that he had addressed this with them before, and he obviously considered it important enough to emphasize again. Then, like the great preacher of righteousness he was, he stated the powerful truth, that those who practice these things will not inherit eternal life in God's Kingdom.

What is most striking about the message Paul gave is that it was not a sermon delivered to unbelievers. He was writing to people who professed to be born-again, Bible-believing Christians, what we might call in our modern vernacular, "church folk." He was obviously very concerned about them getting the message, because, again, he made a point of reminding them that he had addressed these matters on a previous occasion. The obvious reason for this was that he knew some churchgoing folk really do not know the Bible, and they live their life thinking that because God is love, He will tolerate any sort of behavior. But love demands change, love requires commitment, and love expects total consecration of spirit, soul, and body. Anything opposed to that; is anti-God and contrary to His Word.

The silly woman, who continually commits fornication and thinks that she can just say a prayer and God will forgive her and let her come into His presence as though nothing had happened, is on dangerous ground. We know that everyone makes mistakes, but not everyone makes a continual habit of committing sins they know are wrong. We just saw from the Scriptures that Christians who practice sin do not have eternal life within them, which means they are not really saved. When they stand before the Judgement Seat of God, they will be in for a very rude awakening.

So many so-called Christians think they can do whatever they want to with their body, and God is just expected to accept their lifestyle. We see it in movies and television shows that portray church folk, and they commit all manner of wickedness. As distasteful as those programs are, the most heinous factor is that they exist because they reflect what is taking place in many churches today. The Bible says that there is nothing new under the sun, and what exists in our time has manifested in previous eras.

In the days of the early church, there was a heretical movement that arose, a group known as the Nicolaitanes. They believed that sexual immorality was acceptable, and they also practiced idol worship to the spirit of Jezebel, the wicked queen who killed prophets and made the people of ancient Israel to sin. When a modern person hears the term *idolatry* or *idol worship,* usually an image comes to mind of some primitive culture bowing before a statue of some kind. While this is true. it is only a small part of the equation. Those statues of false gods were crafted because the people believed and interacted with them.

I have already explained that these so-called gods were, in fact, demonic spirits. However, since I only touched on this briefly, I will now bring further clarification. These wicked spirits introduced all types of sexual immorality to pagan cultures by perverting God's original plan for sex within the covenant of marriage. All other illicit acts of indecency and lewdness were introduced by these evil spirits, and when human beings engaged in those acts, they did so in honor of those false gods. In some cultures, some of the evil spirits even manifested themselves in those immoral acts along with humans. That is why God strongly condemns sexual immorality. Commuting adultery and fornication is not only a sin against your body; it is idol worship to unclean spirits, and it opens the door for those spirits to take hold of your life.

The Nicolaitanes brought this foolishness into the church, and although they no longer refer to themselves by that name, there are still Nicolaitanes at work in many churches today. Jesus did not mince words when declaring His feelings toward these heretics:

> *Nevertheless I have somewhat against thee, because thou hast left thy first love. Remember therefore from whence thou art fallen, and repent, and do the first works; or else I will come unto thee quickly, and will remove thy candlestick out of his place, except thou repent. But this thou hast, that thou hatest the deeds of the Nicolaitanes, which I also hate.* Revelation 2:4-6

> *But I have a few things against thee, because thou hast there them that hold the doctrine of Balaam, who taught Balac to cast a stumbling block before the*

children of Israel, to eat things sacrificed unto idols, and to commit fornication. So hast thou also them that hold the doctrine of the Nicolaitanes, which thing I hate. Revelation 2:14-15

I know thy works, and charity, and service, and faith, and thy patience, and thy works; and the last to be more than the first. Notwithstanding I have a few things against thee, because thou sufferest that woman Jezebel, which calleth herself a prophetess, to teach and to seduce my servants to commit fornication; and to eat things sacrificed unto idols. And I gave her space to repent of her fornication; and she repented not. Behold, I will cast her into a bed, and them that commit adultery with her into great tribulation, except they repent of their deeds. Revelation 2:19-22

Contained within these passages of scripture are the exhortations and admonitions of the Lord Jesus Christ given to His servant John for the purpose of bringing order and correction to certain churches that existed at the time. Once again, these are not evangelistic sermons delivered to unbelievers, but prophetic declarations give to people who professed to be Christians and who attended Christian churches.

The first passage I quoted (Revelation 2:4-6) concerned a church that had lost its passion and zeal for the Lord. Although Jesus rebuked them for their complacency, He nevertheless commended them for the fact that they had no tolerance for the teachings of the Nicolaitanes. Jesus said, quite emphatically, that He hated those false beliefs. Most people do not think of Jesus as hating anything, but here He states clearly that He has contempt for a doctrine that says you can commit sexual immorality and worship other gods, and then have the audacity to come before the throne of grace, expecting to get something in your time of need. Because the Bible says that Jesus is the same yesterday, today, and forever, what He disapproved of then, He still disapproves of today.

The next set of scriptures that are referenced (Revelation 2:14-15) were words Jesus spoke to another church. This church had allowed the cradle of sin to hold sway in their house of worship. Jesus stated that this particular church had members within it who believed in the teachings of Balaam. Balaam was a false prophet in the Old Testament who was called upon by Balac, a king of the Moabites, to curse the people of Israel. Although Balaam was unable to curse

God's people, the Bible says that he counseled Balac to seduce the Israelites into commiting fornication with the women of Moab and to eat food that had been sacrificed to demon spirits. There is a great spiritual application here involving the eating of foods sacrificed in idolatry. Many times in the Bible God used the concept of eating, tasting, and food as metaphors to signify experiencing spiritual things. For example, when the Bible says, *"O taste and see that the Lord is good"* (Psalm 34:8), it is not implying the physical act of eating God, but rather the spiritual operation of experiencing His presence in your life. So, as the ancient Hebrews performed the physical act of eating pagan foods, they were spiritually partaking of the cup of iniquity that comes from the demonic realm. This process still occurs in our time, when one partakes in watching ungodly programs, listening to music with unwholesome lyrics, or engaging in filthy conversations. Those who do such things are feeding their spirits with idolatry and satanic powers. The book of Revelation tells us, that all of this was being done by church-attending people in those days, and Jesus said that He hated it.

In the final passage (Revelation 2:19-22), we read of another church, and this one had perhaps committed the most egregious act of all. The first church had no zeal for God, and yet they had not crossed the line by accepting false doctrine. The second church had within it members who openly practiced sexual immorality and engaged in practices that constituted idol worship. This last church, however, allowed a false teacher to stand before the congregation and preach the doctrines of the Nicolaitanes.

This was a woman who called herself Jezebel, probably in homage to the wicked wife of King Arab of the Old Testament. This woman certainly had the Jezebel spirit operating in her life, which is a demonic force that promotes idolatry and seeks to silence the true preachers of righteousness. Jesus said that this woman, who had the nerve to refer to herself as a prophetess, deceived people into thinking that it was acceptable to commit fornication and practice idolatry. This kind of depravity still exists in our churches today. How many self-appointed preachers, prophets, and bishops stand in pulpits and preach that homosexuality and lesbianism is pleasing to God! How many so-called shepherds allow secular entertainers who call themselves "life coaches" and "motivational" speakers to stand before congregations and women's conferences and promote sex outside of marriage (as long as you have waited ninety days to get to know each other first)! Sex outside of marriage is wrong, whether it occurs ninety days after you meet a man or nine thousand days after you meet him. How many so-called men of God use their pulpits as pimp mobiles, trying to seduce the silly women in their congregations to sleep with them after the service! These Christian groupies are led astray by hirelings posing as shepherds, spreading deceitful lusts, as they parade up and down the platform. Jesus said of the false prophetess, that she would be judged and would have to lie in the bed she had made, and not her only, but also all those who went along with her. Jesus does not change, and what He judged to be evil in that day He still judges evil in our day.

It is altogether fitting that Jesus dealt most sternly with the false prophetess, for it is the leadership in the church that promotes and engages in such immoral activity, and this results in the congregations engaging in such sinful behavior. Too many preachers in our own time have also been guilty of living ungodly lives, committing fornication with any woman in the church who will give them the time of day. It is a common thing now to hear the story of a preacher who has impregnated some young woman in his church, or of some bishop leaving his wife for his secretary. Instead of such behavior producing righteous indignation within the hearts of God's people, the collective consciousness of many churchgoers is tolerance and acceptance, all in the name of "walking in love." As a result, an entire generation of silly women sit in the pews of the church week after week. Many are deceived into thinking that God will allow this to continue, but as we read in the Scriptures, *"God is not mocked"* (Galatians 6:7), and when a person sows to the flesh, they will reap the whirlwind.

In the Old Testament, during the days before Israel had kings, they were governed by judges. God would raise up these judges to lead and direct His people, to ensure that the nation did that which was right in His eyes. The judges were assisted in guiding the spiritual life of the nation by the priests, the preachers of their day. One of the most famous priests in Israel's history was a man named Eli. His name echoes through time because he was the man who trained the great prophet Samuel, who was also the last judge of Israel before God gave them a king.

Eli is not only famous in history; he is also infamous, and this is because of the conduct of his sons. The Bible says that Eli had two sons, and they were not known for being righteous men. The Scriptures declare of them:

Now the sons of Eli were sons of Belial; they knew not the Lord.
1 Samuel 2:12

Now Eli was very old, and heard all that his sons did unto all Israel; and how they lay with the women that assembled at the door of the congregation.
1 Samuel 2:22

These men were what we might call today, "Pentecostal playboys." They engaged in sexual immorality with the women who gathered at the church. These were a special class of women who had dedicated themselves to do the work of the temple. This custom was initiated during the time of Moses, and certain women would be given the position of taking care of the needs of the Temple. This is comparable to some of our modern-era women's groups. They exist to help take care of certain areas of the church. Although these were supposed to be holy women, focusing on serving the house of God, they were silly women, who allowed themselves to be seduced by the Leviticus libertines, and, in this way, they brought immorality into the holy Temple of God. The Lord ultimately judged these wicked men, sending a prophet to speak to Eli this prophetic word:

And this shall be a sign unto thee, that shall come upon thy two sons, on Hophni and Phinehas; in one day they shall die both of them. 1 Samuel 2:34

Usually, in the trashy erotic novels that deal with scandalous and carnal church folk who engage in all manner of wickedness, the stories do not end in this way. But we are dealing with real life, and in that arena, it is best to believe the report of the Lord. God desires that we come to understand the mysteries of His Kingdom, so that true Christian maturity can spring forth within the Body of Christ. I pray that, as you have read these words and continue to read, that the full counsel of God will come alive in your spirit, so that you can become the vessel of honor He has purposed you to be.

Chapter 11

Eliminating the Weak Male Image

During the decade of the 1930s, at the time of what is considered to be the Golden Age of Hollywood cinema, one of the most prominent movie stars of that era was a man by the name of Clark Gable. Although not as widely known by younger generations today,Gable was once considered to be the king of Hollywood, and he was called the king they needed just then. At a time when the Great Depression had ravaged not only the material goods of people's lives, but also taken away the collective confidence of society, it was said of Gable that his on-screen persona gave reassurance of male strength still being alive and well. So great was his influence in popular culture that in one of his movies where his character revealed that he did not wear an undershirt beneath his regular dress shirt, the sales for T-shirts dropped considerably. He was considered to be what is known as the alpha male, and he represented the standard by which so many men wanted to model themselves.

Not only was Gable's on-screen persona so influential to men, but women also swooned over him and held him and other matinee idols like him to be the standard by which they evaluated potential mates. This concept continues even to this day, for just as those male images served as cultural touchstones for what was considered to be the ideal man, the dominant forces that exist in our own time also seek to plant subconscious ideas within women of what an alpha male is supposed to be.

What is most disheartening about this phenomenon for this modern era is that we live in a less urbane and civilized culture. While earlier decades had their own challenges and problems, the cultural male icons did at least pose a general standard of good taste. Now, some men walk openly in public wearing pants hanging down, showing their behinds, somehow believing themselves to be "cool" and "stylish." Other men have no shame when it comes to using coarse language in the presence of children, justifying their actions by saying that such profanity is good for children to hear, to help prepare them for the realities of life. There are males who consider it to be a sign of weakness to treat women with courtesy and kindness, for fear of being considered the "nice guy," since, as is so often said in our culture, nice guys finish last. There are those of the male gender who consider the Christian life to be something only for women and children, and that the church should only be visited during weddings and funerals. All of this would be sad enough, but compounded on top of these is the fact that so many women think men who think and act in these ways are the real alpha males, while men who seek a higher way of living are thought of as the weaker specimens. All of this exists today because we live in a culture that promotes and exalts the weak male image.

The reason so many males seek to take on this macho image is that they have been brainwashed into thinking that this is the image of the strong masculine man. The even greater tragedy in this equation is how it affects the silly woman. She is drawn to, fascinated by, attracted by, and constantly seeking out this kind of man. Sadly, she is blind to the fact that it is the spirit of this world that has drawn her to the kind of man and that he will rob her of her God-given destiny. I have already explained how the silly woman is often ensnared into destructive and ungodly relationships, being seduced by deceiving spirits. While these spirits bring about much harm, at the root of the problem, there is a desire on the part of the silly woman, to want to attach herself to the weak male image.

You need to understand that Satan, in an attempt to cheat you out of the abundant life Jesus paid the price for you to have, is working on several fronts. He is so subtle at this game that it often seems that he is playing chess, while the Christian is stuck playing checkers. While Satan has dispatched his forces to seek to ensnare you with direct attacks, he is also pulling the strings behind the scenes in the culture to promote a false presentation of what success looks like. It is often said, in a critical way, that the church focuses too heavily on the corruption of the media and on the entertainment world. However, these two forces are dominant in our society, and much of what people think and believe comes from these arenas.

These days people like to buy certain things because they are programmed by advertisers and sales corporations into believing that the products they are pushing will make the consumer happy. To refer back to my previous example, men wanted to be Clark Gable, and women wanted to be with him, in part because he was put before the public and promoted by the power brokers of his day as the ideal of what a man should be. As a society in general, we are constantly being told, whether subliminally or openly, what is appealing and what is not. That, in and of itself, is not a problem, but if the culture that defines what is supposed to be attractive is influenced by Satan, the god of this world, then what you are being spoon fed by that culture is a lie.

Consider the whole concept of the bad boy. The image of the bad boy portrayed in our culture is that of an alpha male who does not play by the rules and lives his life in a carefree and exciting way. This male image is put forth as the ideal man, the kind of man who gets what he wants and does not take anything from anyone because he is so strong and confident. Our society seeks to program people into believing that this is the kind of man who always gets the girl. Why? Because he is dangerous and volatile, and that is supposed to be appealing to women.

The "bad boy" often dresses in a crude fashion, communicates in a coarse speaking style, and all of this is what we are told is what makes women excited, because the bad boy is the, "alpha male." What is behind this propaganda machine is the reality of a male with no purpose or sense of destiny, who, deep down, is so insecure with himself that he must hide that insecurity by telling everyone how great and how strong he is. The wild, adventurous streak he has that is supposed to be thrilling and interesting is a facade that hides a person who is both a danger to himself and those who connect themselves with him. The rebellious streak that seems beguiling to women at the beginning usually leaves a bitter aftertaste of abuse, disrespect, and, sometimes, violence and destruction. And yet many women are fooled into desiring that type of male, when the very idea of a "bad boy" is antithetical to the true concept of a genuinely appealing man.

The term *bad boy* should be a *non sequitur* from the outset. Why would a woman want a boy when she could have a man? And why would a woman want a man who prides himself on being a menace and a cancer on society? Yet many women do, because the prince of this world has seeded this society with a false sense of what a real man should be, causing multitudes of women to walk around as if they have scales over their eyes, preventing them from choosing the right kind of man.

Then there is the image of the man considered by polite society to be powerful and successful, but he cares nothing about the Lord, nor about giving his life over to Jesus. He has the job, the house, the money and all of the other trappings this world considers accomplished men to have, and he considers the things of God to be trivial, unimportant matters that are a waste of his time. He considers Christianity to be something that is for weaker men. He mocks the house of God by saying that church is filled with nothing but women, children, and effeminate males, all foolishly looking to someone they cannot see. This type of male prides himself on how many women he has seduced and belittles the idea of monogamy and fidelity to one special woman.

In spite of men having these ungodly points of view, many women pride themselves on attracting this very type of man to their lives. This is the constant infirmity of the silly woman. As a result of her lack of spiritual perception, she is continually drawn toward and attracted to the weak male image. When a good and decent man seeks to court her favor, she looks upon him with ridicule because she has been brainwashed by the wicked spirits of this age into believing that a good and decent man is boring and, ultimately, unfulfilling.

These challenges, that also exist in the Body of Christ, must be dealt with, and they must be addressed in the light of the Word of God. The Bible is the Guidebook for all the issues of life, including defining what a real man is and what a real man is not. If you are a woman who seeks to have what God wants you to have, you must train yourself to think as He thinks and come into agreement and harmonize with His idea of what a real man is.

The weak male image that is exalted in our society and has even crept into the Church of the Lord Jesus Christ must be torn down and replaced with the standard God has outlined in His Word. We are told by the apostle Paul in these sobering words:

> *(For the weapons of our warfare are not carnal, but mighty through God to the pulling down of strong holds;) casting down imaginations, and every high thing that exalteth itself against the knowledge of God, and bringing into captivity every thought to the obedience of Christ.* 2 Corinthians 10:4-5

Here the believer is informed that God has equipped His Church with the tools necessary to fight the world, the flesh and the devil. Those weapons of warfare are undoubtedly the Holy Scriptures, for the book of Hebrews declares:

> *For the word of God is quick, and powerful, and sharper than any twoedged sword, piercing even to the dividing asunder of soul and spirit, and of the joints and marrow, and is a discerner of the thoughts and intents of the heart.*
> Hebrews 4:12

The prophet Jeremiah, by the Spirit of the Lord, made this declaration:

> *Is not my word like a fire? saith the* L*ORD; and like a hammer that breaketh the rock in pieces?* Jeremiah 23:29

From these two verses, we understand the formula by which God operates. The principles contained within His Word are the spiritual weapons that we need to use to tear down every thought and imagination that produces false images that creep into the Body of Christ. It is also the Word of God that can plant new seeds into the soil of your heart, to reveal to you what a true mighty man of valor is. So, let us once more turn to the Scriptures and receive the inspiration and impartation that comes from heeding the full counsel of the Great I Am.

In taking this journey to eliminate the weak male image and raise up the true picture of the God-kind of man, it is incumbent upon us to go back to the very beginning, or origin, of man, as recorded in the book of Genesis. The information contained within that book is not only full of facts about the origins of life; it is also the pattern by which we, as believers, should frame our world view regarding the building blocks of life. As we understand this pattern and lay a foundation in proper alignment with that pattern, then we can grow into thinking as God would have us to think. From there, you will see what His idea of a real man is, and, based upon that, you will know what kind of man to look for when choosing a mate.

In the account of the creation of the human race, we, as readers of the book of Genesis, are given the special privilege of being granted access to the councils of the Godhead and are allowed to pull back the curtain and take part in one of the greatest conversations that has ever taken place in all of history. The Bible records the dialogue as follows:

> *And God said, Let us make man in our image, after our likeness: and let them have dominion over the fish of the sea, and over the fowl of the air, and over the cattle, and over all the earth, and over everything that creepeth upon the earth. So God created man in his own image, in the image of God created he him; male and female created he them.* Genesis 1:26-27

This is a conversation between God, the Father, God, the Son, and God, the Holy Spirit. We can discern this because God said,*"Let US make man."* The *us* that is referred to here is the Trinity, or what is often referred to as God in Three Persons. Notice what God said about man, that he would be made in His image and after His likeness. Those words *image* and *likeness* mean that man was modeled and crafted to look like and to resemble his Creator, God. That resemblance was not just meant to imply an outward form, but, also, a degree of inward character. God went on to say that man would have *"dominion ... over the earth,"* and that dominion was to reflect how God Himself had dominion over the entire Universe. So the first male image that was established in the world was of a man who would look and act like God Himself.

This man would not only resemble God's outward form, but also carry within him the nature and the character of God. This man would possess the God-kind of faith, and that would allow him to have authority over the world, so that he could be an overcomer in all the issues of life. He would not only be able to master life because of His faith in God, but, even more importantly, he would be able to master himself. Because his spirit would be attuned to God (because he was made in God's likeness), He would walk in temperance and self-control over his body and emotions, thereby living a life that would only do those things pleasing and acceptable to the Creator. This portrait is not only the first male image set in place; it is the model for which a man should strive and the kind of man a woman of worth and value should want to be with.

The Bible delves deeper into this portrait of the spiritual man by giving us further insight into God Himself. Remember that He made the man to both look and act like Himself and then placed him as the original role model of what a real man should be.

The Bible is clear when it declares that God is a Spirit being. This means that He is not a man in the sense of a being human. However, the Bible *does* compare Him to a certain type of man, and that comparison provides us not only insight into Who He is, but also what an ideal man should be. This revelation comes out of the momentous occasion when God delivered the children of Israel from the bondage of Egypt. After the hosts of the oppressors were drowned in the Red Sea, the children of God rejoiced at their triumph. As Moses stood before the people and sang a song of deliverance, he began to make a declaration that described who this God who worked on their behalf was. He said:

The Lord is a man of war: the Lord is his name. Exodus 15:3

This statement, brief in content, but laden with meaning, gives us revelation about the nature of God. Even though God is not a human male, He spoke through Moses and revealed Himself as *"a man of war."* This means that when we seek to form a contextual framework of Who God is, and if we do so by comparing Him to a certain type of man, then we could compare Him to a man of war. The Lord, our great God, is a warrior. He is not just any warrior. He is the warrior against whom all others must be judged. He is not a man of action, but, rather, the Male figure of heroism that is the standard every man must strive for. This statement made by Moses provides us with the knowledge that a real man is, first and foremost, a spiritual warrior.

The war that I am referring to here is not a natural conflict played out on some earthly battlefield; it is a spiritual contest between good and evil. All the natural battles fought in the Old Testament were the result of spiritual conflicts that existed in the heavens. When God delivered His people from their enemies, He was manifesting in the natural what had been won in the Spirit. Based upon this, and keeping in mind the alignment of the real alpha male with the image of God, we see that a real man is one who will fight on behalf of God's righteous causes.

Paul, in writing to his spiritual son Timothy, gave him insight on how he lived his life as a Christian, hoping that Timothy would follow in his footsteps. Even as he prepared to face death, Paul boldly proclaimed his testimony:

I have fought a good fight, I have finished my course, I have kept the faith.
2 Timothy 4:7

These are the words of a true man, one who lived his life as a spiritual warrior, fighting to keep his faith strong.

Life, in and of itself, is a contest, a contest of who will go to the best schools, who will get the job, and who will be promoted. It is a contest of wills. The greatest battle in life is to keep your faith strong so that you are not defeated by the world, the flesh, and the devil. Paul understood this and purposed within himself to fight, to complete his assignment from God and to keep his faith in God so strong that he would not give up nor compromise his Christianity. He took this position because he modeled himself on the strong male image he saw in God. The reason some men fail at achieving this way of life is that they are weak in their spirit, and a weak spirit will always result in a weak man.

It is often pointed out in Christian circles that, within church membership, the dominant gender is that of females. There are more women in the Sunday service, more women who attend the prayer groups, and more women who work in the church in general. This has become so noticeable that even secularist have pointed out the trend. Often, when men are asked why they do not go to church, they offer many reasons, usually pointing the finger of blame at the house of God. They say, "Church is boring; it does not address my issues." Or they insist that regular church attendance is not a very manly thing. All of this finger pointing at the church is a smoke screen and a dodge designed to draw attention away from the fact that these men are just too weak to serve God.

That may seem like a harsh statement, but consider this: To live in this world, you must contend with the reality that the currents of society are constantly seeking to pull you in a direction that is opposed to the will of God. Because of that pull and that pressure, it is easier to make the ungodly choice rather than the righteous one. It takes work and resolve to commit to one woman and stay with that woman through good times and bad. It is easier to go from woman to woman, using them for their bodies instead of consecrating the flesh to be faithful and true to just one. It is a continual battle to walk by faith and not by sight, believing God even when it seems like nothing will come to pass. It is easier just to give up at the first sign of trouble and say, "Well, I guess it didn't work." It requires true strength to humble oneself under the mighty hand of God, putting the male ego on the altar and allowing God to purge that pride with holy fire. It is far easier to keep the pride and live life based on what the carnal nature wants. It takes discipline to get up every Sunday and go to church, be there on time, and stay for the entire service. It is much easier to stay in bed, sleep in, and wake up in the afternoon, in time to watch a football game. Then, after all of that leisure, you can reveal your weakness by accusing the church of not being *macho* enough.

It takes spiritual hunger to go to every service and not just attend on Sunday. It is easier to say, "Well, I went to church on Sunday. Why should I go on Tuesday?" Many men behave this way because, in spite of all of their chest beating and feigned attempts at being *macho,* they are just too weak to take up their cross and say yes to God's will and to God's way.

If it was easy to fight the good fight of faith, more men would be in church. But, because it requires consecration and commitment, some men do not have within them strength to press toward the high calling of God. They could obtain that strength through the help of the Holy Spirit, but they would have to humble themselves and male pride can often cloud sound judgement. Still, this kind of man is often portrayed as the ideal, and many silly women are deceived into forming attachments with these weak male images. If you want a real man, then you need a man of faith, a man who will walk by faith, live by faith, and if necessary, die by faith, a man who never casts aside his confidence in God.

One of the greatest examples of a man of faith is found in the life of Abraham. Here was the kind of man every woman should hope to marry, for he was fully committed to the will of God. If a man cannot commit to God, he will be unable to fully commit to you. Don't be fooled into being yoked together with an unbeliever, for you are only opening the door to Satan to cheat you out of an abundant life.

Because of Abraham's commitment to God, He was committed to his family, his ministry, and his destiny. Even during the seasons when God tested and tried him, in order to develop his character, Abraham stayed true to his Lord. The book of Hebrews provides a beautiful synopsis of Abraham's life, and it is interesting to discover that, within that synopsis, we are shown the ways in which Abraham was tested. In order to be a man of faith, we must all endure and overcome tests. If you desire to join yourself to a true alpha male, you need to see and understand how God develops a male and makes him into a man. The Bible declares:

> *By faith Abraham, when he was called to go out into a place which he should after receive for an inheritance, obeyed; and he went out, not knowing whither he went. By faith he sojourned in the land of promise, as in a strange country, dwelling in tabernacles with Isaac and Jacob, the heirs with him of the same promise: for he looked for a city which hath foundations, whose builder and maker is God.*
>
> *By faith Abraham, when he was tried, offered up Isaac: and he that had received the promises offered up his only begotten son, of whom it was said, That in Isaac shall thy seed be called: accounting that God was able to raise him up, even from the dead; from whence also he received him in a figure.*
>
> Hebrews 11:8-10 and 17-19

Contained within each of these tests were moments when Abraham had to choose obedience toward God in his situation. The first test was to see if Abraham would be obedient to leave his old way of life and follow God, even when He did not yet know all the details. When God saves a man and calls him out of darkness into His marvelous light, that man must decide to follow the Lord all the way. Even if the road may seem to be unclear at times, the strong male image will stay true to the Master's call and continue to walk by faith and not by sight.

Second, Abraham was instructed to look for a city whose Builder and Maker was God Himself. This signifies the seeking of the place where God desires a person to be. If a man has within him the true moral fiber of greatness, he will live a continuous lifestyle of seeking God, to find his place and his purpose in this world.

Finally, there was the greatest test of all, to see whether or not Abraham would offer to God his beloved son Isaac. The Lord commanded Abraham to offer Isaac as a sacrifice. This seemed to mean killing him, and, in this way, destroying any hope of future posterity. At that point, Abraham could have easily faltered or given up, but he decided to hold fast to the promise of God.

Keep in mind that Isaac was to be the one through whom Abraham would be the father of many nations, and because God spoke that specific word concerning Isaac's future, Abraham trusted it. Even if God had to raise Isaac from the dead, that word would come to pass. The kind of man you want the Lord to join you to is a man who, even when the chips are down, will wrap himself around the promises of God and settle in his heart that he will live to see the salvation of his God. This is the portrait of the real alpha male, a man of integrity, a man of faith, a man of God.

In conclusion to this chapter and this section of the book, I want to share something with you that comes from the book of Ruth. Ruth was a woman who had the great privilege of being a part of the family lineage from which Jesus was to be born. Although she had to go through much to receive her blessings, she did ultimately attain them. Her story began by describing how she married into the family of an Israelite couple who had two sons. The family lived during a time of famine, and the Bible shares with us these words regarding the their lives:

> *Now it came to pass in the days when the judges ruled, that there was a famine in the land. And a certain man of Bethlehemjudah went to sojourn in the country of Moab, he, and his wife, and his two sons. And the name of the man was Elimelech, and the name of his wife Naomi, and the name of his two sons Mahlon and Chilion, Ephrathites of Bethlehemjudah. And they came into the country of Moab, and continued there.*
> *And Elimelech Naomi's husband died; and she was left, and her two sons. And they took them wives of the women of Moab; the name of the one was Orpah, and the name of the other Ruth: and they dwelled there about ten years.*
> *And Mahlon and Chilion died also both of them; and the woman was left of her two sons and her husband.* Ruth 1:1-5

These scriptures, if read in a casual manner, seem of no great spiritual significance. However, we must always keep in mind what the Bible says: that all scripture is given by the inspiration of God. Contained within each verse is information that is relevant to our spiritual development. In these passages, we are told about this family that migrated from Israel to the country of Moab, to escape a famine that had ravaged the land. We are also informed of the fact that the sons of this family had married two Moabite women, and one of them was named Ruth.

In the process of time, both the father and the sons died, leaving Naomi alone with her two daughters-in-law. The father, more than likely, died of old age, but it is strange that the two sons, who, more than likely, were in the flower of their manhood, also died. It is worth noting that the names of all of these participants are given, and each name in the Bible contains a meaning. The names of these two sons meant sickness and weakness.

God was about to do something great in the lives of Ruth and Naomi (which we will examine in a later chapter), but this great change could not occur with those weak male images in their lives, nor could those men help take the family to the next level that God had in store for them. If you want to rise to the next level that God has prepared for you, you must decide what kind of a woman God wants you to be. If you desire for the Lord to bless you with a true man of valor, you must be sure that every imagination of weak male images is cast out from your mind. I have not written these words merely to curse the darkness, but, rather, to light a candle that will point you toward becoming your better self.

As we now take our journey into looking at the virtuous woman, I encourage you to reach for that person God called you to be, and receive the spark of divine illumination that has the power to take you into your glorious future.

Part Three

The Virtuous Woman

Chapter 12

Portrait of a Lady

Shall I compare thee to a summer's day?
Thou art more lovely and more temperate. William Shakespeare

One of the most beautiful and poignant fairytales that have ever been told is the story of Pygmalion and his statue that came to life. According to the myth, as it has come down through history from the Greek poet Ovid, Pygmalion was a famous sculptor who was considered to be one of the greatest artisans of his day. So powerful was the scope of his genius and so deep was his devotion to his craft that his work was all-consuming, so much so that he had time for nothing else. Unlike most men, he was not easily wooed by the women he came into contact with. In fact, he considered the women he encountered to be inadequate to his standard of worth and beauty. So, as the result of necessity being the mother of invention, he decided to sculpt a statue of his ideal woman. Pouring out all his skill, his technique, his energy and his passion, he toiled and labored over every detail, to bring his vision into manifestation. Finally, at the end, his statue was complete. As he gazed upon its wonder, he realized that his ideal woman was more glorious than even he had imagined in his mind.

In the process of time, as Pygmalion would spend his quieter hours gazing upon the stature, he could not help but wish that his creation would come alive. So great was his desire that he longed and prayed for his dream to come true ... until one day his petition was heard. The goddess Aphrodite came and touched the statue, and, to the sculptor's amazement, life began to break forth. Suddenly, before his very eyes, stone and mortar became flesh and bone, and the ideal image of one artist transformed into a living creature of such loveliness and beauty that it beggared all description. Pygmalion instantly fell in love with the woman, soon after they were married, and, like all good fairy-tales should end, the two lived happily ever after.

Of course that story is exactly that—a story. It is a fable out of the stuff of dreams and legends. But like all good stories, it contains within it a message and an idea that can inspire us to pursue a greater truth. This simple tale of a man who created his ideal woman and was allowed to see that idea come to life has a strong Christian element to it. The Chief Architect and Fashioner of things is none other than God Himself. His hands, the Bible tells us, stretched out the heavens. It was based upon His design schematics. God also designed the Tabernacle in the wilderness built by Moses. It was through God's art that man was made man. God fashioned him to embody the image of His own Person.

Throughout the Bible, there are numerous references that liken God to a great craftsman, molding and shaping His children to be more like Him. Perhaps the most direct reference comes from the words of the prophet Jeremiah, when he heard God speak to him:

> *The word which came to Jeremiah from the LORD, saying, Arise, and go down to the potter's house, and there I will cause thee to my words. Then I went down to the potter's house, and, behold, he wrought a work on the wheels. And the vessel that he made of clay was marred in the hand of the potter: so he made it again another vessel, as seemed good to the potter to make it.*
> *Then the word of the LORD came unto me, saying, O house of Israel, cannot I do with you as this potter? saith the Lord. Behold, as the clay is in the potter's hand, so are ye in my hand, O house of Israel.* Jeremiah 18:1-6

This passage of scripture speaks directly to the fact that God is the Master Potter. Just as clay is formed into something beautiful, so, too, are we who seek to be changed into His image. We are molded and fashioned by the Potter's hands. Because of the principle that says, "Out of the mouth of two or more witnesses, let every word be established," let us look at the New Testament to see if the Lord also spoke in these terms under the New Covenant.

In Paul's second letter to Timothy, we read of how God looks upon His chosen people and the way in which He deems them fit for service. Once again, we are confronted with a spiritual comparison that is very similar to what we read in Jeremiah. The Bible declares:

> *Nevertheless the foundation of God standeth sure, having this seal, The Lord knoweth them that are his. And, let every one that nameth the name of Christ depart from iniquity. But in a great house there are not only vessels of gold and of silver, but also of wood and of earth; and some to honour, and some to dishonour. If a man therefore purge himself from these, he shall be a vessel unto honour, sanctified, and meet for the master's use, and prepared unto every good work.* 2 Timothy 2:19-21

Paul was speaking to his protégée, Timothy, and telling him that every person who professes to be a follower of Jesus should live a life free from iniquity. He then compared the Church of God to a great household, one that contains within it vessels of high quality and also vessels of a lesser quality. If a person will consecrate their life unto God, they will be a vessel of the higher quality, one that is prepared to be used by God for His good work.

Based upon these two scriptural references, the concept of God as the Potter and us as the clay is clearly seen. If you desire to live a life of quality service toward God, you must choose to be a quality vessel. Just as there were vessels of varying degrees in the house, there are varying degrees of peoples in the Church. The silly woman is the vessel of wood and earth, while the virtuous woman is the vessel of gold and silver. If you desire to be the virtuous woman, you must allow the Potter to form you in His mold and use you for His glory.

The question becomes: What is God's idea of the perfect woman? When I use the word *perfect,* I am not referring to someone being infallible, but, rather, being complete and mature in their relationship with God, always going from one level of glory to another. So, once again, who is this virtuous woman? If God could describe in detail how He would sculpt the ideal female vessel of honor, what would she look like? What kind of a woman would she be? Fortunately for us, we have been given a portrait of a divine lady in the Bible.

I want to now draw your focus to the famous passage of scripture that speaks about the virtuous woman. This description is found in the last chapter of the book of Proverbs, and I wish now to quote the entirety of it to you.

Often, when the virtuous woman is discussed in Christian circles, only certain sections of the chapter are cited. However, in order to appreciate the depth of the revelation that comes in the middle and the end of the chapter, one must start at the beginning. It is by laying the foundation that a full range of insight can be gleaned, to bring an understanding of who the ideal woman God speaks about really is:

> *The words of king Lemuel, the prophecy that his mother taught him. What my son? and what, the son of my womb? and what, the son of my vows? Give not thy strength unto women, nor thy ways to that which destroyeth kings.*
>
> *It is not for kings, O Lemuel, it is not for kings to drink wine; nor for princes strong drink: lest they drink, and forget the law, and pervert the judgement of any of the afflicted. Give strong drink unto him that is ready to perish, and wine unto those that be of heavy hearts. Let him drink, and forget his poverty, and remember his misery no more.*
>
> *Open thy mouth for the dumb in the cause of all such as are appointed to destruction. Open thy mouth, judge righteously, and plead the cause of the poor and needy.*
>
> *Who can find a virtuous woman? for her price is far above rubies. The heart of her husband doth safely trust in her, so that he shall have no need of spoil. She will do him good and not evil, all the days of her life. She seeketh wool, and flax, and worketh willingly with her hands. She is like the merchants' ships; she bringeth her food from afar. She riseth also while it is yet night, and giveth meat to her household, and a portion to her maidens. She considereth a field and buyeth it: with the fruit of her hands she planteth a vineyard.*
>
> *She girdeth her loins with strength, and strengtheneth her arms. She perceiveth that her merchandise is good: her candle goeth not out by night. She layeth her hands to the spindle, and her hands hold the distaff. She stretcheth out her hands to the poor; yea, she reacheth forth her hands to the needy. She is not afraid of the snow for her household: for all her household are clothed with scarlet. She maketh herself coverings of tapestry; her clothing is silk and purple.*
>
> *Her husband is known in the gates, when he sitteth among the elders of the land. She maketh fine linen, and selleth it; and delivereth girdles unto the merchant. Strength and honour are her clothing; and she shall rejoice in time to come. She openeth her mouth with wisdom; and in her tongue is the law*

of kindness. She looketh well to the ways of her household, and eateth not the bread of idleness. Her children arise up, and call her blessed; her husband also, and he praiseth her.

Many daughters have done virtuously, but thou excellest them all. Favour is deceitful, and beauty is vain: but a woman that feareth the LORD, *she shall be praised. Give her of the fruit of her hands; and let her own works praise her in the gates.* Proverbs 31:1-31

These are truly some of the most poetic and meaningful words that have ever been recorded by the hand of humankind. I encourage you to read that chapter through several times ... until the truth of those words become engrafted into your spirit.

For my part, in helping you to see that these words become a reality in your life, the Lord has impressed upon me to use this chapter as the template for the remaining chapters of the book, looking at all the facets of the virtuous woman, and, in so doing, building on the foundation of revelation that is contained in Proverbs 31.

To begin, it is important to start at the beginning. This chapter immediately brings us into the mind of a king, and we are even provided with this man's name—Lemuel. From the standpoint of biblical scholarship, we do not know much about who Lemuel was, nor where his kingdom might have been. Some Bible expositors have advanced the theory that Lemuel was just another name for Solomon, but there is no concrete evidence to support this theory. Because the Bible provides no hard evidence that would connect him with Solomon and because most of the writings of Proverbs are attributed to Solomon and no other names are mentioned, I will take the Bible at face value and refer to Lemuel as a distinct person. Whoever he was and wherever he came from, King Lemuel was undoubtedly a blessed ruler because he had a very wise mother.

It has been said by sages of old that a mother is the first teacher of her child. After all, that child began life in her womb. Everything a mother feeds her children—both spiritually and naturally—has a direct impact on the growth and development of that child. This mother, in Proverbs 31, fed her spirit with the Word of God, which Jesus said is *"the bread which cometh down from heaven"* (John 6:50). What did the Master say to the devil when He was tempted in the wilderness:

But he answered and said, It is written, Man shall not live by bread alone, but by every word that proceedeth from the mouth of God Matthew 4:4

One of the greatest truths to ensure spiritual victory and help you walk in continuous revelation is to always feed your spirit and your soul on the Word of God. The mother of King Lemuel understood this truth and purposed within herself to teach her son the ways of God. She went about this task by instructing him on key elements of wisdom that came from a prophecy that she obtained. Whether that prophecy was given directly to her or whether she obtained it from another source, the point is that she obtained it and embraced the power of the prophetic word and how it could change her son's life.

It is quite sad that in this modern era of Christianity, prophecy is simply thought of by some as a declaration by a preacher to someone about getting a new house or some other material possession. Prophecy, in its highest and deepest form, is a supernatural declaration from the Lord to His servants, to deliver a message of divine revelation regarding the present or the future. This particular prophetic word, taught to King Lemuel by his mother, was a message about what it takes to be a great and noble leader.

It is altogether fitting that God would choose to record these words, given through the heart of a mother, because all good parents want the best for their children. This mother understood that her son had a divine assignment to rule over a kingdom and to use all his strength toward that task. Therefore she began to decree the words of the prophecy.

The first thing the prophecy declared was a warning for the young man not to give his strength to women, nor to those vices which destroy kings. I have already examined how God has given women a great ability to influence the affections and the passions of men, and history throughout the ages has recorded accounts of great leaders brought down because of lusting after the wrong kind of woman. This mother was determined that this would not happen to her son, so she declared this prophecy over his life, to give him a glimpse of the future companion he would one day encounter.

It is always God's desire, not only to give us words of warning, but also to provide words of encouragement. These heavenly exhortations are meant to inspire us to wait on the promises of God, even when we are tempted to lay hold of the wiles of the devil. Therefore, this mother continued to give her son the word of the Lord, and instructed him on those things he must avoid if he was to be a successful ruler.

It is fascinating that the prophecy began with the advice to avoid the wrong type of woman and then led into a visual portrait of the right kind of woman, the virtuous woman. The prophecy declares that this kind of woman is the rarest of treasures, and, therefore, is not easily found. Her worth and value are so great that the cost of obtaining her is very high. The Bible puts her value at *"far above rubies"* (verse 10), considered to be one of the most precious jewels in the entirety of the ancient world. This woman's value was so high that the king needed to understand it would cost him something to attain her. He would have to wait for her, pray about finding her, be in the right place to notice her and be prepared as a man who was worthy of her hand and of her love.

Most importantly, the king would have to understand that the value of this woman would be so great that, without her in his life, he would never be a leader of fame and renown. He would come to the understanding that all the seeds of greatness that were planted within him could only come to harvest by the watering of this woman's love. Not only would it cost the king a high price to be with her. She, too, would have to pay a high price to become this woman. This is the other reason the Scriptures imply how difficult it is to find this woman. Too few females really pay the price to become this woman of virtue. Some don't pay the price because they don't understand what the price is. Others don't pay because the cost is to great. God does not give cheap thrills, and He will not cast His pearls before those who place no value on them (see Matthew 7:6).

This woman is special. She is unique because she was sculpted and fashioned by God Himself. If your desire is to become this woman, you must understand all that she is. With that being said, let us now examine this chapter and see the workings of the Holy Spirit in creating this daughter of Zion. All the great things this woman is able to do and accomplish, she does by starting with a specific revelation. She understands one great truth, and from that seed springs forth her harvest of success. This golden key of knowledge is her template, and that key is to be found in this next chapter.

Chapter 13

Perceiving that Your Merchandise Is Good

Cogito ergo sum. [I think, therefore I am.] Renee Descartes

One of the greatest tools that God has given you in order to live a life of faith and victory is the ability to have a positive perception of yourself, based upon what God's Word says about you. The virtuous woman's foundation for successful living is in understanding her value as a child of God and in recognizing all the ways He has equipped her to live the abundant life in Christ Jesus.

Many religious people equate spirituality with a total emphasis on God's role in the life of the believer. They naively assume that God does everything. If He wants something great to happen in their lives or if He wants them to think great thoughts, He will just force these things upon them. This, however, is not true Spirit living, nor is it in accordance with a proper understanding of how the Lord works. The victorious Christian life is one in which a person will yield their life to God, so that He can teach them how to cooperate with Him. The partnership between the two will produce dynamic results.

True faith is you working with God in order to achieve a great result. You do your part, by doing what you can and know to do. As that takes place, then God will do His part, by doing what only He can do, so that the blessings can flow in a continual stream.

The great apostle Paul brought forth revelation regarding this principle in his first letter to the saints at Corinth. When he spoke about the contributions that both he and Apollos brought to the ministerial work at Corinth, he declared:

> *I have planted, Apollos watered; but God gave the increase. So then neither is he that planteth any thing, neither he that watereth; but God that giveth the increase. Now he that planteth and he that watereth are one: and every man shall receive his own reward according to his own labour. For we are labourers together with God: ye are God's husbandry, ye are God's building.*
>
> 1 Corinthians 3:6-9

From this passage we understand that the believer must do his or her part by planting and watering, and then one can expect God to bring forth the harvest. The key is understanding what the Bible clearly states: that we are workers together with Him.

It is also important to note that Paul said we are God's "husbandry." This means "a land that is cultivated to produce a harvest." So, not only does God look at us as workers together with Him, but we are also the soil through which He brings forth a harvest of blessings for all the world to see. This is for the purpose of displaying His power. If you do not do those things that are in your power to do, then you block God from doing the things that only He can do in your life.

The number one priority you have in life is to plant within yourself seeds of a healthy, godly, and victorious self-image of who you are in Jesus Christ. If you do not see yourself as more than a conqueror, you hinder God from making you into an overcomer. If you do not water your spirit with thoughts of health and healing, you block God's healing promise from manifesting in your life. If you do not see yourself as prosperous, you cause a blockage to occur in the realm of the Spirit that will hinder the provision of God from materializing in your life. You plant, you water, and then you watch God give the increase. The firsts seeds to plant in your heart are the ones that allow you to see yourself as an overcomer.

There is another passage of scripture that reaffirms the point I am attempting to make. It is one of the most quoted and famous passages in the entirety of the Scriptures. Even though that is the case, let us look at it once more, this time with fresh eyes, able to see another facet of revelation. The Bible declares:

I can do all things through Christ which strengtheneth me.
Philippians 4:13

Usually, when this verse is quoted, it is with an emphasis on Christ doing the thing that needs to be done. But look at how Paul started the verse. He began by saying, *"I can."* He understood that in order to have true faith in God, he must have faith in himself, what God had placed within him, and what God could do through him. Paul saw himself in a positive way, because Christ was in him. Because Christ was in him, he had "the goods" on the inside of him to accomplish whatever he needed to do.

John, the beloved disciple of Jesus, also emphasized this point in one of his epistles:

Ye are of God, little children, and have overcome them: because greater is he that is in you, than he that is in the world. 1 John 4:4

The victory comes in knowing that you have greatness within you. Why? Because the Greater One lives in you. Unless you put those seeds into your thoughts and meditate upon them, you will always fall short of the best that God has for you.

We are also given these words from the book of Proverbs:

For as he thinketh in his heart, so is he: Eat and drink, saith he to thee; but his heart is not with thee. Proverbs 23:7

Continuous confirmations from the Scriptures make the message crystal clear. If you want to make a success of your faith, you must cooperate with God to make it happen, and the first step in that collective enterprise is to think the right thoughts about yourself. Your perceptions determine your reality. If you perceive correctly, you will walk in perfect faith. If your perception is negative and dark, that is what you will manifest in your life. Faith is a substance that can work for your good or for your destruction. If you believe incorrectly about yourself, that substance will produce a negative reality. If you believe positively about yourself, then that substance will produce a glorious reality. You have to perceive that your merchandise is good, and this is what makes the virtuous woman the person she is.

The woman of virtue understands her value as a child of God, and, because she places her worth within that context, she realizes that she has been made by God, equipped by God, and empowered by God to live life at her fullest potential. She is a confident and capable human being, not based on her own ability, but on what God is able to do with her and through her. She has embraced the principle in the Bible that declares:

> *And this is the confidence that we have in him, that, if we ask any thing according to his will, he heareth us: and if we know that he hear us, whatsoever we ask, we have the petitions that we desired of him.* 1 John 5:14-15

Notice that the verse speaks about the confidence of the believers. That spiritual and emotional strength is not founded upon self, but upon Christ. And, because it is founded in Christ, the believer is able to think positively about themselves. The virtuous woman knows who she is, and she has caught the revelation of her eternal self-worth because of Christ (Who is the hope of glory) in her. With that in mind, let us return once more to Proverbs 31 and examine how this woman is described, in the light of the foundational truth that we have to build upon:

> *Who can find a virtuous woman? for her price is far above rubies. The heart of her husband doth safely trust in her, so that she will have no need of spoil. She will do him good and not evil all the days of her life. She seeketh wool, and flax, and worketh willingly with her hands. She is like the merchants' ships; she bringeth her food from afar.*
> *She riseth also while it is yet night, and giveth meat to her household, and a portion to her maidens. She considereth a field, and buyeth it; with the fruit of her hands she planteth a vineyard. She girdeth her loins with strength, and strengtheneth her arms. She perceiveth that her merchandise is good, her candle goeth not out by night.* Proverbs 31:10-18

From the beginning of this prophetic teaching, we read how the mother started with a question that implied how complex it is to find a virtuous woman. Why is this such a difficult quest? Because this woman is of such high caliber that her worth and value is greater than rubies. She is valuable because she has what it takes to deal with the situations and phases of her life.

When the modern ear hears the word *virtue* or *virtuous,* usually the thoughts that come to mind are ones of purity and propriety. While that is true, it is only part of the diamond. The other facets of the jewel must be examined, so that the greater revelation can come forth.

In the original Hebrew, the word translated *virtue* means "strength, wealth and valor." The part of the word that deals with strength is not exclusive to the physical domain. It is more focused on strength in the area of resources, riches, and the substance of wisdom and knowledge. These definitions provide further insight into understanding the text.

The Bible shows that this woman has everything within her to satisfy the needs of her husband. So stimulated and intoxicated is this man by his woman that every need he has—whether it be emotional, physical or spiritual—she has the wealth of goods within her to meet. He understands this so fully that he trusts in her abilities completely, and he knows that because she is a woman of God, she will always do what is right and good for him and the rest of the family.

It is interesting that the Bible also says he will now have no need of *"spoil."* This indicates that he does not need to look outside of his home for fulfillment from any other woman. He understands that his wife has "the goods" to take care of all that concerns him.

But the Bible goes further and deals with this woman's skills in managing both her home and her business. When the Scriptures speak of her household and her maidens, it is informing us that this woman possesses within her the ability to take care of a home and manage a business. She has mastered good time management and the proper management of her family's finances. She is, therefore, productive and wealthy enough to purchase property and to know exactly what to do with that property.

This woman is a living miracle in every way. Not only does she have the goods to satisfy her husband, and not only does she has the goods to balance home life and work life, but the Bible even compares her to a merchant shipping vessel. Those types of ships were used in transporting supplies from one area to another, and when someone used the term "merchants' ships," it was understood that it was a vessel that was filled with resources. This woman was like a ship filled with resources to meet a multitude of needs. Truly, she was a vessel of honor fit for the Master's use.

Some may read Proverbs 31 as an allegorical fable. They might say, "It's not possible for one woman to be able function in all of these offices." I have personally heard ministers stand and proclaim that Proverbs 31 is not talking about one woman, but, rather, is a composite of many women. These unscriptural and overtly sexist points of view clearly do not agree with God's thinking.

First, the Bible is very clear when it says that this prophecy is about a particular woman and not some composite of many women that someone met over the years.

Second, God would not have put these things in the Bible if it were not possible to become this woman. Any woman has the potential to become like this woman mentioned in Proverbs 31, if she is willing to pay the price. To start the process of paying that price, you have to begin where the woman in the scriptures began. This woman was able to produce the goods by, first, having a proper perception within herself, that her merchandise was good.

When the Bible uses the term *merchandise* in this chapter, it is referring to the woman. She was the merchandise, and she recognized that she was good, because God had made her good and had put good things within her.

All of this revelation from God's Word ultimately leads me to pose this particular question to you: Do you perceive that your merchandise is good or, to put it more bluntly, do you like yourself? When you wake up in the morning and look at yourself in the mirror, do you like the person you see in the reflection? Before you put on the makeup, before you put on the wig, before the fake eyelashes and all the other artificial trappings, do you like who you see staring back at you? By no means am I suggesting that those things are wrong. It is certainly not unholy to wear makeup and other things that enhance your beauty. But it is important to ask yourself: Are you seeking to enhance the already beautiful person you are? Or are you trying to become a completely different woman because, deep down, you really don't like who you are?

The cosmetic surgery industry has made billions of dollars, mainly because people do not like the person God made them to be. Young girls bleach their skin in a vain attempt to change their complexion, to be like someone else, trying to fit into another person's mold. Women feel pressured to make themselves look like the models and actresses that appear on the cover of magazines, in an attempt to look like what society considers to be attractive. All of these actions are a direct insult to God, because if He made you to look the way you do, He did so for a reason. And, if what He made was pleasing to Him, then it should be pleasing to you as well. The issue is learning to like yourself the way God designed you.

Some people believe that it is wrong to like themselves. They mistakenly equate liking themselves as somehow being prideful and unscriptural. And because human beings tend to go to the extremes in many areas, some are either very vain or very insecure about who they are. God calls us to a balanced way of life in which we appreciate the person He created us to be. It is not wrong to like yourself. As a matter of fact, the Bible teaches that you should not only like yourself; you should love yourself.

In the gospels that record the life and ministry of Jesus, we are told of an account in which one of the learned men of His day came to inquire of Jesus. The man asked the Lord about the commandments, and from the answer Jesus gave, we learn a great truth. I want to quote the story as it is told in Saint Mark's gospel:

> *And one of the scribes came, and having heard them reasoning together, and perceiving that he had answered them well, asked him, Which is the first commandment of all?*
> *And Jesus answered him, The first of all the commandments is, Hear, O Israel; The Lord our God is one Lord. And thou shalt love the Lord thy God with all thy heart, and with all thy soul, and with all thy mind, and with all thy strength: this is the first commandment. And the second is like, namely this, Thou shalt love thy neighbor as thyself. There is none other commandment greater than these.* Mark 12:28-31

Jesus stated that we have a command, not only to love God, but also to love our neighbor. And the only way we can truly love our neighbor is to first love ourselves. In fact, the measuring rod for determining how you love your neighbor is the way in which you love yourself. If you do not have a healthy appreciation and self-respect for the person God made *you* to be, then you will not be able to appreciate anyone else who comes into your life.

You may be at the point of believing God for a husband, but, for some reason, you are not seeing that prayer answered. If so, I ask you to examine yourself and see if you are truly in the position of faith that you need to be, in order for this man to come into your life. You cannot expect a man to love and appreciate you, if you don't first love and respect yourself.

Then there is the factor of always comparing oneself to another woman. This is one of the great challenges of our society because we live in a culture that tries to impose on us what is attractive and what is not. Women are often conditioned by the culture to believe that men, all men, are attracted to a certain type of woman. This so-called ideal female usually has a certain type of body and a certain physical charisma. When many women, especially younger ladies, look at that and compare themselves to that image, they become discouraged. You need to do as the virtuous woman in Proverbs 31 and look at your merchandise as *"good."* God created you and gave you the body you have for a reason.

Because God made you the way He did, you should be content and happy with who you are. You need to develop a habit of declaring what the writer of Psalm 149 said:

> *I will praise thee; for I am fearfully and wonderfully made: marvelous are thy works; and that my soul knoweth right well.* Psalm 139:14

You may not be as tall as a model on a magazine cover, but God said that when He made you, He made you wonderful. You might not have naturally long hair like some other woman you admire, but do not envy her. Be thankful for who God made you to be and understand this: God has the right man for you, a man who is attracted to just the kind of woman you are.

Men are not monolithic creatures. Not all men like the same type of woman. Just because you may not have what someone else has, you do have what you need to have in order to appeal to the man God has ordained for you to be joined to. Think about that virtuous woman once again, and consider what the Bible says regarding her relationship with her husband. He did not lack anything in his marriage, because she had within her and about her what it took to satisfy her man. You do not need to be every man's ideal woman, because all men are not the same. Just be happy with the woman God created you to be, and know that there is a man of God out there who will desire you and be excited by who you are. When you use makeup and other such trappings, don't do it to try to hide what God made. Instead, use it to further shine the light on the masterpiece of creation you truly are.

Another aspect of the virtuous woman's success is that she understands her value in the area of courtship and dating. Because she recognizes the power of this principle in perceiving that her merchandise is good, she does not feel any pressure to compromise her godly standards in choosing a mate. The spirit of this world that dominates our modern culture says that being abstinent and saving oneself for marriage is out of style and arcane. Women are told that they will have to compromise and give their bodies to men for the purpose of finding out if they are sexually compatible with a certain person. All of this seeks to manipulate the mind into thinking that a man will not wait and that the only way to catch him is to be open to engaging in sexual intercourse before marriage. The virtuous woman knows that these are lies from Hell, and she understands that she is worth waiting for. If a man truly wants to be with her physically, he will follow God's pattern of first being joined with her in holy matrimony.

The virtuous woman also knows that she does not have to dress in revealing and provocative clothing in order to get a man's attention. This woman respects and values herself enough to know that her body is the Temple of the Holy Ghost, and she does not have to impress men by showing off what God gave her. She knows that it is important for her to be respected as a person and not simply as a physical object, and she would rather leave some things to the imagination, as opposed to exposing herself for all to see. She does this because she perceives that her merchandise is good, and she is worth waiting for.

When thinking about the virtuous woman, also consider the following factors: We read in Proverbs 31 how industrious she is, not only in her home life, but also in her business. She is a successful entrepreneur whose business has increased so much that she even has a full-time staff to assist her. This woman has been raised up by God to know her mission in life, not only as a homemaker, but also as a businesswoman. She is successful in both of these arenas because she understands that God has equipped her with the tools she needs in order to achieve results. Here, we see, once again, that, because she perceives that her merchandise is good, she is ever-increasing. Her increase is the result of her continually feeding on the Word of God, for notice very carefully what the text says:

> *She perceiveth that her merchandise is good: her candle goeth not out by night.*
>
> Proverbs 31:18

This "candle" represents the Word of God. The virtuous woman knows her value because she has found herself in the Word. Remember, in the Parable about the Ten Virgins, that each of them had a lamp. The five who were wise kept oil in their lamps, but the five who were foolish did not. The lamp, in that story, also represented the Word of God. Foolish virgins fail to keep themselves full of the Word.

Here in Proverbs we read about the candle, the Word. It is *"a lamp unto [our] feet; a light unto [our] path"* (Psalm 119:105). The virtuous woman never allows the Word of God to grow dim within her. She continually reads and meditates upon the truths of the Scriptures. She sees herself as good because that is what the Bible says she is. She recognizes that she has the seeds of greatness within her because the Bible says she does. And she understands that whatever God has called her to do in this life, He has empowered and anointed her to do it.

One of the greatest examples of this principle is found in the life of Mary, the mother of Jesus. She was called by God to carry forth this divine assignment, and the Bible says of her:

> *And in the sixth month the angel Gabriel was sent from God unto a city of Galilee, named Nazareth, to a virgin espoused to a man whose name was Joseph, of the house of David; and the virgin's name was Mary. And the angel came in unto her, and said, Hail, thou that art highly favoured, the Lord is with thee: blessed art thou among women.*
>
> *And when she saw him, she was troubled at his saying, and cast in her mind what manner of salutation this should be.*
>
> *And the angel said unto her, Fear not, Mary: for thou hast found favour with God. And, behold, thou shalt conceive in thy womb, and bring forth a son, and shalt call his name Jesus. He shall be great, and shall be called the Son of the Highest: and the Lord God shall give unto him the throne of his father David: and he shall reign over the house of Jacob for ever; and of his kingdom there shall be no end.*
>
> *Then said Mary unto the angel, How shall this be, seeing I know not a man?*
>
> *And the angel answered and said unto her, The Holy Ghost shall come upon thee, and the power of the Highest shall overshadow thee: therefore also that holy thing which shall be born of thee shall be called the Son of God. And, behold, thy cousin Elisabeth, she hath also conceived a son in her old age: and*

this is the sixth month with her, who was called barren. For with God nothing shall be impossible.

And Mary said, Behold the handmaiden of the Lord; be it unto me according to thy word. And the angel departed from her. Luke 1:26-38

Reading these thrilling words about this momentous occasion has the power to change your entire way of thinking. This young woman received a supernatural visitation from a messenger of Heaven, and the divine being informed Mary that she had been chosen by God Himself to bring forth His Son Jesus. This news astounded Mary, and she asked how this could be possible because she was a virgin. Then the angel gave her what was, perhaps, the greatest news: she had been empowered by the Holy Ghost to bring this miracle to pass.

To bring forth a crescendo to this message, the angel declared that with God nothing would be impossible. Mary then understood that she had what she needed and that her merchandise was truly good. In that spirit of faith, she said, *"Be it unto me according to thy word."* I believe it is time for you to start making that same declaration over your life. Start seeing who you are (a valued treasure worth more than silver and gold) and what God has given you. Begin to perceive that your merchandise is good, and watch the good things of God materialize in your life.

Now that we have established the importance of the power of proper perception, let us proceed to learning how you can and must position yourself in the right place to receive your promised inheritance.

Chapter 14

Gleaning in the Right Field

There are three things that matter in property – location, location, location.
– Harold Samuel

As we continue to probe deeper into our study of the virtuous woman, I want to begin this chapter by looking once again at the description recorded in the Bible. Revelation from God's Word is constantly progressive, and, as a result of this, the truths of the Scriptures continue to speak to us. If we look closely at the text and meditate upon it, line upon line and verse by verse, then the power of the revelation found there will continue to enlighten our path. That being established, let us go once more into the breach and draw out the living water that comes from the counsel of the Almighty. The Bible declares regarding the woman of virtue:

Who can find a virtuous woman? for her price is far above rubies. The heart of her husband doth safely trust in her, so that he shall have no need of spoil. She will do him good and not evil all the days of her life. She seeketh wool and flax, and worketh willingly with her hands. She is like the merchants' ships; she bringeth her food from afar. She riseth also while it is yet night, and giveth meat to her household, and a portion to her maidens. She considereth a field and buyeth it: with the fruit of her hands she planteth a vineyard. She girdeth her loins with strength, and strengtheneth her arms. She perceiveth that her merchandise is good: her candle goeth not out by night.

She layeth her hands to the spindle, and her hands hold the distaff. She stretcheth forth her hands to the poor; yea, she reacheth forth her hands to the needy. She is not afraid of the snow for her household: for all her household are clothed with scarlet. Proverbs 31:10-21

This is the portrait of the woman who has it all. She has her spiritual life established upon a sure foundation because of the way in which she has consecrated herself to the Lord, thus making her a virtuous woman. She has a beautiful marriage, with a husband who adores her. And, because he is so enraptured by who she is, he has no desire to seek any type of fulfillment outside of her love. She is a businesswoman *par excellence,* not only working and creating goods and selling them, but also being her own boss, owning the company. God has given her the power to get wealth to such a high degree that she can afford to hire staff for her house and her company.

The prosperity in this woman's life overflows so strongly that, not only is she a successful entrepreneur, but she is also a humanitarian of the first order. Her philanthropic work allows her to display the love and compassion of God to those who are suffering and in need. There is not one area of her life that is not productive, and she is always increasing in the manifestation of the abundant life the Lord has promised for all His children.

During the latter part of the twentieth century and even leading into the twenty-first, there was a great cultural debate as to whether a woman could have all of the trappings of life. Could she obtain and maintain a successful career and still have a stable and healthy family? Prognosticators and pundits have speculated as to whether it was possible for a women to be successful, accomplished, and able to exists as her own unique individual and still find a husband with whom she could build a loving and meaningful relationship, one built on mutual respect and affection. While the media and the culture still seek the definitive solutions to balance these issues, the Bible provided the answers even before people asked the questions.

The feminist movement that came to prominence in the twentieth century would have been totally unnecessary if people had just looked to the Bible. Just think, that long before there was even talk of a woman's liberation movement, the Word of Almighty God already gave the portrait of the truly liberated woman. This woman allows the Holy Spirit to order her steps, and where the Spirit of the Lord is, there is real liberty.

God put these things in His Word to show us that it is possible to have it all. The key is: It must be done according to His divine timing and His divine pattern. It is incumbent upon us, as believers, to learn His ways.

In the previous chapter, we looked at the first step to becoming this woman – developing a positive perception of yourself based upon what God's Word says about you. The second step is just as important as the first, and, like the first, is recorded in Proverbs 31 in the prophecy of the virtuous woman.

The scripture that contains the second golden key to unlocking the door of blessing is a verse that is often glossed over by the casual reader. However, by now I trust that you have gone beyond reading any verse in the Bible in a casual way. I trust that you are seeking to read each text carefully to discover all its worth. The verse that has the treasure for this portion of our study says:

> *She considereth a field, and buyeth it: with the fruit of her hands, she planteth a vineyard.* Proverbs 31:16

On the surface, this scripture might seem to be nothing more than information regarding this woman's business activities, and yet, there is an important principle hidden within the text. The Bible, as a whole, is a book comprised of natural events and circumstances, but it contain a spiritual meaning. Throughout the Scriptures, God uses places, concepts and settings, as metaphors for understanding how to live a Spirit-led life. There is a long thematic structure all through the Scriptures of harvest fields and lands, symbolizing spiritual work or ministry to the Lord.

Some of the examples in scripture that speak of fields are strictly allegorical and represent the world and how the believer is called to work in a particular part of the world. At other times, as is the case in Proverbs 31, the mention of the field is speaking of a natural occurrence and, at the same time, represents a spiritual principle.

Perhaps the most famous version of the latter came from the lips of Jesus Himself, when He compared the world to a harvest field. We are given the account of that event in the Gospel according to Saint Matthew:

> *And Jesus went about all the cities and villages, teaching in their synagogues, and preaching the gospel of the kingdom, and healing every sickness and disease*

among the people. But when he saw the multitudes, he was moved with compassion on them, because they fainted, and were scattered abroad, as sheep having no shepherd. The saith he unto his disciples, The harvest truly is plenteous, but the labourers are few; pray ye therefore the Lord of the harvest, that he will send labourers into his harvest. Matthew 9:35-38

Jesus was explaining to His disciples the need for ministers to go into the world and bring people to a saving knowledge of Him. He used the metaphor of a harvest field and of laborers to symbolize the world and the ministers. Thus, He was both establishing and reaffirming the scriptural principle of the field symbolizing a person's work—whatever that work might be.

The field is also symbolic of other areas of our lives. Just as natural fields produce different types of products, so, too, in the realm of the Spirit. The place a person chooses to invest their life in will determine what type of return they get on their investment.

So, going back to the virtuous woman, we see that she is making a decision regarding her business. She is looking to invest in some property, and she wants to make sure that the piece of land she purchases will yield her a suitable return. That was the reason she considered the matter. *Consider* is another word for meditate. To put it even more succinctly, she was seeking the Lord, by considering what field she should invest in.

The Bible goes on to say that she planted a vineyard, and, based on how prosperous the Bible describes her, we can discern that the field she invested in has brought forth a harvest. This woman understands the principle of choosing the best location through which her harvest is divinely favored to come forth. The spiritual application the Lord would have you to see from the concept of working in the right field is this: You must always allow the Holy Spirit to lead you into the right place at the right moment, for there you can have divine appointments and receive all that God has ordained for you to have.

In this natural sphere that we call human existence, our lives consist of meeting appointments. Whether the appointment is to be at school, at work, or even a visit to the doctor, the life that we live consists of making our scheduled appointments. Not only do we need to be aware of being on time for our appointments; we must also be mindful to be at the right location where that appointment is designated to take place. If your general medical practitioner gave you a referral to see a specialists regarding a specific problem you are having in your body, and the doctor's office makes the appointment for you to go to a specific location for the consultation, but you decide to go somewhere else (because you assume that it doesn't matter which doctor you see), you might not get the proper care. If you are hired by a certain company to do a job, that company will probably assign you to a specific location, and you are expected to be at that location to fulfill your duties. Once all of that is established, if you decide to go to another site owned by the same company (because you assume that as long as you are working for the company, what difference does it make which location you are in?), you might find yourself very disappointed when you fail to receive the paycheck you were expecting—all because you were in the wrong place. These principles are realities in the natural world, and they are also realities in the spiritual world.

Your Christian experience on this side of eternity is made up of a series of divine appointments, and your success or failure as a Christian will be determined by whether or not you meet your divine appointments. A divine appointment is a designated moment in eternity in which God has you in a certain place at a certain time. In that specific place and at that specific time you can grow in your relationship with Him and receive the blessing you need for that period of your life. However, too many Christians believe that because God is omnipresent and has the ability to do whatever He wants to do, He will bless them no matter where they are or when. Too many Christians naively believe that they can go to any church they want, because they say to themselves, "Well, God is everywhere." But the plain fact of the matter is that the church of your choice might not be the church God has chosen for you. Too many so-called Spirit-led Christians believe that they can choose any job they want in any city they want, without consulting the Lord as to whether or not their decisions is the appointed place He has designated for them to be in. Then, to add insult to injury, after refusing to acknowledge God in their decisions, they still expect Him to bless them in their decisions. Bible-based Christianity does not work that way, and God is not the fool some try to make Him out to be.

Many times in life, God will call you to a certain place to meet your divine appointment, and if you want to be blessed, you had better be at that location. The Scriptures bear this out. One of the greatest examples of this principle comes from the lips of the Lord Jesus Himself. After our Lord rose from the dead, He appeared to His disciples and spoke to them about the great promise, that one day they would be baptized with the Holy Spirit. But, in order for this to happen, they had to position themselves for the miracle. Therefore, Jesus spoke to them and said:

> *And, behold, I send the promise of my Father upon you: but tarry ye in the city of Jerusalem, until ye be endued with power from on high.* Luke 24:49

Jesus gave His followers a great blessing to look forward to, the mighty baptism of the Holy Spirit. This experience was to radically change their lives and propel them into fulfilling their divine destinies. But, in order to fulfill that divine destiny, they first had to position themselves in a divine destination. The Master was very specific. They should go to Jerusalem and wait at a specific location for the promise to come to pass. God made sure that we understood this revelation because He saw to it that another verse in the Bible mentioned His instructions. That verse is found in the Acts of the Apostles:

> *And, being assembled together with them, commanded them that they should not depart from Jerusalem, but wait for the promise of the Father, which, saith he, ye have heard of me.* Acts 1:4

Upon hearing these orders, the disciples could have said, "Well, why do I have to wait in Jerusalem for the promise to come to pass?" They could have said, "Why can't I be wherever I want to be, because God is everywhere. He can bless me anywhere." Thankfully, they did not choose to think in that carnal and immature way, and the whole world has been the beneficiary of their obedience. When the disciples put themselves in the designated location, at the appointed time, the outpouring came:

> *And when the day of Pentecost was fully come, they were all with one accord in one place. And suddenly there came a sound from heaven as of a rushing mighty wind, and it filled all the house where they were sitting. And there appeared unto them cloven things like as of fire, and it sat upon each of them. And they were all filled with the Holy Ghost, and began to speak with other tongues, as the Spirit gave them utterance.* Acts 2:1-4

If these disciples had not been at the assigned location, they would have missed their appointed moment, and they would never have been able to turn the world upside down with the Gospel of Jesus Christ. Your life, from beginning to end, is made up of divine appointments. Even your last moment on this side of eternity is appointed, for the Bible tells:

> *And as it appointed unto men once to die, but after this the judgement.*
> Hebrews 9:27

If the moment of your death is set in eternity, then you can be sure that in between birth and death, there are many appointed moments in your life. If you miss your appointments, by being in the wrong place or not being on time, you will rob yourself of your appointed miracles. The early followers of Jesus understood this. Not only did Jesus give them the instruction, but He also lived out the example to them in His own ministry. He always had the mindset of being at the place where God the Father had ordained for Him to be. It was because of this that Jesus always produced results in His life and ministry.

One of the most famous accounts in the Bible that illustrate this point is found in the story of Jesus meeting the woman at the well in Samaria. Because Jesus understood that His purpose on this earth was to set people free from the powers of darkness, everything He did and every place He went was always designed with that purpose in mind. God wanted to send a revival to the people of Samaria, and Jesus recognized that He had a divine appointment in that place. In the gospel according to Saint John, we read the following words concerning Jesus and the woman at the well:

> *When therefore the Lord knew how the Pharisees had heard that Jesus made and baptized more disciples than John, (though Jesus himself baptized not, but his disciples,) he left Judea, and departed again into Galilee.*
> *And he must need go through Samaria. Then cometh he to a city of Samaria, which is called Sychar, near to the parcel of ground that Jacob gave to his son Joseph. Now Jacob's well was there. Jesus therefore being wearied with his journey, sat thus on the well: and it was about the sixth hour.*
> *Then cometh a woman of Samaria, to draw water: Jesus saith unto her, Give me to drink. (For his disciples were gone away unto the city to buy meat.)*

Then saith the woman of Samaria unto him, How is it that thou, being a Jew, askest drink of me, which am a woman of Samaria? for the Jews have no dealings with the Samaritans.
Jesus answered and said unto her, If thou knewest the gift of God, and who it is that saith to thee, Give me to drink; thou wouldest have asked of him, and he would have given thee living water.
The woman saith unto him, Sir, thou hast nothing to draw with, and the well is deep: from whence then hast thou this living water? Art thou greater than our father Jacob, which gave us the well, and drank thereof himself, and his children, and his cattle?
Jesus answered and said unto her, Whosoever drinketh of this water shall thirst again: but whosoever drinketh of the water that I shall give him shall never thirst; but the water that I shall give him shall be in him a well of water springing up into everlasting life.
The woman saith unto him, Sir, give me this water, that I thirst not, neither come hither to draw. John 4:1-15

This began, not only a wonderful change in the life of this particular woman, but also one of the greatest revivals in the history of the world. For later, after this woman's life had been changed by Jesus, she initiated a move of God that reached the entire region. None of this would have happened had not something triggered the event. The trigger is mentioned in the text, but is often glossed over by many who read the account. God tells us how this miracle began:

And he must needs go through Samaria. John 4:4

Some who read that will scoff and say that Jesus probably just had to pass through there on His way to Galilee. One could read it that way, but our aim is to rightly divide the Word of Truth, and examine why God puts these pieces of information in the Bible in the first place. Primarily, we must understand that nothing that is in the Bible is there by accident. God included everything, even the smallest details, for a specific purpose. So then, we could read verse four and interpret it as nothing more than geographical information about having to go through one location to get to another. Or we could think as God thinks and read the verse as a marching order from Central Command in Heaven. Jesus had an assignment in Samaria, and He had to go there to fulfill His mission.

Consider the fact that the Bible takes the time to even mention the name of the city, the location of the well, and the historical significance of that particular spot. These things are mentioned in the Scriptures to let you know that location is important. Where you go to church is important. Where you sow your financial seeds is important. What city you live in is important. And what job you take is important. It is your responsibility to make sure that you are in the place God wants you to be in, so that you can live a successful and productive life.

Consider also these words that our Lord spoke when He taught His disciples so long ago:

> *The field is the world; the good seed are the children of the kingdom; but the tares are the children of the wicked one.* Matthew 13:38

Jesus looked out at the chasm of creation called earth and, as He endeavored to teach His disciples how to master this experience called life, He made a comparative analysis. He compared the world to a great harvest field. If life is one giant field, then you need to be working and living in the right field so that you can receive your harvest.

You may be at a crossroads in your life right now, wondering why things are not happening for you in the way you want them to. You may question God, asking Him why you not yet married. You may be crying out to the Father, wondering why you are not growing in spiritual development. You might have grown frustrated in your professional life and are trying to figure out why you are not fulfilled in your job. I believe the Lord is revealing something important to you now. It is time to come to an awareness that you must position yourself in the right places, so that you can meet your divine appointments. God is calling you and exhorting you to elevate your thinking and do as the virtuous woman in Proverbs 31. Consider the fields you plan to invest in. It is vital for your personal growth and development that you plant yourself in the right field. Only then will you see the abundant life that God has made provision for you to have.

Now I want to draw your attention back to the story of Ruth. Hers is the perfect example of a virtuous woman. For those who would put forth the idea it is not possible for one female to embody all the characteristics of the woman described in Proverbs 31, the story of Ruth completely refutes that claim. Within the life of Ruth we find the supreme manifestation of everything that was spoken of in the prophetic word given by the mother of King Lemuel. Ruth is the ultimate heroine and a woman whose heavenly graces carried her forward into achieving a position in God that has made her name famous and given her a place of honor, so that an entire book bears her name and tells her story.

Ruth was the woman for all seasons and the complete portrait of the godly lady. Her life was of such significance that God saw fit to devote an entire book of the Bible to her story. Even though the book of Ruth is small, compared with other volumes, it contains all the facets of the human condition. Within its pages we find loss and gain, joy and sorrow, brokenness and redemption, and one of the greatest love stories in all of world literature. Most profoundly, we discover within Ruth's story how one can become the virtuous woman and how the power of choosing the right field can forever bless your life.

I touched on a certain aspect of Ruth's story when I quoted a portion of the first chapter. However, for the sake of looking much deeper at the text, I wish to quote the entirety of chapter one and allow the Holy Spirit to open your understanding to behold the majesty of how He directs and uses a person's life for His glory. With that said, let us once more break the Bread of Life and read what the Word says:

> *Now it came to pass in the days when the judges ruled, that there was a famine in the land. And a certain man of Bethlehemjudah went to sojourn in the country of Moab, he and his wife, and his two sons. And the name of the man was Elimelech, and the name of his wife Naomi, and the name of his two sons Mahlon and Chilion, Ephrathites of Bethlehemjudah. And they came into the country of Moab, and continued there.*
>
> *And Elimelech Naomi's husband died; and she was left, and her two sons. And they took them wives of the women of Moab; the name of the one was Orpah, and the name of the other Ruth: and they dwelled there about ten years. And Mahlon and Chilion died also both of them; and the woman was left of her two sons and her husband.*
>
> *Then she arose with her daughters in law, that she might return from the country of Moab: for she had heard in the country of Moab how that the Lord*

had visited his people in giving them bread. Wherefore she went forth out of the place where she was, and her two daughters in law with her; and they went on the way to return unto the land of Judah.

And Naomi said unto her two daughters in law, Go, return each to her mother's house: the Lord *deal kindly with you, as ye have dealt with the dead, and with me. The* Lord *grant you that ye may find rest, each of you in the house of her husband. The she kissed them; and they lifted up their voice, and wept.*

And they said unto her, Surely we will return with thee unto thy people.

And Naomi said, Turn again, my daughters: why will ye go with me? are there yet any more sons in my womb, that they may be your husbands? Turn again, my daughters, go your way; for I am too old to have an husband. If I should say, I have hope, if I should have an husband also to night, and should bear sons; would ye tarry for them till they were grown? would ye stay for them from having husbands? nay, my daughters; for it grieveth me much for your sakes that the hand of the Lord *is gone out against me.*

And they lifted up their voice, and wept again; and Orpah kissed her mother in law; but Ruth clave unto her.

And she said, Behold, thy sister in law is gone back unto her people, and unto her gods: return after thy sister in law.

And Ruth said, Intreat me not to leave thee, or to return from following after thee: for whither thou goest, I will go; and where thou lodgest, I will lodge: thy people shall be my people, and thy God my God. Where thou diest, will I die, and there will I be buried: the Lord *do so to me, and more also, if ought but death part thee and me. When she saw that she was steadfastly minded to go with her, then she left speaking unto her.*

So they two went until they came to Bethlehem. And it came to pass, when they were come to Bethlehem, that all the city was moved about them, and they said, Is this Naomi?

And she said unto them, Call me not Naomi, call me Mara: for the Almighty hath dealt very bitterly with me. I went out full, and the Lord *hath brought me home again empty: why then call ye me Naomi, seeing the* Lord *hath testified against me, and the Almighty hath afflicted me?*

So Naomi returned, and Ruth the Moabitess, her daughter in law, with her, which returned out of the country of Moab: and they came to Bethlehem in the beginning of barley harvest. Ruth 1:1-22

The book of Ruth opens during a time of transition in the national life of the Jewish people. Long gone were the days of Moses and Joshua, when those men led the chosen nation from one mighty conquest to another. And the time of the great reign of men like David and Solomon, who led a united nation to glory and splendor, had not risen upon the scene. The children of Abraham lived during anxious times, always seeming to go through one challenge after another. The crisis that afflicted the nation at this particular time was a terrible famine that swept through and ravished homes and families. One particular Jewish family was so adversely affected by this crisis that they decided to leave their beloved Promised Land and journey to the country of Moab. In this way, Elimelech, along with his wife and two sons, went to live as strangers in a strange land.

In Moab, among people who worshiped false gods and lived a totally different way of life, this godly family tried to build a new life for themselves. But, as with all things in this world, time, that great arbitrator, caught up with Elimelech, and he died, leaving his wife Naomi a widow with nothing but her two sons.

Having the support of two sons would have been of comfort to any grieving widow, but Naomi's sons were not like the mighty men of old who rushed on the city of Jericho and overcame the enemies of God. They possessed neither the endurance or the capacity for achieving great things. Even their names meant "sickness" and "weakness." They were so emaciated in their spiritual capacity to understand how they ought to live in this world that they did that which was against their moral heritage; they married women of Moab.

Ever since God had brought His people out of Egyptian bondage, He had desired to keep them consecrated for His divine purposes. One of the ways to ensure this was to command the Israelites not to marry people who worshiped false gods. However, where sin did abound, grace did much more abound (see Romans 5:2). In this time of the Old Covenant, in which only the Jews could be called the children of God, the Lord was about to give a preview of how He would make a way for any and all who wished to be adopted into His family. Through what was about to take place, He would show that what the devil meant for evil, God could turn around for His glory.

The two women who were joined to these men were named Orpah and Ruth. Even though they were both outsiders to the household of faith, Ruth was very special. She had within her the desire and determination to rise above her past and look toward the future God had in store for her. She had been born as a woman of Moab and raised with the values of that nation. She was not born into a godly home, one that had godly values. Therefore, she came from a field that would yield no fruit. This shows us that no matter where you may start in life, God can position you in a place of blessing—if you choose to follow Him.

Even though Ruth came from an ungodly environment, she must have learned some valuable lessons along the way from the godly example of her mother-in-law. So deeply affected was she by this that when Naomi decided to return to Israel after her two sons died, both Ruth and Orpah decided to go with her. Under normal circumstances, this might have seemed to be a natural thing, but these were not normal circumstances.

As they prepared to take their journey, Naomi began to evaluate her life, and as she considered her condition, she had a change of heart concerning letting her daughters-in-law come with her. Looking around at all she had lost, she suddenly considered her life to be a failure. So despondent was she about her existence that she thought God had forsaken her and that her future was nothing to look forward to. That caused her to reason with her daughters-in-law that there was no benefit to staying with her. She was no longer able to bear children, so there would be no more sons for the women to marry. Even if she could have conceived and borne sons, she reasoned, would the women waste away their youth waiting for her babies to grow into manhood?

Naomi thought of herself as a woman forsaken, lost, with no present or future hope. Orpah was convinced by this and decided to turn back to her old life. She left Naomi, but, the Bible says, *"Ruth clave unto her"* (verse 14). Despite Naomi's negative prognostics regarding her life, there was something about the woman that made a deep impression upon Ruth. Maybe it was the way Naomi carried herself, or perhaps it was the quality of the relationship she'd had with Elimelech, or perhaps all of the above, but there was something special about the woman.

At the time in which this family lived in Moab, great stories of how God had wrought mighty miracles for Israel circulated among the other nations of the ancient world. The people of Moab undoubtedly heard how the Great I Am had decreed His blessings upon the seed of Jacob. Maybe Naomi expounded upon those testimonies in her time with her sons and their wives. Whatever was said by Naomi to her family spoke directly to Ruth's spirit, and it caused something to come alive inside of her. Even though Naomi considered herself forsaken, Ruth saw something very different.

At that critical juncture in her life, Ruth weighed her options. She looked at the field of her old life in Moab and thought about the field that awaited Naomi in her home country of Israel, and she considered which field to invest in. After much careful consideration, Ruth chose to align herself with Naomi and everything that Naomi represented and told her mother-in-law that she would not leave her.

Ruth's commitment to Naomi was very strong. She said that wherever Naomi went, she would follow. Wherever Naomi lived, she would live. In whatever place Naomi died, she would commit herself to die in that place as well. Ruth had so purposed in her heart that she was a new person with a new life that she even declared that whatever people Naomi took as her own, those would be her people as well. And, most importantly, Ruth declared that the God Naomi worshiped would be the God she worshiped and served. Such decisions and resulting declarations form a portrait of a true follower of Jesus.

Christianity cannot be defined as saying a prayer and then halfheartedly attending church when it is convenient for you to do so. Being a disciple of the Lord Jesus is not choosing the church of your choice and casually practicing your faith as the mood suits you. Living a life led by the Holy Spirit is not saying, "I will do what God wants me to do, say what God wants me to say, and go where God wants me to go, as long as it does not interfere with my plans for my life." Life in Christ is a complete giving of yourself in total obedience in all things.

You must understand that what Ruth was doing when she said those powerful words to Naomi was displaying the requirements for discipleship in the program of God. If you want to become the virtuous woman, you must commit to doing all that God requires of you. That call may cost you having to move to a place that is unfamiliar to you. That call may cost you giving up some friendships, because those relationships will keep you from fulfilling your destiny. It may even cost you walking by faith and not by sight, when it looks like all hope is lost. Just as Naomi appeared to have nothing to offer Ruth, there will be times when it will look as if faith is not producing anything for you. However, you must plant your feet on the Solid Rock that is Jesus Christ and say, as Ruth did to Naomi, "Your God will be my God."

These choices may cost you to have to wait on God for Him to send you the right mate, because you require a season of preparation to be ready for that great man to come into your life. These decisions for Christ might cost you having to move halfway around the world, to work in a place where it may seem like nothing productive is taking place. But if you wait on the Lord and keep your confidence in Him, you will not be put to shame.

There is another aspect to this story of Ruth that bears reflection. It concerns Naomi and her relationship with her daughter-in-law. One of the things the Word of God teaches us is that there are many aspects of the Old Testament that are types and shadows of what God has done under the New Covenant (which is found in the New Testament portion of the Bible). This means that, while all the stories we read about in the Old Testament are historically true and completely accurate, they are also used as metaphors to help us understand how we are to live as Christians under the New Covenant.

Under the New Covenant, each believer has the ability to develop a relationship with the Holy Spirit, for the purpose of following His direction and leading into our Promised Land of blessing. Ruth stands as a type or a model of the virtuous woman that all Christian ladies should aspire to be. Naomi represents the Person of the Holy Spirit Who leads the believer and helps to mentor and guide them into being at the right places at the right time, to meet their divine appointments. If you develop your relationship with the Holy Spirit by daily communion with Him in prayer and study of the Word, He will order and direct your steps. He will lead you to the right house of worship, where you can grow and mature in the ways of the Almighty. The Holy Spirit will (if you allow Him to) lead you to the right place, where, at the appointed time, you will be able to meet the man of your dreams.

If you develop a sensitivity to hearing the voice of the Holy Spirit, He will direct you to the career path that is best for you and brings out your gifts and talents, all the while providing you with joy and financial increase. All of this can and will happen if you say to the Holy Spirit what Ruth said to Naomi, "Where You lead, I will follow."

The first chapter of Ruth ends with the two women arriving in Israel with Naomi still feeling saddened by her past misfortunes. But, thanks be unto God,

Who always gives His people victory, Naomi was about to discover that, as Ruth began to work in the field that God had called her to, she would produce a harvest that would cause all the pain of the past to grow strangely dim, in the light of God's glory and grace.

In the next chapter, we read:

> *And Naomi had a kinsman of her husband's, a mighty man of wealth, of the family of Elimelech; and his name was Boaz. And Ruth the Moabites said unto Naomi, Let me now go to the field, and glean ears of corn after him in whose sight I shall find grace.*
>
> *And she said unto her, Go, my daughter.*
>
> *And she went, and came, and gleaned in the field after the reapers: and her hap was to light on a part of the field belonging unto Boaz, who was of the kindred of Elimelech. And, behold, Boaz came from Bethlehem, and said unto the reapers, the LORD be with you.*
>
> *And they answered him, the LORD bless thee.*
>
> *Then said Boaz unto his servant that was set over the reapers, Whose damsel is this?*
>
> *And the servant that was set over the reapers answered and said, It is the Moabitish damsel that came back with Naomi out of the country of Moab: and she said, I pray you, let me glean and gather after the reapers among the sheaves: so she came, and hath continued even from the morning until now, that she tarried a little in the house.*
>
> *Then said Boaz unto Ruth, Hearest thou not, my daughter? Go not to glean in another field, neither go from hence, but abide here fast by my maidens. Let thine eyes be on the field that they do reap, and go thou after them: have I not charged the young men that they shall not touch thee? and when thou art athirst, go unto the vessels, and drink of that which the young men have drawn.*
>
> *Then she fell on her face and bowed herself to the ground, and said unto him, Why have I found grace in thine eyes, that thou shouldest take knowledge of me, seeing I am a stranger?*
>
> *And Boaz answered and said unto her, It hath fully been shewed me, all that thou hast done unto thy mother in law since the death of thine husband: and how thou hast left thy father and thy mother, and the land of thy nativity, and art come unto a people which thou knewest not heretofore. The LORD recompense*

thy work, and a full reward be given thee of the Lord *God of Israel, under whose wings thou art come to trust.*

Then she said, Let me find favour in thy sight, my lord; for thou hast comforted me, and for thou hast spoken friendly unto thine handmaid, though I be not like unto one of thine handmaidens.

And Boaz said unto her, At mealtime come thou hither, and eat of the bread, and dip thy morsel in the vinegar. And she sat beside the reapers: and he reached her parched corn, and she did eat, and was sufficed, and left.

And when she was risen up to glean, Boaz commanded his young men, saying, Let her glean even among the sheaves, and reproach her not: and let fall also some of the handfuls of purpose for her, and leave them, that she may glean them, and rebuke her not.

So she gleaned in the field until even, and beat out that she had gleaned: and it was about an ephah of barley. And she took it up, and went into the city; and her mother in law saw what she had gleaned; and she brought forth, and gave to her that she had reserved after she was sufficed.

And her mother in law said unto her, Where hast thou gleaned today? and where wroughtest thou? blessed be he that did take knowledge of thee. And she shewed her mother in law with whom she had wrought, and said, The man's name with whom I wrought to day is Boaz.

And Naomi said unto her daughter in law, Blessed be he of the Lord*, who hath not left off his kindness to the living and to the dead. And Naomi said unto her, The man is near of kin unto us, one of our next kinsman.*

And Ruth the Moabitess said, He said unto me also, Thou shalt keep fast by my young men, until they have ended all my harvest.

And Naomi said unto Ruth her daughter in law, It is good, my daughter, that thou go out with his maidens, that they meet thee not in any other field. So she kept fast by the maidens of Boaz to glean unto the end of barley harvest and of wheat harvest; and dwelt with her mother in law. Ruth 2:1-23

How wonderful is the Lord, and His ways are truly marvelous. As Ruth took the first steps toward a new life in the Lord, He began to orchestrate a sequence of events that needed to take place in order for her destiny to come to pass. This chapter began with a description of the man who would come to play a large role in the continuing narrative of the text, as he took his place among the great giants of the faith. The man that was spoken of would have a great impact upon the life of Ruth, ultimately becoming her dearly beloved husband. And, because Ruth serves as an example or the model of what a virtuous woman should be, this man is a representation of the type of man God would bless the virtuous woman with as a husband. This man stands as the example of what you should look for in a husband and how you should direct your prayer in seeking the Lord to bless you with the right mate.

The man the Bible speaks of was named Boaz, and in every way possible, he was the polar opposite of the weak male Ruth had been married to when she dwelt in Moab. We must start with his name, for names in the Bible were extremely important. Because God took the time to give us the names of these historical figures, it is essential for us to appreciate the fact that He did so for a reason. The meaning of the names exists to provide spiritual insight into the ways in which the Kingdom of God operates.

This man was named Boaz, and that name means "strength." As a result of her obedience to God, Ruth was about to be blessed with a man who did not operate in weakness, but rather in strength. And, because this story is recorded in the Bible, how we define words should be in a biblical context. God defines strength as total dependency upon Him and not upon self.

The apostle Paul highlighted this point in his letter to the saints of Ephesus:

> *Finally, my brethren, be strong in the Lord, and in the power of his might.*
>
> Ephesians 6:10

A real man will define his masculinity by his relationship with Christ and by living his life based upon the standards that Jesus laid out in His Word. True male strength is displayed by the man whose confidence is built, not on his own ability, but in the power of God's ability to make of him who He wants him to be.

The second thing we discover about this man is that he was a kinsman of Elimelech, meaning a blood relative of the family. There is a spiritual correlation here that must be applied to your life as well, and it is this: If you, as a woman of God, are asking the Lord to bless you with a mate, then you need to be sure that you ask Him to send you a man who is of the household of faith. If you profess to be a woman of faith and if you declare that you are a part of the family of God, then the man you marry must also be a part of the same spiritual family. You cannot be a Christian and marry a man of another faith. Nor can you be a Christian and marry a man whose faith is not as strong and committed as yours. If you join yourself to a man of lukewarm commitment toward God, you are attaching yourself to a weak male image. And when that takes place, when times of testing and trial come, that man's faith will fail him and fail you. You should want a man of strong faith, strong devotion, and a strong determination to become all that God has called him to be. That kind of a man will always be blessed by God.

Even if that man starts out with nothing but his faith, if he keeps his eyes on Jesus, He will make that man into a person with the power to get wealth, so that God's covenant may be established in the earth. You should desire a man of vision, for without a vision that man will perish and you with him. You should believe God for a man of faith, because his faith will see him through every trial, and, out of weakness, God will make him strong. You should pray for a man of commitment, someone committed to his faith, committed to his love for you, and, most importantly, committed to his God. All of these attributes were found in Boaz.

God was preparing to bring Ruth in Boaz's direction and join these star-crossed lovers together for a divine purpose. The way in which this all came together is the pattern to follow on how the Lord wants to direct your life, so that you can get all you desire from Him.

The Scriptures tells us that Ruth first inquired of Naomi as to whether or not she should go into a certain field and work to get a harvest. Naomi gave her blessing, and off Ruth went. The guiding principle from this portion of the text is to live your life in constant fellowship with the Lord and with His guidance and blessing. Ask God before you decide to take that new job. He may have something better for you. If you wait on Him, seeking the Lord as to whether or not you should join the church that is just up the street from your house, he will show you. Just because that particular house of worship is conveniently located to your home does not mean it is the place where you will be properly developed spiritually. The church God has for you might be two hours from where you live, but if you invest in the right field, you will get your harvest.

This was what took place in the life of Ruth. As she worked in the field God had ordained for her, she caught the eye of the most eligible bachelor in the land, none other than Boaz himself. He noticed her working and was instantly captivated by her. Even within that casual piece of information, there is a great principle to be learned: Too many Christians are so encumbered by all of the cares of this life that they make no time to really give themselves to God and to His work. Jesus Himself saw the severity of this problem and provided the answer when He spoke to the multitude:

> *But seek ye first the kingdom of God, and his righteousness; and all these things shall be added unto you.* Matthew 6:33

Many are too busy seeking other things, rather than seeking God and His Kingdom. They are seeking a mate, seeking social status, seeking career advancement. Jesus said that this is how the children of this world operate. The wise children of the Father understand that when they put Him first, the blessings will find them, or He will direct them to the blessings.

You might be preoccupied seeking a mate, when God has been trying to get you to devote your free time to be more faithful to your church. Maybe He is calling you to work with the choir or the usher board, and you are resisting because you are too busy trying to further your career goals. What you need to understand is that God would not be asking these things of you if He did not intend to bless you with them. Maybe if you start being more faithful to your church and get involved in those areas where there is a need, you might very well meet the man of your dreams. Maybe if you volunteer to work as an usher for the services, you might make the business contact you need, to take your career to a whole new level.

You may be very busy trying to get someone to notice you, and God is trying to get you to pay more attention to Him. If you put God first, you will not have to look for your husband. God will make sure he finds you. Everything you want is found in the field that God has called you to work in, and if you work that field, you will reap your harvest.

After Boaz noticed Ruth, he began to inquire about who she was and what her story was. As a man of honor, he wanted to be sure that she was free to be courted and that she was worth the effort of courtship. Once he was told what he needed to know, he then began to approach Ruth. He not only introduced himself to her, but he informed her that every provision she needed would be met by his authority.

Naturally, Ruth was overcome by this display of generosity, and she began to ask how it was that she had obtained such favor. Boaz could have pointed to any number of wonderful attributes that Ruth possessed, but he chose to emphasize her character and her commitment to Naomi. Here is another treasure among the jewels of this story. In this world that we live in, there is more emphasis placed on physical beauty than on any other attribute of a person. Because of this, some women believe that, because they meet the physical requirements of what society considers to be attractive, they have an advantage over everyone else. However, the harsh truth of the matter is that attractive people are a dime a dozen. There are millions of them, and if you base your worth on your physical appearance, you are setting yourself up for disappointment. It takes more than a pretty face to get the attention of a true man of God.

Also, beauty fades, your body will change and, as a result, your ego cannot be tied to your looks. A very astute novelist once wrote that the charms of a passing woman are in direct relation to the swiftness of her passing. To put it more simply, if you think the world will revolve around you because you have a pretty face and a pleasing shape, you are sorely deceived. There are thousands of other women in this world who have pretty faces and pleasing shapes. If you want to stand out and gain the attention of a man who wants more than some physical plaything, you need to remember the words of Proverbs 31:

> *Favour is deceitful, and beauty is vain: but a woman that feareth the LORD, she shall be praised.* Proverbs 31:30

Boaz may have initially been drawn to Ruth by her outward appearance, but what caused him to pursue her love was her godly character. If you want the right man to pursue you in the right way, you need to be a woman who honors the Lord, for that is the woman who will receive all the praise worth receiving.

When Ruth returned to Naomi and related to her all that had happened, the elder woman knew that God was at work. She began to pronounce blessings upon her daughter-in-law and, most importantly, to further advise her on how to continue to position herself in the right field, so that what God had started, He could finish. The Lord was truly at work in Ruth's life, just as He is working in your life as you read this book.

A great miracle was about to take place for Ruth, and a wedding was on the horizon. Whatever you are believing God for is drawing nigh to you as well, as you glean in the right field. But, as the poet once said, "The course of true love doth not always run smooth, for there are other steps that must be taken before the joys can commence." In between the flowering of love at first sight and the ringing of the wedding bells, there is preparation that must take place. Let us climb the mountain of God higher and discover how one must adorn themselves in readiness for the fulfillment of the promise.

Chapter 15

Adorning Yourself Modestly

I had no idea of the character. But the moment I was dressed, the clothes, and the make-up made me feel the person he was. I began to know him, and by the time I walked onto the stage he was fully born. —Charlie Chaplin

History has shown, so that it can be clearly stated without fear of contradiction or hyperbole, that the Church of the book of Acts was the greatest example of what Christianity should be that has ever existed. That Church was the model Church; it was the exemplary Church, and it set a quality of godly character that has never been matched since. Since those days of the early apostles, subsequent generations have seen great moves of God and experienced mighty revivals, but the people who birthed the Christian movement had a communion and a fellowship with the Holy Spirit that kept them in a continual stream of holiness and purity. When deception and venality sought to creep into that great movement, it was quickly cut down and torn up at the roots, so that no corrupt fruit could grow in God's garden.

One of the outstanding characteristics that made the early Church so remarkable was that they were taught and understood the principle of moderation. It has always seemed that the believers who came after those glorious days struggled with this spiritual concept. Religious movements have gone from one extreme to another, while, at the same time, falling short of the fullness of God's glory. History has shown so clearly how the church of the Middle Ages grew to such a place of temporal power and influence that even kings and other sovereigns would tremble before it. But that absolute power gave rise to unbridled corruption, and those who were supposed to be spiritual leaders lived more ungodly than the vilest pagans.

Then, when the great Protestant Reformation came upon the scene, God's power flowed through the earth once more, bringing change and blessing. But in that move, men grew too dogmatic, and they fought and argued among themselves, causing the problem of denominationalism that exists to this day. All the while, the Holy Spirit, has been calling the Church back to the words of Paul:

Let your moderation be know unto all men. The Lord is at hand.

Philippians 4:5

God wants His children to live under the revelation of the balanced life.

One of the main areas in the church where this needs to be understood is in the area of clothing and dress. One of the greatest moves of God to ever take place in the world was known as the Holiness Movement. At the beginning of the twentieth century, believers began to catch the revelation of consecrating themselves unto the Lord. They began to preach and teach sanctification, purity and being set apart from the corruption of this world. That spiritual intensity that emphasized moral purity shook the world and helped usher in the great Charismatic renewal that brought the power of Pentecost to a whole new generation.

So deep was the spiritual fervor that churches began to be filled, not only with the glory of God, but also with a people who presented themselves with decency and propriety in the way in which they came into the House of the Lord. Preachers dressed in a way that presented the image of dignified statesmanship. Choirs were adorned to look both regal and tasteful. Families came into the place of worship looking their very best, to praise and magnify their majestic Lord.

Then, however, the pendulum swung too much to one side into extremism, and the old leaven of the Pharisees began to replace the manna from Heaven. Religious leaders began to preach strange doctrines. These were delivered with very good intentions, but they ultimately produced a bondage mentality that was not in keeping with the liberty of the Holy Spirit. It was taught across pulpits, for example, that in order to be truly pious, a person had to be materially broke and live as lowly as possible without financial success. Holiness was presented in a perverse extreme that banned women from wearing makeup and jewelry and forced them into wearing clothing that made them look and feel unlike the royal queens God made them to be. While some embraced these notions, mainly because their faith was so strong that it outweighed these contradictions, others could not. Some began to turn away from the faith, wanting to be free from the chains imposed upon them. And, just as it was two thousand years before, the leaven of the Pharisees brought a breach in the moving of the Holy Ghost.

In the process of time, some began to see the handwriting on the wall, and they started to preach reform. They proclaimed that God was not opposed to makeup and jewelry and that He took pleasure in the prosperity of His children looking their best and also having the best. Change came, and what a wonderful change it was! Christians embraced a new freedom, while, at the same time, conforming to general standards of good taste and keeping God's glory in the services.

Then, again, the pendulum swung to the extremity of the other side, and the spirit of the world began to creep in. People began presenting themselves in a manner that communicated "anything goes." Choirs traded in their robes for ripped jeans and T-shirts, and praise teams threw away their suits and dresses, in order to look like rock stars and rappers. The "come as you are" blessing that genuinely sought to bring people to the Lord became a distorted monster, in which the House of God became just another Studio 54, and the parishioners turned into clubgoers. All the while, God was calling His people back to His truth: *"Let your moderation be known before all men. The Lord is at hand."*

The Holy Spirit wants His Church to be both a holy Church, and a glorious one. He desires that we look our best and be free to express ourselves, while, at the same time, refusing to look and present ourselves like the world. He wants a Church that does not look like a Soul Train music festival, nor a Grammy Awards telecast. He wants a Church that looks like a rehearsal room for the day in which all of His people will be adorned in royal attire for the great Marriage Supper of the Lamb. He wants to raise up a generation of women who will become the virtuous ones who are ambassadors for Christ and radiate the glory of God both within and without. In essence, the Father wants His daughters to understand the principle of adorning themselves modestly.

The Lord does not want His people to live under the bondages of the past; nor is He interested in seeing His Church use their liberty as an occasion to do just anything that suits them. You must understand how you can and should present yourself before the Lord and also before the world. Some might say. "God doesn't care either way how I adorn myself," but nothing could be further from the truth. If you profess to be a child of God, then you represent your heavenly Father. And no father wants his daughter to dress in just any fashion; nor does he want his daughter to look like she is oppressed or downtrodden. A good father wants his daughter to be treated like a queen, and he wants her to act like she is a queen and present herself in the manner of a queen. If a human father feels that way, how much more your heavenly Father!

As a Christian, you represent Jesus to the world. The Bible declares:

> *Now then we are ambassadors for Christ, as though God did beseech you by us: we pray you in Christ's stead, be ye reconciled unto a God.* 2 Corinthians 5:20

If you profess Jesus as Lord of your life, that means He has a say in how you present yourself in this life. As His representative on the earth, your presentation to the world should reflect His character and bring glory to His name. This means that we need to look once more at the Word of God and see if we can define godly adornment from a biblical perspective. So, let us again break the Bread of Life and draw from the well of living water.

In the battle for establishing scriptural veracity concerning proper adornment, two Bible references have been at the frontlines. These passages of scripture have been misused and abused by preachers for decades to oppress women and perpetrate a false sense of piety. The passages of scripture both come from the New Testament, and they read as follows:

> *In like manner also, that women adorn themselves in modest apparel, with shamefacedness and sobriety; not with broided hair, or gold, or pearls, or costly array; but (which becometh women professing godliness) with good works.*
> 1 Timothy 2:9-10

> *Whose adorning let it not be that outward adorning of plaiting the hair, and of wearing of gold, or of putting on of apparel; but let it be the hidden man of*

the heart, in that which is not corruptible, even the ornament of a meek a quiet spirit, which is in the sight of God a great price. 1 Peter 3:3-4

If one were to read these scriptures and casually take them at face value, it is possible to assume that God prohibits a woman from using makeup and jewelry. Because these scriptures have caused such controversy in the Body of Christ, some have just chosen to ignore them altogether and proceed with wearing what they want. However, both of these approaches are wrong and miss what God is trying to say through the writings of these apostles.

The first approach to looking at these verses is wrong because if you take a scripture and pull it out of the Bible and base an entire doctrine on that verse, you open yourself up to error. A person can make the Bible say whatever they want it to say—if they fail to interpret it properly. In the history of the Church, entire movements with very strange doctrines have come forth because of a failure to properly interpret the Bible. This is why Paul admonished his protégée Timothy to adhere to this principle:

Study to shew thyself approved unto God, a workman that needeth not to be ashamed, rightly dividing the word of truth. 2 Timothy 2:15

Notice what Paul did *not* say. He did not tell Timothy to just read the Word, but, rather, to study it. Study implies work and being diligent to dig deep into the Bible, to see what the Scriptures are truly saying. If an individual just casually reads the Scriptures without laboring to understand proper context, they can impose their prejudices and biases into the Word and make it say what they want it to say. This is why Paul also told Timothy to *"rightly divid[e] the word of truth."* There is a right way to understand the Bible and a wrong way to understand it. Wrong understanding produces wrong believing, and wrong believing produces confusion, bondage. and deception—all of which are contrary to the will of God.

The second approach that people take in regard to these verses is as detrimental as the first. To ignore the Scriptures and take "the ostrich approach," sticking our heads in the sand, is an affront to and a total disrespect toward God. The Lord did not allow men and women over the centuries to lay down their lives to make sure that we have the Bible today, just so that we could ignore passages that are difficult to understand. Every verse in the Bible is important, and God has them recorded for our remembrance. He said:

> *All scripture is given by inspiration of God, and is profitable for doctrine, for reproof, for correction, for instruction in righteousness.* 2 Timothy 3:16

The verse is very clear. There is not one verse in God's Word that should be ignored. It is all necessary to our ability to live in the full counsel of His knowledge. Therefore, it is incumbent upon each of us, as God's people, to properly understand what our Lord wants us to know.

This brings us back to these verses.

> *In like manner also, that women adorn themselves in modest apparel, with shamefacedness and sobriety; not with broided hair, or gold, or pearls, or costly array; but (which becometh women professing godliness) with good works.*
> 1 Timothy 2:9-10

> *Whose adorning let it not be that outward adorning of plaiting the hair, and of wearing of gold, or of putting on apparel; but let it be the hidden man of the heart, in that which is not corruptible, even the ornament of a meek and quiet spirit, which is in the sight of God a great price.* 1 Peter 3:3-4

In order to understand what God was saying through these verses, it is helpful to first begin by establishing what God was not saying. If you eliminate the impossible, as well as the improbable, then whatever remains will ultimately guide you to the truth.

Through the generations, these texts have been used to promote the idea that God prohibits women from wearing makeup and elaborate and beautiful clothing. This could not be the case because when we look at the totality of the Bible, we find references that attest to the truth, that God is very much in favor of ornate and lavish adornment. One of the most outstanding examples of this revelation comes from none other than the book of Revelation. The vision that God gave John, the beloved disciple, has been recorded for all posterity, to give us a preview of the end of this age and the beginning of the ages to come. In one of John's visions, the Lord showed him a picture of the new Jerusalem that

He will prepare for His people. Before John began to describe what he saw, he compared how the city was designed to that of a bride preparing herself to greet her future husband. As we read the words from the text, it can be clearly discerned how no one in all the universe loves beautiful adornment more than our great God. Here now are the words of the Holy Spirit, given to the apostle John:

> *And I saw a new heaven and a new earth: for the first heaven and the first earth were passed away; and there was no more sea. And I John saw the holy city, new Jerusalem, coming down from God out of heaven, prepared as a bride adorned for her husband. And I heard a great voice out of heaven saying, Behold, the tabernacle of God, is with men, and he will dwell with them, and they shall be his people, and God himself shall be with them, and be there God.*
>
> Revelation 21:1-3

> *And he carried me away in the spirit to a great and high mountain, and shewed me that great city, the holy Jerusalem, descending out of heaven from God, having the glory of God: and her light was like unto a stone most precious, even like a jasper stone, clear as crystal; and had a wall great and high, and had twelve gates, and at the gate twelve angels, and names written thereon, which are the names of the twelve tribes of the children of Israel: on the east three gates; on the north three gates; on the south three gates; and on the west three gates. And the wall of the city had twelve foundations, and in them the names of the twelve apostles of the Lamb.*
>
> *And he that talked with me had a golden reed to measure the city, and the gates thereof, and the wall thereof. And the city lieth foursquare, and the length is as large as the breadth: and he measured the city with the reed, twelve thousand furlongs. The length and the breadth and the height of it are equal. And he measured the wall thereof, an hundred and forty and four cubits, according to the measure of a man, that is, of the angel. And the building of the wall of it was of jasper: and the city was pure gold, like unto clear glass. And the foundation of the wall of the city were garnished with all manner of precious stones. The first foundation was jasper; the second, sapphire; the third, a chalcedony; the fourth, an emerald; the fifth, the sardonyx; the sixth, sardius; the seventh, chrysolyte; the eighth, beryl; the ninth, a topaz; the tenth, a chrysoparsus; the*

> *eleventh; a jacinth; the twelfth, an amethyst. And the twelve gates were twelve pearls: every several gate was one of pearl: and the street of the city was pure gold, as it were transparent glass.*
>
> *And I saw no temple therein: for the Lord God Almighty and the Lamb are the temple of it.* Revelation 21:10-22

If fine jewelry and lavish adornments were unholy and profane, someone neglected to inform God about it. He seems to think that there is nothing ungodly about such things, for He adorned His city with the finest jewels and the greatest craftsmanship ever.

To further emphasize God's desire to bring this message to us, He moved upon the heart of John to compare the arrangement of the city to the way in which a bride prepares herself for her future husband. The fact that this particular imagery was included in the narrative is meant to engraft this point in us: while religious traditions may seek to keep women bound, God does not.

We are also provided with another example of this principle, this one in the life of the great King David. David was the most outstanding monarch in the Old Testament and one of the greatest leaders in world history. Although he accomplished so much in his life, there remained yet one desire that was left unfulfilled: the building of a great tabernacle for the Lord his God. David was told by God that he would not build the temple, but that his son Solomon would carry on that work in his stead. In spite of what seemed to be a disappointment for the mighty king, David made sure that everything required to construct such a great edifice was in place. The Bible has preserved this information for us:

> *Furthermore David the king said unto all the congregation, Solomon my son, whom alone God hath chosen, is yet young and tender, and the work is great: for the palace is not for man, but for the* Lord *God. Now I have prepared with all my might for the house of my God the gold for things to be made of gold, and the silver for things of silver, and the brass for things of brass, the iron for things of iron, and wood for things of wood; onyx stones, and stones to be set, glistening stones, and of divers colours, and all manner of precious stones, and marble stones in abundance. Moreover, because I have set my affection to the house of my God, I have of mine own proper good, of gold and silver, which*

I have given to the house of my God, over and above all that I have prepared for the holy house. Even three thousand talents of gold, of the gold of Ophir, and seven thousand talents of refined silver, to overlay the walls of the house withal: the gold for things of gold, and the silver for things of silver, and for all manner of work to be made by the hands of artificers. And who then is willing to consecrate his service this day unto the LORD? 1 Chronicles 29:1-5

David was a man of intense passion. His zeal was one of the great qualities of his character. Although it would cause him trouble from time to time, for the most part he knew how to channel his passion in the right direction. The Bible lets us know that there was nothing David was more passionate about than seeing the house of God built. He wanted, not just a building, but a place so magnificent in beauty and grandeur that he ensured that the very best materials were secured for that effort. He set aside the gold, the silver, and all the precious jewels of his kingdom, so that the temple of God would look like a place befitting the residence of the Creator of all things.

So passionate was David's love for God's temple that he even made sure that when Solomon was ready to build the structure, he would have the very finest artists and craftsmen at his disposal, not only for the construction, but also for its decoration. And God did not object to any of these provisions David made. If the Lord was pleased to have a building adorned splendidly, how much more does He want His children to look and feel their best!

There may be those who dismiss such notions by pointing out the fact that in both of the aforementioned scriptural references, what was being decorated in so splendid a fashion was a building and a city. The key to the door of revelation is to realize that in both instances these were tabernacles meant to serve as dwelling places for the Lord. And, under the New Covenant that exists in this present Church age, we, as believers, are now the temple of the Lord. The Bible declares it:

Know ye not that he are the temple of God, and that the Spirit of God dwelleth in you? 1 Corinthians 3:16

What? know ye not that your body is the temple of the Holy Ghost which is in you, which ye have of God, and ye are not your own? 1 Corinthians 6:19

If God saw fit to have the temple under the Old Covenant decorated with jewels and makeup, how much more should not the temple under the New Covenant be adorned in like fashion? God wants you to look your best, to wear your best, and to adorn yourself in a way that makes you feel like the royal treasure you are. Abstaining from wearing makeup and nice clothing does not make one more holy and sanctified than anyone else. The Kingdom of God is not without you, but within you, and if anyone in this world should look like royalty, it should be the children of the King of kings and Lord of lords! If you want to wear makeup, by all means, wear it, and if you choose not to wear it, then don't. The point is that it's not a problem with God, and it does not have to be a problem with His Church. God will never violate His Word; nor will He contradict His Word. It is impossible for God to lie, and it is improbable that He would put an image before us of someone or something to emulate and then place a prohibition on attaining that image.

Going back to Proverbs 31, we are given this valuable information regarding the virtuous woman:

She maketh herself coverings of tapestry; her clothing is silk and purple.

Proverbs 31:22

The Word states that the virtuous woman makes herself to look lovely and stylish, just as a craftsman would decorate an ornate piece of tapestry. It also says that she wears clothing made from the finest fabrics and the most beautiful colors. God would not include this in His Word and then turn right back around and denounce it in another book of the Bible, particularly those books in the New Testament that deal with our New Covenant rights as Christians. God is not a fool, and He is far too intelligent to contradict Himself. Men may misinterpret what God has said, but just because someone does so does not mean that their interpretation is right.

Now that we have eliminated the impossible and removed the improbable, let us turn our attention back to the two passages of scripture that come from the writings of Peter and Paul. To begin, I want to quote again the passage from Peter's epistle. This time, instead of quoting just the section that has been used to stifle and oppress women, I want to start with the beginning of the chapter, where Peter began the teaching. Coming in on the middle of a conversation can often lead to confusion because you don't have the proper context. Looking at the complete message will allow us to truly see what God wants us to know:

> *Likewise, ye wives, be in subjection to your own husbands; that, if any obey not the word, they also may without the word be won by the conversation of the wives; while they behold your chaste conversation coupled with fear. Whose adorning let it not be that outward adorning of plaiting the hair, and of wearing of gold, or of putting on apparel; but let it be the hidden man of the heart, in that which is not corruptible, even the ornament of a meek and quiet spirit, which is in the sight of God of great price. For after this manner in the old time the holy women also, who trusted in God, adorned themselves, being in subjection unto their own husbands; even as Sara obeyed Abraham, calling him lord: whose daughters ye are, as long as ye do well, and are not afraid with any amazement.* 1 Peter 3:1-6

After reading the totality of Peter's teachings, the context for his exhortation becomes more clear. This is a message about husbands and wives and particularly regards a marriage situation in which the wife is saved and the husband is not. Peter was writing this part of his epistle to show women who were in that situation how they could be a godly influence for winning their man to the Lord.

Peter started by encouraging the women to honor and respect their husbands in spite of their sinful condition. He then explained that maintaining a spiritual atmosphere of respect and affection toward these types of men can have a positive impact, helping them to experience the love of God, as it is displayed in the conduct of their wife.

Peter next stressed the point that it would not be through placing emphasis on their physical appearance that would change the heart of their man. As is usually the case, a man will marry a woman he is attracted to, so for those women who are saved to try to use their physical beauty to win their husband to the Lord would be counterproductive.

Peter told women who found themselves in this situation to work especially on their spirit, which he referred to as *"the hidden man of the heart."* If the wife will make sure her inner self is strong in the Lord, God will be able to use her spiritual example as a catalyst for change to take place in the marriage.

Next, Peter referred back to spiritual mothers of the past whose faith in God had allowed them to take on the nature of love, and this gave them the ability to treat their husbands in such a way as to move their hearts in a positive direction of obedience toward God. This is not a message banning makeup or any other grooming or clothing adornment. It is, rather, a teaching meant to stir women in troubled relationships, to focus mainly on keeping their hearts pure before God, in order to be a positive role model for their husbands to see the true power of a saved life. God does not want His daughters bound by religious dogmas; He wants them free, and whom God sets free is free indeed.

This brings me to the words of Paul that I referenced from his first letter to Timothy. In order to properly interpret this verse, one must have a solid understanding of the context in which this entire letter was written. Paul wrote this letter to his son in the faith, to help guide him on how to instruct the members of his congregation to live godly lives. Throughout the two letters, Paul wrote to Timothy, there are constant admonitions to not become too excessive, partaking of the things of this world. One of the greatest examples of this principle is found in this particular passage:

> *But they that will be rich fall into temptation and a snare, and into many foolish and hurtful lusts, which drown men in destruction and perdition. For the love of money is the root of all evil: which while some coveted after, they have erred from the faith, and pierced themselves through with many sorrows.*
>
> 1 Timothy 6:9-10

What Paul was doing here was establishing a principle as to how Timothy should minister to those members of his parish who were very wealthy. They needed to look at money in the right context. Paul understood that those with great wealth could be open to temptation from the devil, to get so caught up and consumed by their material gain, that they could become susceptible to different types of sins. The root of their fall would not be the money they possessed, but the fact that the money would possess them, because of their love for it.

Some theologians have misappropriated this passage to promulgate the idea that God is against financial prosperity, in the same way some have misappropriated the passage about modest adornment to suggest that God is against makeup. Both of these notions are wrong. In this passage, the message was about moderation in one's thinking about money. What God was saying was not to become so infatuated with money that it becomes your god. God is not against money; He just wants to make sure that money does not become a person's object of worship.

This same principle can also be applied to the following verses located in the same book of 1 Timothy:

> *But refuse profane and old wives' fables, and exercise thyself rather unto godliness. For bodily exercise profiteth little: but godliness is profitable unto all things, having promise of the life that now is, and of that which is to come.*
>
> 1 Timothy 4:7-8

Just as with the teaching Paul gave concerning money, throughout the centuries, some theologians have taken this passage and used it as a talking point to promote the idea that God is against physical exercise. However, if they would examine the verse in the light of the totality of God's Word, they would realize their folly in such notions. God wants us to take care of our physical bodies, for they are the temple of the Holy Ghost. We bring glory and honor to Him when we make sure that we take care of His dwelling place. Once again, we are not reading a message that is against something, but, rather, putting something into its proper context.

During the era in which this letter was written, there was a great emphasis placed on the glorification of the human body. These were the days of the gladiators and games that showcased men with idolized physics put on display for the masses to see them engage in mortal combat. It was the time in which palaces and temples were adorned with sculptors that showcased gods and goddesses in striking poses to draw attention to their physical beauty. It was also a moment in history when pagan women would lavishly cover themselves in makeup and jewelry as a symbol that displayed their social status and to express their unbridled lust for material goods. The Lord did not want His daughters to have such vain imaginations, so he had Paul include that ordinance in the letter. Thus, Timothy would know how to help the Christian women keep the right perspective.

This was why Paul began his exhortation placing the emphasis on women being shamefaced and having sobriety. Of course, in our time, these words can carry with them a negative connotation, but remember that we are reading from an English translation of the Bible that was made by the people of a prior century, and they were translating words from the original Greek.

The King James Version of the Bible, from which I have quoted and referenced throughout this entire book, was first printed in the year 1611. As a result of the translation being done by people of another century, some of the modern usages of our English words differ from the way the words were used in the seventeenth century. Also, it is important to understand the original meaning of the words in Greek in order to grasp the full revelation of what God is endeavoring to say to us.

When the people of Elizabethan England heard the words *shamefacedness* and *sobriety*, they did not think in terms of someone not liking themselves. Those words were used to imply "a sense of reserved dignity, of not being a show off, or too gaudy." They were meant to suggest "a form of carrying oneself with a gracefulness that bespoke of elegance and good taste." When the translators looked at the original Greek, they saw that the idea to be conveyed was "a sense of modesty," once again, "of not being a gaudy show off." With the passing of time, the word *shamefacedness* has come to mean "someone with low self-image," but it was not so in Paul's time.

Having all this information at our command, we can now re-examine the text and rightly divide the word of truth. In addition to quoting the verses in 1 Timothy again, this time I will include verse 8 for further clarification:

> *I will therefore that men pray every where, lifting up holy hands, without wrath and doubting. In like manner also, that women adorn themselves in modest apparel, with shamefacedness and sobriety; not with broided hair, or gold, or pearls, or costly array; but (which becometh women professing godliness) with good works.* 1 Timothy 2:8-10

Paul began by stating that it was his desire that men would take the position of being people of prayer, using the lifting up of their hands as a means of glorifying God at all times. We must think about the word *prayer* and its core meaning. Although it can be expressed in various ways and there are different levels of it, prayer, in its most basic definition, is "communication with God." Paul places emphasis on the hands, and the hands are the primary part a person uses to express their non-verbal communication. In essence, therefore, Paul was saying he desired that men would live lives in continual communication with God, using the lifting up of their hands as a symbolic gesture of the fact that they have consecrated their entire bodies unto God. The symbolism of their raised hands communicates both to God and the world that they are devoted to their Lord.

Next, Paul turned his attention to the women and began with the phrase, *"In like manner."* This wording implied that he wanted the women to take what he was getting ready to say and keep it in the same context of what he had said in the previous verse. So, with the context of using your body as a way to communicate with God and showing that you are committed to Jesus Christ, you should dress in a way that expresses that commitment. Keep a reserved and humble state of mind, and do not use your clothing and decorations to exalt yourself, as secular women do. Let your adorning be done in a way that promotes godliness and holiness.

The prohibition is not against the makeup or the nice clothing; it is against a vain and arrogant state of mind that says, "I will dress any way I want, even if it does not express a life set apart for God's service." If prayer is communication with God and Paul said that we should approach the way we dress in the same manner, then you must communicate a holy life to God through your attire. The leaders of the holiness movement went off course in this area. They thought that, in order to be holy and pure, women had to look as plain as possible. What they failed to realize was that it was not these things that caused a person to be unrighteous; it was the condition of the heart. If a person's heart is pure before God, they will present their outward appearance in a way that is both grand and elegant, while, at the same time, being holy and sanctified.

This now leads us to address the other side of the equation with regard to proper adornment for Christian women. We now see that God is not against women wearing makeup, jewelry, or beautiful clothing. In fact, the Bible encourages the believer to decorate themselves in a lovely way, for such things bring glory to God, as long as they are kept in the right perspective. God calls His people to freedom, but along with freedom there comes responsibility as well. As children of God, we have the liberty to enjoy the natural things of this life, but that liberty cannot be abused by turning our lifestyle into something that is contrary to the character of Christ.

The Bible admonishes us:

> *For, brethren, ye have been called into liberty; only use not liberty for an occasion to the flesh, but by love serve one another.* Galatians 5:13

> *For so is the will of God, that with well doing ye may put to silence the ignorance of foolish men: as free, and not using your liberty for a cloke of maliciousness, but as the servants of God.* 1 Peter 2:15-16

Both of these references were written to Christians, because God understood that freedom must be coupled with sobriety. Once a person realizes that they have a degree of liberty in a certain area, if they are not mature in their emotions, they will go too far to the extreme side of that freedom and end up being a slave to their carnal desires. This is why Paul wrote to the church in Galatia, insisting that the freedom given to them by God was not meant to be used to serve their carnal flesh, but should be used to be a blessing to their fellow man. Peter, in his epistle, also exhorted the believers not to use their liberty to hide ungodly intentions that bring a reproach upon the Church of the Lord Jesus Christ. We have seen this unfortunate problem manifested in the way some Christians dress today. Because of the teachings of certain preachers who encourage people to come as they are, some took that to the extreme and not only came as they were, but stayed as they were, still looking and dressing like the children of this world. This is exactly what Peter warned *against* in his writings.

There are too many foolish people in our world who promote the ignorant idea that the Church is nothing more than another social club, no different than any secular meeting place where people gather for entertainment. This notion is, of course, untrue, but the sad fact remains: many Christians give this idea credence by the way in which they present themselves. Many churches today look like clubs where the people, from the pulpit down to the pews, look like they are going to a disco rather than a revival. The Bible is very concise as to why this takes place. Just as Peter spoke of a cloak of maliciousness that hides wrong intentions, so, too, in the church, is the trend to promote this club-like attire, a desire to hide the fact that some Christians really want to look like the world. They have not properly separated their thinking from the thinking of this world, and, as a consequence, they wish to make the church conform to the world.

God does not want any of His children, especially His daughters, lowering their standards by dressing like the children of this world. This goes back, once again, to the woman written about in Proverbs 31. Every aspect of her character and lifestyle is presented before us, including the way she adorns her physical body. We looked at one aspect of this in an earlier section of this chapter. I want to quote that scripture once again, this time going further and gathering further insight as to how the woman of God should present herself:

> *She maketh herself coverings of tapestry; her clothing is silk and purple. Her husband is known in the gates, when he sitteth among the elders of the land. She maketh fine linen, and selleth it, and delivereth girdles unto the merchant. Strength and honour are her clothing; and she shall rejoice in time to come.*
>
> Proverbs 31:22-25

This extraordinary woman is so blessed by God that she owns and wears the very best clothing that money can buy. She even has her own clothing line and not only make clothes for herself, but she sells her products to the local retailers of her day. The key to all of this success is found in verse 25. It says that strength and honor are her clothing, and this causes her to rejoice in the God she serves.

Why would the Bible take the time to emphasize moral characteristics such as strength and honor and then relate that to clothing? The reason is that the Lord is showing a connection between the two concepts. What God is saying is that how you dress and present yourself to the world should reflect the strength of your relationship with God and your level of consecration to Him. When you truly are in connection with your heavenly Father, you will have His divine nature working within you. And, along with that divine nature, will come a moral sensitivity that will cause you to know that certain attire is not becoming on a Christian lady.

Just because you *can* do something does not mean that you *should* use that liberty and risk bringing a reproach upon yourself and the God you serve. When you first clothe your inner being with the strength of the Lord and put on your spiritual robe of righteousness, then your outer attire will be an honorable presentation for all to see the quality of your Christian witness. The apostle Paul put it this way when he wrote to the Christians in Rome:

> *The night is far spent, the day is at hand: let us therefore cast off the works of darkness, and let us put on the armour of light. Let us walk honestly, as in the day; not in rioting and drunkenness, not in chambering and wantonness, not in strife and envying. But put ye in the Lord Jesus Christ; and make not provision for the flesh, to fulfill the lusts thereof.*
>
> Romans 13:12-14

There is an epidemic sweeping the Body of Christ in which acts of adultery, fornication, and other unseemly practices are running rampant among professing Christians. Too many people who call themselves saints are behaving like anything but that, by fulfilling every form of lust that Satan plants in their head. One of the main reasons for this is that too many make provision for the flesh by dressing in seductive and ungodly clothing. Women can be seen now on Christian television wearing tight, ripped jeans and short skirts, and showing cleavage that should only be seen by their husbands in the privacy of their bedroom. These provisions for the flesh, which contribute to people fulfilling their lusts, are there because the saints have not put on the spiritual garment of the character of Christ.

It is taught subliminally in our culture that when women dress in revealing clothing that makes them strong and powerful because they are freely expressing their sexuality. They say they are liberating themselves from the shackles of oppression, the control of a Puritan subculture of bygone values that wanted to stifle their freedom and individuality. But these are all lies from the pit of Hell, and they run contrary to the heart of God.

You, as a Christian woman, only diminish your power by dressing provocatively; you do not enhance it. You cheapen and denigrate yourself and your moral standing by presenting yourself in the same form and fashion as a Hollywood video girl or a common woman of the night. This is why Paul said that the night is *"far spent,"* and it is time to cast off the attire of the harlot and put on the silk and colors of the virtuous woman.

The way in which you dress and present yourself to the world should communicate strength, regality, and moral power, all of which can only be found in the Lord and in conforming your total life to Him. The great man Paul also placed emphasis on this point when He declared in his letter to the Ephesians these powerful words:

Finally, my brethren, be strong in the Lord, and in the power of his might. Put on the whole armour of God, that ye may be able to stand against the wiles of the devil. Ephesians 6:10-11

Satan would love to trick you into thinking that, as a Christian, it is acceptable to dress any way you please because God knows that your heart is in the right place. This is what is meant by *"the wiles of the devil."* It is a trap to start you down the path of, not just looking like the world, but ultimately acting like the world as well. Your dress and manner should bring honor not shame to God. It is not honorable to see women looking like video vixens, reality television stars, and disco partygoers professing that Jesus is their Savior and Lord. It is a hurtful thing for God to have to see His daughters looking like lounge singers offering up praises to Him that should come forth from vessels adorned in a godly fashion. In this day and hour, God is calling His Church to come out of the ways of darkness and be clothed in the full Gospel, which will not only change the inside, but will also be reflected in how you present yourself on the outside.

In the end, it all comes back to the beginning and the verse that we started with:

Let your moderation be known unto all men. The Lord is at hand.
Philippians 4:5

God is calling His people to a balanced and complete life, established in the understanding of the full counsel of His Word. He wants you to look your best, wear your best, and present yourself in the best way that works for you. If that includes makeup and jewelry, that's no problem for Him, and if it does not include those things for you, that's also no problem for Him. What your heavenly Father wants is for you to keep those things in the right perspective, never becoming vain or high-minded, being of no heavenly good to the Master. The key is clothing yourself inwardly with strength and honor, so that when you prepare to dress yourself outwardly, you will adorn yourself as the woman of virtue He has chosen you to be.

Chapter 16

Purity, the Source of True Passion

We are helped with the knowledge that love is there yet, for the two are in each other's arms. Riches take wings, comforts vanish, hope withers away, but love stays with us. Love is God. – Lew Wallace

The ways and the plans of God are always the best solution to every situation and produce the most prosperous outcome for all who are involved. That is not a new or deep statement, but, although it goes without saying, it is still something that Christians need to remind themselves of from time to time. In spite of hearing such sentiments declared from pulpits and podiums, so much so that they have almost become cliches, there is still something very powerful about understanding the fulness of that principle.

We live in an age in which the world, the flesh, and the devil work constantly to try to convince us otherwise. Actually it goes all the way back to the garden of Eden, where Satan tempted Adam and Eve and deceived them into believing that what he had to offer them was a far greater experience than what God had given them. That same strategy is continually being played out in our time by the adversary of our souls. Although the tactics may be a little different and they may flow from different weaponry, the same lie is repeated over and over again.

This lie seeks to sway Christians into feeling as if there is something missing in living a righteous life and that only by following the devil's plans can one fill that gap in their souls. In ancient times, this lie came from the lips of the serpent in the garden, but now we have movies, television, and social media platforms that seek to promote a false reality about the true nature of this human experience. It seems that practically every form of media entertainment and secular dialogue attempts to send subliminal messages to our minds that say: The way of life the devil offers is more thrilling, more interesting, and more exciting than living a life in service to the Lord. This conflict is perhaps played out even more forcefully in the arena of love, sex, and marriage.

God, in His Word, has laid out a specific way in which these concepts should be defined, understood, and practiced in our lives. But all we need do is turn on the television, and it seems that almost all the sitcoms and the dramas promote approaching these topics from a view that is anti-God and anti-Bible. God says that sexual relations between men and women should be conducted only within the covenant of holy matrimony. And, as our Creator, He defined the terms of holy matrimony as an agreement between one man and one woman, living together with God as the center of their union. On this foundation rests the key to fulfilling the needs and desires of both the flesh and the soul.

Modern soap operas, movies, and reality shows try to present an opposing view to these parameters God has established. So much of what is presented on these platforms involves people engaging in adultery, fornication, and all manner of other sexual perversions. This is not by accident, but rather by an unholy design. The enemy is desperately seeking to make the alternative look so attractive and so appealing that Christians will begin to think that what the world permits and tolerates somehow liberates you and makes you a more well-adjusted individual.

The body politic is constantly saturated with images of people going from one sexual partner to another, and we see the characters in movies engaging in adulterous affairs and secret liaisons, and it is produced in a way that looks exciting. Because the institution of marriage has become so demeaned and belittled in our society, characters on these shows who are married are often portrayed as either miserable or sexually and emotionally frustrated.

When the world does address the subject of marriage and tries to speak of it in a positive way, the idea of two people waiting and saving themselves for each other for their wedding night is ridiculed. Instead, we hear the often crude and tasteless analogy: "You have to test drive the car before you buy," as if to compare something as sacred as marriage to a simple business transaction. Not only do such foolish notions help contribute to the horrendous divorce rate, as people feel like they can trade in their partner like they trade in a car when and if they tire of it, something is not working right, or they are drawn to a newer model. It also sends a signal to the young people of our world that, unless you engage in premarital sex, you can never be sure you will be happy once you are married. These tactics by the devil are carried out every single day, and it is sad to say that many Christians are led astray into believing the same lies as the world does.

This leads us back to the truth that declares: God's ways are the best. Although the world offers one thing, what God offers is far better. Not only are the promises of God far better than the temptations of this world; but God is also honest with us by showing His people the full picture. The reason sin looks so appealing to the natural eye is that it *is* appealing, and it *does* feel good. Some religious people try to hide this fact. Thank God, the Bible tells us the truth and gives us the entirety of it.

One of the prime examples of this transparency comes from the life of Moses. The name Moses has come down through the annals of history as being one of the great prophets, a man who was mighty in word and deed. Much has been said and written about him throughout the ages, but of all that has been spoken and written, one important fact of his story is often overlooked. It has to do with the point in his life when he had to decide what kind of life he would live. Would he follow the path of righteousness? Or would he walk the wide road that leads to destruction? It was a choice that required great searching of the heart, because both sides had something to offer.

The Bible deals with this fact in a very honest way, when it says concerning Moses:

> *By faith Moses, when he was come to years, refused to be called the son of Pharaoh's daughter; choosing rather to suffer affliction with the people of God, than to enjoy the pleasures of sin for a season.* Hebrews 11:24-25

Moses looked across the chasm of the valley of decision and realized that he would have to choose which road he wanted to travel. If you are a believer in Christ, you are among the blessed, but it is not as cut and dried as some might think. The Bible very specifically states that Moses not only rejected sin; he also recognized the *pleasures* of sin. Still, in spite of those recognized *pleasures*, he chose the way of God. Yes, there is pleasure in sin. If there were not, then no one would engage in it. But the mature person understands that pleasure only lasts for a season, and, once that season is over, the aftertaste will be more bitter than you can imagine.

It may feel good to have multiple sex partners for a while, but after the fun and games come sexually transmitted diseases, rejection, and wounded hearts that might never mend. It may feel good to have an affair with a married man, but after the thrill has worn off, then comes a broken home, shattered lives, and seeds that have been sown that will come back and haunt you in ways that are too frightening to imagine. The soap operas, the movies, and the romance novels do not tell this part of the story. Even if they do dramatize consequences, it is done in such a stylistically artificial fashion that it doesn't even come close to the realities of life. The Bible, on the other hand, "gives it to you" as forcefully and honestly as possible, so that you can make the right choices, choosing the more excellent way.

Even in understanding the truth behind the pleasures of sin, there is a higher revelation that God wants to bring to you. Many people are deceived into believing that the commandments of the Bible are put in place to withhold pleasure from us. These people have been fooled into thinking that God is trying to restrict them from happiness, stimulation, and joy. Nothing could be further from the truth. Even though many focus on the pleasures of sin, there are also pleasures in righteousness. On both sides of the spectrum, there is pleasure. The difference is that, while the devil's pleasures last for a season, God's pleasures last for eternity.

The psalmist declared this truth to us in one of the most beautiful statements ever recorded:

> *Thou wilt shew me the path of life: in thy presence is fulness of joy; at thy right hand are pleasures for evermore.* Psalm 16:11

There is a pathway of living that says: If you follow the Lord and do things His way, you will experience pleasure that is far beyond even the moon and the stars. God is not trying to restrict you from fulfilling the needs of your body and your soul, but He wants you to fulfill those needs in His way. Why? Because His ways are best for all of us.

Christianity, throughout the ages, has been falsely accused of being stiff, boring, and devoid of any sort of passion. Scoffers and mockers have sought to paint the Christian life as an existence in which having fun is a sin. And, because these malcontents are motivated by Satan, they only equate fun with committing sin. But the Kingdom of God is *"righteousness, and peace, and joy in the Holy Ghost"* (Romans 14:17). This is especially true of marriage.

The institution of marriage is under assault today as never before. Not only is the biblical definition of marriage being denied and redefined in our culture, but the idea of a commitment to one person for the rest of your life is now being looked upon as an archaic and restrictive way of living. Secularists are writing books and manifestos, promoting the idea that young women should not even desire to get married. Reality shows are promoting families with men having multiple spouses and women having live-in boyfriends. All the while, no one is refraining from having sex, and that is all part of Satan's plan. If he can convince people that it is better to engage in fornication outside of God's proscribed form of marriage, then he can destroy our entire society.

What Satan does not tell people is that there is more joy and passion in holy matrimony than in any ungodly relationship he can invent. God is the Creator of sex. He is the Author of passion. If anyone knows about sexual pleasure, it is the One Who made it in the first place.

The Bible is the guidebook for every aspect on how to live a successful, productive, and passion-filled life. That includes how to have pleasure in relationships. There is no other book in all the world that is filled with more love, more romance, and more intensity of feeling than the Word of the Almighty God. If you will follow God's programs and do things under His covenant, you will have a pleasure-filled life that outweighs anything this world has to offer. This is a revelation that the Proverbs 31 woman understands.

One of the greatest portraits of a loving and romantic relationship is found in the example of this woman and her husband. Although I have quoted these verses in previous chapters, I want to draw your attention to them again. The Bible declares:

> *Who can find a virtuous woman? for her price is far above rubies. The heart of her husband doth safely trust in her, so that he shall have no need of spoil. She will do him good and not evil all the days of her life.* Proverbs 31:10-12

Her children arise up, call her blessed; her husband also, and he praiseth her. Many daughters have done virtuously, but thou excellest them all. Favour is deceitful, and beauty is vain: but a woman that feareth the Lord, *she shall be praised. Give her of the fruit of her hands; and let her own works praise her in the gates.* Proverbs 31:28-31

This is the portrait of a godly marriage that all Christians should embrace and aspire to emulate. Here we see a stable and loving family in which there is spirituality, productivity, and an ever-increasing stream of harvest and blessing in every area. This woman is not only strong in her relationship with the Lord, and not only does she also have a successful business, but her home is also filled with the presence of God. Just as the Scriptures, in the book of Psalms, speaks about the joy that comes when the presence of God is manifested, we are given a glimpse of that promise manifesting through marriage.

This woman has children who wake up every day and are so filled with the joy of the Lord that they recognize the special blessing of their mother's love for them. Because they have caught this revelation in their hearts and minds, they do not curse and disrespect their mother; they esteem her highly and call her blessed. Her husband is so contented and complete in his relationship with her that he lives his life always singing her praises.

Many women hear nothing but criticism and attacks from their husbands, but because God is at the center of this marriage, this woman hears nothing but affirmation and affection from the man she is joined to. She has the heart of her husband, both passionately and completely, and because he is so enraptured by her, he has no need for the love of any other woman. This is what the psalmist meant when he said that in God, there are *"pleasures forevermore."*

Too often Christians equate those words only with spiritual blessings, but God desires to bless His children in every area, including physical pleasure. As I stated before, God is the Author of physical intimacy, and yet the church has let the devil run rampant with the lie that sexual pleasure can only be found in the world. When men and women follow God's blueprint for relationships and build on the right foundation, He will bless their union with physical pleasures that far surpass any perversion that this world has to offer.

Satan has very skillfully sown the lie that Christianity is rigid and cold and that sex in marriage is only for the purpose of having children. But God *is* love, and love is romantic and passionate. When we put God first and do things according to His ways, He will bring true passion into the marriage bed.

Consider the following scriptures from the Word of God which show that our Lord is very much in favor of His people experiencing physical passion:

> *The song of songs which is Solomon's Let him kiss me with the kisses of his mouth: for thy love is better than wine. Because of the savour of thy ointments thy name is as ointment poured forth, therefore do the virgins love thee. Draw me, we will run after thee: the king hath brought me into his chambers: we will be glad and rejoice in thee, we will remember thy love more than wine: the upright love thee.* Song of Solomon 1:1-4

> *I have compared thee, O my love, to a company of horses in Pharaoh's chariots. Thy cheeks are comely with rows of jewels, thy neck with chains of gold. We will make thee borders of gold with studs of silver.*
> *While the king sitteth at his table, my spikenard sendeth forth the smell thereof. A bundle of myrrh is my well-beloved, unto me; he shall lie all night betwixt my breasts. My beloved is unto me as a cluster of camphire in the vineyards of Engedi.*
> *Behold, thou art fair, my love; behold, thou art fair; thou hast dove eyes. Behold, thou art fair, my beloved, yea, pleasant; also our bed is green.*
> *The beams of our house are cedar, and our rafters of fir.*
> Song of Solomon 1:9-17

> *I am the rose of Sharon, and the lily of the valleys.*
> *As the lily among thorns, so is my love among the daughters.*
> *As the apple tree among the trees of wood, so is my beloved among the sons. I sat down under his shadow with great delight, and his fruit was sweet to my taste. He brought me to the banqueting house, and his banner over me was love.*
> Song of Solomon 2:1-4

These are not words from a Harlequin romance novel; these are words quoted directly from the Word of God. These scriptures convey feelings of intensity, desire, and physical intimacy that no other writer has ever been able to match. God is the ultimate Poet Laureate of Love, because He writes true love, born of the spirit and rooted and grounded in holiness.

The entire book of Song of Solomon is filled with amorous language. Because of it, some have questioned whether it should have even been included in the Cannon of the Holy Scriptures. But God saw fit to ensure that this text was preserved for future posterity, to show us the power of righteous love in all of its dimensions. Many theologians and commentators have placed the sole emphasis of this book on the fact that the relationship described in its text is merely put in place to serve as an allegory for Christ and His love for the Church. While that framework of thinking is true, to only emphasize that point fails to see the complete message the Holy Spirit wants to speak to the Church. God could have used another example that could have functioned as an illustration for His love for His people, but He intentionally chose to use a romance between a man and a woman to convey, not only a theological message, but a practical one as well.

The theological side of this message is the part that speaks of Christ and His love for the Church. The practical side of the message is the understanding that a romance between a man and a woman that is built on the foundation of a theological covenant will produce the greatest physical pleasure that anyone could imagine. You cannot have one without the other. God is not only concerned with feeding your spirit; He also wants your natural desires to be met as well. You cannot afford to seek to satisfy your natural desires outside of the covenant of marriage, for when you go outside of God's laws, you will produce tragic results.

God put the Song of Solomon in the Bible to reveal His truth to us. Even if we were to ignore the Song of Solomon (because we were embarrassed by its content), we would still have to deal with scriptures like those found in the book of Proverbs:

> *Let thy fountain be blessed: and rejoice with the wife of thy youth. Let her be as the loving bind and the pleasant roe; let her breast satisfy thee at all times; and be thou ravished always with her love.* Proverbs 5:18-19

Here is a verse from the very first book of the Bible that proves the point I am attempting to make here:

And they were both naked, the man and his wife, and were not ashamed.
Genesis 2:25

God is not embarrassed to address the issue of sex and romance, and neither should His Church be. He wants us to understand that the devil does not have the market on pleasure. It is within the plan of God that a person experience real pleasures and real joy. The key ingredient was given to us in this scripture in Genesis, where it says, *"the man and his wife."* It does not say, "the man and his girlfriend ...," nor does it say, "the man and his fiancée." It says, *"the man and his wife."* Not only were they open before each other; there was no shame in their exposure, because they were man and wife. If you are seeking real love, true romance, and intense passion, then you need to get on the Lord's side and do things according to His program and not the world's way.

Usually, in the area of relationships that are established for the purpose of marriage, there is a pattern the world tends to follow. A man and a woman meet (usually through some social setting they just "happen" to find themselves and the other person in). Once they meet and establish a rapport, they begin the dating process. This process involves dinners, outings, walks home and, sadly, sexual relations. After a few romantic *rendezvous,* the initial intoxication of attraction wears off, and the two part ways. Soon afterward, both the man and the woman will have met someone else through either the same or some other social scenario, and the process will start all over again, ending in the same results.

Generally, what tends to be the case is this: after a decade has passed on the dating scene, going through the same merry-go-round of process that I described, a person will then become more selective in their choices, looking for someone who can provide them with a degree of both excitement and stability, and then they get married, or, as the world would say, they settle down.

The problem with this process is that after so many bad relationships, after so many sexual encounters, and after so many hurt feelings, by the time you enter into marriage, you have so much emotional baggage from the past that it makes the present a struggle which many never overcome. And this is what the world considers to be an acceptable path to finding a mate. The tragedy in all of it is that many Christians have adopted these worldly ways of dating, including the premarital sex. They date this person and that person, each time sleeping with them, and they still go to church and sing in the choir and weep at the altar, and wonder why God has not blessed them. God will not cast His pearls before those who put no value in them. Nor is He the author of confusion. If you want His blessing, you have to do things His way, and His ways are found in His Word.

The Bible is a very intriguing book in that God chose a certain period in world history, with particular groups of people, with distinct customs and traditions, to tell the story of redemption. Everything in the Bible is recorded for our learning and to help us approach living in this natural world with a supernatural methodology. Often this supernatural approach is contained within the customs and the traditions of the people of biblical times. Even though God condemned certain traditions, there were others that He was very much in favor of.

At times, God allowed the historical figures who are written about in the Scriptures to carry out their traditions for us to see as types and shadows of things to come, and to instruct us on how to apply the principle of the tradition to our own personal lives. In the case of marriage, particularly as it relates to God's chosen people, men and women did not date multiple people until they stumbled upon a compatible person. Instead, marriages were often arranged by godly parents. Men and women did not look to "fall in love," but as they were brought together, they appreciated the wisdom of their parents' choice and learned to love each other. Usually, it was the heads of families who made the marriage arrangements for the young people, and, because they knew their children better than anyone else, they knew what they needed in a mate. The elders of the two families would come together, work out the necessary details, and only then bring the young man and woman together to be married.

To the ear of the so-called "liberated" and "independent" young woman of the twenty-first century, this all seems, at best, out of style, and, at worst, barbaric and crude. Who in the civilized world would want to engage in such archaic rituals practiced by primitives? But this arrogant and unlearned view is what produces so much trouble for so many young women today. They go out looking for a suitable man, hoping to find romance. They get very excited at the first man who charms them and get too emotionally attached, only to end up with a broken heart and a scarred soul. When the next man comes along, they go through the same process, with the same results, not realizing that these men are not looking for them to open their heart, but only to give their bodies to be used for physical pleasure. How sad that many who fall into this trap are professed Christians who do not understand the ways in which God works concerning relationships!

Going back to the concept of arranged marriages and how it was a commonplace practice in Bible days, God allowed that practice to exists and to be recorded in His Word, so that we could understand that it was a type and shadow of how God wants to work on behalf of His children today. We live in a world of dating apps, chat rooms, and professional matchmaking, all the while not realizing that God is the very best Matchmaker. He knows the right person for you, and if you will trust Him and follow His leading, He will arrange your marriage for you, just as the elders of old did for their children.

There is a wealth of revelation in this statement that Jesus made:

> *And he answered and said unto them, Have ye not read, that he which made them at the beginning made them male and female, and said, For this cause shall a man leave his father and mother, and shall cleave to his wife: and they twain shall be one flesh? Wherefore they are no more twain, but one flesh. What therefore God hath joined together, let no man put asunder.* Matthew 19:4-6

Jesus stated the obvious: that men and women were created by God, and given the fact that He is the Manufacturer, He knows the product better than anyone else could. He knows who is the best person for you, and you can save yourself a great deal of time and effort by letting your heavenly Father lead you to the right mate, instead of going from man to man looking on your own. There is nothing like allowing God to guide your footsteps and arrange the connections in your life that need to take place.

Consider King David, who has become famous among the heroes of faith. His life was filled with victory after victory, because he always inquired of the Lord as to what he should do. The only times in his life when he experienced defeat were moments when he was not in the place he should have been, and he had taken it upon himself to decide what he should and should not do. He acknowledged this in one of his psalms:

> *The steps of a good man are ordered by the Lord: and he delighteth in his way.* Psalm 37:23

Most people are so stubborn and impatient that they prefer to be the master of their own lives, rather than letting Jesus take control. God did not intend for you to have to stumble over one bad relationship after another before you find the right mate. Because He knows what is best for you, why not allow Him to order your steps and arrange your marriage?

Jesus' statement, *"What therefore God hath joined together, let no man put asunder,"* implies that God arranged the marriage in the first place. He ordained a specific man to be joined to a specific woman, and brought them together to be joined in holy matrimony. With that foundation established within the marriage, the husband and the wife experience true passion and genuine euphoria.

Yes, God knows you better than anyone, and He knows what your body needs. If you seek His guidance, He will arrange for you to meet the right person, one who can meet those needs. And, because God is not limited by distance or resources, He has all the tools at His disposal to bring all the pieces into place to get you to the man of your dreams.

We see this principle beautifully displayed in the life of Isaac and how God arranged his marriage to Rebekah. It is one of the most glorious love stories in all of human history, and it is a picture of how God can bring two people together—no matter the circumstances that stand between them. The Bible devotes an entire chapter to the account of how these two came together, and although it is quite lengthy, I want to share it with you.

Faith comes when we hear and read the Word of God and when we read with an understanding of the people and the customs of their day. These serve as shadows and symbols forged in the sands of time and that point the way to receiving our own inheritance. So, without further ado, here is the tale as it is recorded in God's holy Word:

> *And Abraham was old, and well stricken in age: and the Lord had blessed Abraham in all things. And Abraham said unto his eldest servant of his house, that ruled over all that he had, Put, I pray thee, thy hand under my thigh: and I will make thee swear by the Lord, the God of heaven, and the God of the earth, that thou shalt not take a wife unto my son of the daughters of the Canaanites, among whom I dwell: but thou shalt go unto my country, and to my kindred, and take a wife unto my son Isaac.*

And the servant said unto him, Peradventure the woman will not be willing to follow me unto this land: musts I needs bring thy son again unto the land from whence thou camest?

And Abraham said unto him, Beware thou that thou bring not my son thither again. The Lord *God of heaven, which took me from my father's house, and from the land of my kindred, and which spake unto me, and that sware unto me, saying, Unto thy seed will I give this land; he shall send his angel before thee, and thou shalt take a wife unto my son from thence. And if the woman will not be willing to follow thee, then thou shalt be clear from this my oath: only bring not my son thither again. And the servant put his hand under the thigh of Abraham his master, and sware to him concerning that matter.*

And the servant took ten camels of the camels of his master, and departed; for all the goods of his master were in his hand: and he arose, and went to Mesopotamia, unto the city of Nahor. And he made his camels to kneel down without the city by a well of water at the time of the evening, even the time that women go out to draw water.

And he said, O Lord *God of my master Abraham, I pray thee, send me good speed this day, and shew kindness unto my master Abraham. Behold, I stand here by the well of water; and the daughters of the men of the city come out to draw the water: and let it come to pass, that the damsel to whom I shall say, Let down thy pitcher, I pray thee, that I may drink; and she shall say, Drink, and I will give thy camels drink also: let the same be she that thou hast appointed for thy servant Isaac; and thereby shall I know that thou hast shewed kindness unto my master.*

And it came to pass, before he had done speaking, that, behold, Rebekah came out, who was born unto Bethuel, son of Milcah, the wife of Nahor, Abraham's brother, with her pitcher upon her shoulder. And the damsel was very fair to look upon, a virgin, neither had any man known her: and she went down to the well, and filled her pitcher, and came up.

And the servant ran to meet her, and said, Let me, I pray thee, drink a little water of thy pitcher.

And she said, Drink, my lord: and she hasted, and let down her pitcher upon her hand, and gave him drink.

And when she had done giving him drink, she said, I will draw water for thy camels also, until they have done drinking. And she hasted, and emptied her pitcher into the trough, and ran again unto the well to draw water, and drew for all his camels. And the man wondering at her held his peace, to wit whether the LORD *had made his journey prosperous or not.*

And it came to pass, as the camels had done drinking, that the man took a golden earring of half a shekel weight, and two bracelets for her hands of ten shekels weight of gold; and said, Whose daughter art thou? tell me, I pray thee: is there room in thy father's house for us to lodge in?

And she said unto him, I am the daughter of Bethuel the son of Milcah, which she bare unto Nahor. She said moreover unto him, We have both straw and provender enough, and room to lodge in.

And the man bowed down his head, and worshiped the LORD. *And he said, Blessed be the* LORD *God of my master Abraham, who hath not left destitute my master of his mercy and his truth: I being in the way, the* LORD *led me to the house of my master's brethren.*

And the damsel ran, and told them of her mother's house these things. And Rebekah had a brother, and his name was Laban: and Laban ran out unto the man, unto the well. And it came to pass, when he saw the earring and bracelets upon his sister's hands, and when he heard the words of Rebekah his sister, saying, Thus spake the man unto me; that he came unto the man; and, behold, he stood by the camels at the well. And he said, Come in, thou blessed of the LORD; *wherefore standest thou without? for I have prepared the house, and room for the camels.*

And the man came into the house: and he ungirded his camels, and gave straw and provender for the camels, and water to wash his feet, and the men's feet that were with him. And there was set meat before him to eat: but he said, I will not eat, until I have told mine errand.

And he said, Speak on.

And he said, I am Abraham's servant. And the LORD *hath blessed my master greatly; and he is become great: and he hath given him flocks, and herds, and silver, and gold, and menservants and maidservants, and camels, and asses. And Sarah my master's wife bare a son to my master when she was old: and unto him hath he given all that he hath. And my master made me swear, saying, Thou shalt not take a wife to my son of the daughters of the Canaanites in whose land I dwell: but thou shalt go unto my father's house, and to my kindred, and take a wife unto my son.*

And I said unto my master, Peradventure the woman will not follow me. And he said unto me, the LORD, before whom I walk, will send his angel with thee, and prosper thy way; and thou shalt take a wife for my son of my kindred, and of my father's house. Then shalt thou be clear from this oath, when thou comest to my kindred; and if they give not thee one, thou shalt be clear from my oath. And I came this day unto the well, and said, O LORD God of my master Abraham, if now thou do prosper my way which I go: behold, I stand by the well of water; and it shall come to pass, that when the virgin cometh to draw water, and I say unto her, Give me, I pray thee, a little water of thy pitcher to drink; and she say to me, Both drink thou, and I will also draw for thy camels: let the same be the woman whom the LORD hath appointed out for my master's son. And before I had done speaking in mine heart, behold, Rebekah came forth with her pitcher on her shoulder; and she went down unto the well, and drew water: and I said unto her, Let me drink, I pray thee. And she made haste, and let down her pitcher from her shoulder, and said, Drink, and I will give thy camels drink also: so I drank, and she made the camels drink also. And I asked her, and said, Whose daughter art thou? And she said, The daughter of Bethuel, Nahor's son, whom Milcah bare unto him: and I put the earring upon her face, and the bracelets upon her hands. And I bowed down my head, and worshiped the LORD, and blessed the LORD God of my master Abraham, which had led me in the right way to take my master's brother's daughter unto his son. And now if ye will deal kindly and truly with my master, tell me: and if not, tell me; that I may turn to the right hand, or to the left. Then Laban and Bethuel answered and said, The thing proceedeth from the LORD: we cannot speak unto thee bad or good. Behold, Rebekah is before thee, take her, and go, and let her be thy master's son's wife, as the LORD hath spoken. And it came to pass, that, when Abraham's servant heard their words, he worshiped the LORD, bowing himself to the earth. And the servant brought forth jewels of silver, and jewels of gold, and raiment, and gave them to Rebekah: he gave also to her brother and to her mother precious things. And they did eat and drink, he and the men that were with him, and tarried all night. And they rose up in the morning, and he said, Send me away unto my master. And her brother and her mother said, Let the damsel abide with us a few days, at the least ten; after that she shall go.

And he said unto them, Hinder me not, seeing the LORD hath prospered my way; send me away that I may go to my master.

And they said, We will call the damsel, and enquire at her mouth. And they called Rebekah, and said unto her, Wilt thou go with this man? And she said, I will go.

And the sent away Rebekah their sister, and her nurse, and Abraham's servant, and his men. And they blessed Rebekah, and said unto her, Thou art our sister, be thou the mother of thousands of millions, and let thy seed posses the gate of those which hate them.

And Rebekah arose, and her damsels, and they rode upon the camels, and followed the man: and the servant took Rebekah, and went his way.

And Isaac came from the way of the well Lahairoi; for he dwelt in the south country. And Isaac went out to meditate in the field at the eventide: and he lifted up his eyes, and saw, and, behold, the camels were coming.

And Rebekah lifted up her eyes, and when she saw Isaac, she lighted off the camel. For she had said unto the servant, What man is this that walketh in the field to meet us? And the servant had said, It is my master; therefore she took a vail, and covered herself.

And the servant told Isaac all things that he had done. And Isaac brought her into his mother Sarah's tent, and took Rebekah, and she became his wife; and he loved her: and Isaac was comforted after his mother's death.

Genesis 24:1-67

No poet, playwright, or psalmist could craft a more beautiful love story than that. It is a narrative full of scope, grandeur, and the richness of revelation that could only come from the heart of God. The sheer level of detail that the Lord has provided for us is a telling factor, and every piece of information is placed here for a divine purpose and for a divine lesson.

Even though Isaac and Rebekah only had one encounter before they were married, they were comforted by the truth of knowing that God had orchestrated their steps, and it was His good pleasure for them to be joined together as husband and wife.

Many Bible scholars and theologians have read this historic account and looked at it solely from the standpoint of the story serving as a type and shadow for the end of the age, when Christ will take the Church as His Bride in the great Marriage Supper of the Lamb. Abraham was a type and shadow of God the Father. Isaac represented Jesus as His only begotten Son. The servant, who was commissioned to find the bride, represented the blessed Holy Spirit Who goes forth and prepares the Church for the wedding.

Of course, Rebekah is the representation of the Church, prepared as a bride adorned for her husband. All of these interpretations are valid and in accordance with the entirety of the Scriptures, but as with all things contained in the Bible, there are many levels of revelation. The Song of Solomon is a book that serves an allegorical function that teaches us about the nature and the dimension of Christ and His love for His Church, but there is another facet in that diamond. That majestic book is also a document that records the lives of real people with real emotions, and God not only used their lives to tell His story, but also to show us that He wants Christian marriages to be full of romance and passion.

This same principle is applicable to the story we read here in Genesis because it serves a multifaceted purpose. It is both a spiritual allegory and a story of real people who had real desires and hopes for their future. Underneath the lofty theological context, there is a genuine love story based on purity and intensity and on being led by the Holy Spirit. If we understand that and learn from the lives of Isaac and Rebekah, the blessings they received we can receive as well. So let us think about this text and look at the humanity, as we study the history and receive the spirituality.

This account in Genesis, at its most basic human core, is the story of a woman. Although she does not enter the narrative until halfway through the tale, the idea of her and the power of what she represents is felt throughout the chapter. She is the virtuous woman and, because she perceived that her merchandise was good and she gleaned in the right field, God not only blessed her, but gave her a destiny that ultimately led to the changing of the course of human history.

But, before all that grandeur, there was just a young woman. This woman was like any other young woman who existed in ages past or ages to come. She had hopes and dreams and expectations for her future. She was also a woman of great courage, sincerity, and purity of spirit, soul, and body. She was a woman of virtue, and that made her a woman of destiny. To anyone and everyone who will give their life wholly and unashamedly to the Lord, He will not only open the window of blessing over their life, but He will also provide them the opportunity to be used in fulfilling divine purposes for His glory.

The Bible specifically tells us that this woman was a virgin, chaste and pure, untouched by any man. The Lord provided us with this information because it symbolized her consecration to God, and it is a representation of how believers should present their bodies, holy unto the Lord. Though it is not fashionable in our society for people to remain virgins until their wedding night, it is important to keep yourself pure before God in order to remain in the place of sensitivity to the will of God manifesting in your life.

The devil presents only the short-term pleasure of sin. What he does not tell you is that sin opens the door for you to become controlled and influenced by the powers of darkness. The devil understands that the more you give yourself to sin and allow Satan to place a stronghold over your life, the weaker your relationship with God becomes. This spiritual weakness stops the channel of God's blessings from manifesting in your life, and, even more damaging, it disqualifies you from being used in the depth of power and influence that God would have you to walk in. This is why so many young people become entangled by the wiles of the devil. They are extremely vexed by the pressure and the temptation from this world's culture to engage in all manner of fornication. Much of the Church has failed, not only to tell young people that this peer pressure is motivated by Satan, but they have also failed to fully explain the full consequences of a lifestyle of practicing sin. God wants to use His children to change the world and make an impact upon society that changes the cultural direction of that society. But, in order for this mighty revival to take place, God requires yielded vessels who have consecrated their lives to Him.

Just because God can use anybody does not mean that He will just use anybody. Certain assignments require deeper levels of commitment, and there are certain blessings that will only come about by specific sacrifices that test your character and integrity.

It is not always a simple matter to preserve yourself and save your body for marriage. It may cost you some nights alone. It may cost you moments in which certain men, because of your standards, will pass you by. There may even be seasons in which it seems as if you might never get married, and it would be easier to compromise your values and satisfy the desires of your flesh. But if you give yourself to sin, it will cost you. It will cost you time, maybe even years. It will cost you energy. It may even cause you to miss the fulfillment of your divine destiny. Rebekah understood this even in that ancient time. Just as there is pressure in this day, there was pressure in her day as well. Even as there are temptations today where you are, there were temptations in the places Rebekah lived. The devil works in every age, walking about, seeking whom he may devour, trying to rob God's children of the fulfillment of their destiny.

Whatever you do, do not throw away your virtue, and do not allow your purity to be cast aside. It could cost you more than you imagine. God will not fail you, and if you do things according to His plan, He will give you the victory.

As God was testing and preparing Rebekah, He was also working on her behalf, to bring all her desires to fruition. As she was doing her part in living upright before the Lord, He was making preparation in another country that would propel her toward seeing His salvation.

The Bible tells us that when Rebekah had come into her adulthood, God's servant Abraham was needing to find a wife for his son Isaac. Abraham was, of course, the great patriarch who was called by God to leave the land of his childhood and journey to a place God would direct him to. Abraham obeyed the voice of God and journeyed to the chosen land, and the Lord blessed His servant by allowing his wife to give birth to a son, the child Isaac.

Isaac was not just any child; he had a great destiny upon his life. He was called by God to be the one who would carry on the legacy of faith that God had given to Abraham, his father, and it would be from Isaac's loins that a great nation of people would come forth and be a great blessing to all the world. As it has so often been said: Every great man requires the love and the help of a great woman, and this is something that Abraham understood.

Abraham recognized that, in order for his son Isaac to fulfill his destiny, he would need to be joined to a certain type of woman. A holy nation could only be birthed by a holy mother. A royal priesthood could only come forth from the womb of a queen of purity. A people of purpose could only go forward by the words given to them from a woman whose tongue always spoke the law of kindness. Herein is a great truth you must understand for your own life: You may be at a point in your life when you are believing God for some great thing to break forth for you. It may be meeting and marrying a mighty man of faith.

Or it could be the opening up of a new opportunity to advance in your career. Whatever it is, you need to understand the biblical principle that says: *"Unto whomsoever much is given, of him shall be much required"* (Luke 12:48). You have no right to expect some great man to come into your life if you have not paid the price to do what is right in the sight of God. You have no business expecting a miracle to come to pass in your life if you have not submitted yourself fully to God's will.

When Abraham needed a wife for his son, he called his servant to him and told him to go look for a certain type of woman. Abraham instructed his servant to avoid the women who dwelt in the places where false gods were worshiped. He would not have his son marry a strange woman and abort the plan God had for the whole family. The servant was commanded to go to a certain place and seek out a specific type of woman, showing once more that you have to position yourself in the places that God wants you to be in, if you expect to obtain His blessing.

In tune was the master's wishes, the man made a journey, arriving at the designated spot for the divine appointment to take place. There he offered a prayer unto God. His petition was not just any random request; he prayed a God-inspired prayer that you should pray when believing God for a mate. The man lifted his voice to the Lord and cried out that He would send the woman who was chosen by Him to be the perfect bride for Isaac. This is all recorded for our learning, and it tells us that there is a person appointed by God to be your spouse. If you let Him give you His choice for you, then, not only will He order your steps so that you may meet this person, but everything will come into alignment to bring the two of you together.

The Bible tells us that no sooner had the servant ended his prayer than Rebekah arrived, and she said and did everything needed to confirm to him that she was the woman of virtue chosen by God Himself to be the wife of Isaac. She did not need to go on ten blind dates or sleep with five or six men to find Mr. Right. All she needed was faith in God and being led by the Holy Ghost.

After the initial meeting between the two, Rebekah took the servant to her home to meet her family. Upon meeting them and after having a time of fellowship, the man relayed to them why he had come and who had sent him. After hearing that Rebekah had been chosen to be the bride for Isaac, the family understood and accepted the fact that this was the Lord's doing, and no one could stand against it.

Still, even with that great truth established, there was one more test that had to be passed. It is true that when God sets things in motion in your life for your good, no other force can stand against it. Although some may try, the Word promises that when the enemy comes in like a flood, the Lord will lift up a standard against him (see Isaiah 59:15). There is only one person in the world who can truly hinder you from receiving your miracle, and that is *you*. Whether it is fear, unbelief, pride, or preconceived notions that are not in line with God's will, your own inability to fully align yourself with the divine plan can rob you of your blessing.

Very often your greatest test is the one that comes right before the breakthrough, and this is, sadly, where many give up. It is interesting that the Bible includes within the narrative that just before Rebekah was scheduled to depart with Abraham's servant to go and meet Isaac, her family tried to insist that she stay for a period of time, so that they could spend more time with her. On the surface, this may have seemed like a reasonable request, but in the world of the spirit, this would have delayed the divine timing of God's schedule. There are moments in life when you will have to decide to follow the plans and timing of God, even when other alternative choices seem to be good and valid.

One of the greatest ministers of the Gospel of the Lord Jesus Christ in recent generations was the Rev. Dr. Billy Graham. His ministry touched the world, and his personal life was a model of godly integrity that continues to serve as an example to subsequent generations. Other than his personal relationship with Christ, the essential component that made Dr. Graham so successful in both professional and private achievement was his wife, Ruth Bell Graham. Theirs was a love story that was truly ordained by God.

But, as he told it, there were moments when it seemed as if their life together would not blossom to its full maturity. When the two of them were young students at Wheaton College, they began a friendship that grew into genuine love. Both of them sensed the call of God upon their lives, to serve the Lord in Christian ministry, but there was a slight difference in how they saw themselves fulfilling that call. Ruth had been born in China, the child of missionary parents, and she had long had a strong desire to become a missionary and devote her life to work outside of the United States. She admired those great female pioneers who sacrificed love in order to go and change the world.

Dr. Graham, on the other hand, believed that God had called him to be an evangelist who would travel the world, but have his home base in America. He knew in his heart that God had called Ruth to be his wife, and, in spite of this seeming conflict of interest, he did not pressure her, but he trusted the Lord to speak to her heart.

Serving God as a missionary is a noble and godly pursuit, but if it is not the perfect will of God for you, you will not fulfill your divine destiny. Ruth had a difficult decision to make: Would she serve God the way she wanted or the way He wanted. Fortunately for her, for Billy Graham, and for the world, she chose to submit fully to the plan of God and became Ruth Graham. Although she did not become the missionary stateswoman that she desired to be, her obedience led to the saving of more souls than she could have imagined. Without her love and support, Billy Graham would never have been able to be as effective as he was, and the Kingdom of God would not have advanced in such a powerful way.

Rebekah faced a similar dilemma. She could have very easily insisted that she remain with her family for a few more days, and that certainly would have been a reasonable thing for her to do. But when she heard the call of God spoken through the mouth of Abraham's servant, she responded to that call and chose obedience over comfort. Although it was a sacrifice for her to do so, had she not made that decision, she would have missed her moment. Not only did she keep her divine appointment; but her family began to decree a blessing over her, prophesying that she would be the progenitor of untold millions, and that her descendants would always be victorious over their enemies.

In this way, Rebekah took her journey with the man of God, and they eventually came to the place where Isaac was waiting. When she saw her husband-to-be, the Bible says that she covered herself with a vail before she went to meet him. There is a great spiritual application in this little detail. The covering of the vail symbolized the purity of the relationship and the fact that not everything should be so exposed before marriage. Far too many not only give their bodies to others before marriage; they allow the courtship process to be cheapened by a lack of propriety. Things can become very vulgar and obscene in relationships, and some move too fast by not establishing the proper foundation of connecting on a spiritual basis. When Rebekah covered herself, she was establishing that this romance would be built on purity, and it was the purity that led to the passion. After the foundation was established, then the wedding commenced, and the two became one and experienced comfort and love in a way that has forever changed the world. This is the glory of God in manifestation, bringing two hearts together as one.

This is not a message advocating that a group of men in some back room choose your mate. It is a message that seeks to compel you to allow God to be your Matchmaker. Let Him order your steps and lead you through the course of true love.

This brings us back once more to the book of Ruth, for we see the same principle of godly courtship played out in her story. In our study of her life, we saw how God had directed her steps to lead her to leave her old way of life and enter into the place that He had prepared for her. As a result of her relationship with her mother-in-law, Naomi, Ruth was led by God to meet Boaz, who was one of the greatest men of his era.

After her initial encounter with Boaz, Ruth returned to Naomi and relayed to her the details of the meeting. The mother-in-law rejoiced because she could see the hand of God at work in this meeting, and she knew that He was getting ready to bless Ruth with a husband. Naomi also understood that in order for the plan of God to fully come to pass, the foundation of purity and godliness had to be established in the relationship. Boaz must understand that Ruth was a woman of virtue. He was a direct descendant of Isaac, and this meant that from his loins would come the next link in the linage that would ultimately produce Jesus, the Savior of the world. Therefore Boaz needed a virtuous woman to walk beside him as he continued the legacy of faith put in place by his forefathers.

Naomi counseled Ruth concerning what she needed to do next, and this also serves as a spiritual teaching to show you how important it is to be led by the Lord in relationships. We left the story at the end of Ruth 2, and now I wish to quote some verses from the remaining two chapters of the book. The Bible declares to us:

> *Then Naomi her mother in law said unto her, My daughter, shall I not seek rest for thee, that it may be well with thee? And now is not Boaz of our kindred,*

with whose maidens thou wast? Behold, he winoweth barley to night in the threshingfloor. Wash thyself therefore, and anoint thee, and put thy raiment upon thee, and get thee down to the floor: but make not thyself known unto the man, until he shall have done eating and drinking. And it shall be, when he lieth down, that thou shalt mark the place where he shall lie, and thou shalt go in, and uncover his feet, and lay thee down; and he will tell thee what thou shalt do. And she said unto her, All that thou sayest unto me I will do. And she went down unto the floor, and did according to all that her mother in law bade her. And when Boaz had eaten and drunk, and his heart was merry, he went to lie down at the end of the heap of corn: and she came softly, and uncovered his feet, and laid her down. And it came to pass at midnight, that the man was afraid, and turned himself: and, behold, a woman lay at his feet.

And he said, Who art thou?

And she answered, I am Ruth thine handmaiden: spread therefore thy skirt over thine handmaid; for thou art a near kinsman.

And he said, Blessed be thou of the Lord, my daughter, for thou hast shewed more kindness in thy latter end than at the beginning, inasmuch as thou followedst not young men, whether poor or rich. And now, my daughter, fear not; I will do to thee all that thou requirest: for all the city of my people doth know that thou art a virtuous woman. Ruth 3:1-11

Here, once again, we are provided with a loving and tender portrait of how the Lord arranged and orchestrated events, to bring two hearts together as one. Just as with the story of Isaac and Rebekah, the Bible has provided us with details regarding ancient courtship customs that serve as spiritual metaphors for how the ways of God are established in our lives.

The chapter began with Naomi telling her precious daughter-in-law that it was her desire that Ruth be provided rest from her toil and labor. The idea of rest is symbolic of a place of tranquilly and abundance, where we, as believers, enter into our Promised Land. Just as there are times of sowing (and sometimes one must sow in the midst of heartache and tears), after all of the toil comes the harvest, where the saint enters into the rest that is provided for all God's children.

Naomi told Ruth that Boaz was their near kinsman, signifying that Boaz was also of the household of faith, and because he held true to the same values as they did, he was the best man to give Ruth the life she deserved. Therefore, the elder instructed the younger to go and prepare her body and dress appropriately and make her way down to the location known as "the threshingfloor," where Boaz was working.

The threshingfloor was a place where the wheat and barley gathered from the field would be tested and purified so that all of the impurities (commonly known as chaff) could be removed. There is also a spiritual lesson for us in this. Just as Ruth had to prepare herself for this pivotal moment, so must you, when you are about to step into your divine destiny. You must be sure that you are in constant fellowship with the Holy Ghost, just as Ruth was with Naomi. By spending consistent devotional time in prayer and in the reading of God's Word, you can keep yourself pure and clean and allow the anointing to continually work in your life. Then, as you go forth, adorning yourself in the manner becoming a Christian lady, you will be led, not only in meeting the right man, but the courtship with him will take place on a deeper level.

Most modern romances are experienced in the shallow waters of the heart. Many people come together purely out of soulless infatuation, and couples only see each other through rose-colored glasses. As a result, by the time they enter into marriage, they still have not worked out the things that most often lead to the breakdown of a marriage.

The meeting that was to take place at the threshingfloor symbolized that the relationship was going to be tried and tested so that anything that could have caused a hinderance to the plan of God would be eliminated. This is why premarital counseling is so important. This is why it is essential that you base your romance on praying together and studying God's Word together, so that He can work out of both of you those things that could cause problems down the road.

Ruth took heed to all of Naomi's advice, and we are to follow her example in being led by the Holy Spirit. Just as Ruth said to Naomi that all that she had said she would do, so must our declaration be when our Lord speaks to us.

Ruth went forward and presented herself to Boaz as was customary in that day. It has been said of the women of that time that they would go to the foot of their husband's bed, gently raise the covers, and get in. Because Ruth and Boaz were not yet married, Naomi instructed Ruth to simply go to Boaz and uncover his feet. Anytime the Bible speaks about feet or footsteps, it usually has to do with the paths of life that we choose to take. When the apostle Paul instructed the believers at Ephesus to have their *"feet shod with the preparation of the gospel of peace"* (Ephesians 6:15), he was saying to be sure that the path of life that you take is ordained according to the plan of righteous living, which will ultimately produce lasting peace.

When Ruth was instructed to uncover Boaz's feet, she was fulfilling a custom that stood as a metaphor, to ensure that the man she would be joining herself to was determined to walk in the steps God had ordained for him. Too many women marry men with little or no idea of what they believe about God, or whether or not they see Him leading their lives. When women join themselves to men like that, they cause themselves to become spiritually blind. When a woman is connected to a man with no spiritual perception, his blindness affects her, and they both fall into the ditches of this world. When Ruth uncovered the feet of Boaz, she was ensuring that he understood that all of his days and every step he took were to be placed in God's control.

As Ruth continued to follow the proscribed orders, Boaz woke up and was startled to find a woman at his feet. Even though he had met Ruth before, his state of mind was somewhat perplexed at the moment, possibly as the result of his revelries that had taken place earlier in the evening. It is interesting to consider this in light of the fact that when Adam first saw Eve in the garden of Eden, he knew instinctively and instantly that she was his wife. In a time in which man knew noting of the ways of sin, everything was clear. Now, however, after the fall from grace, mankind sees through a glass darkly, and sometimes fear and unbelief can hinder the child of God from recognizing a blessing when it is standing right in front of them. All of these factors, no doubt, contributed to Boaz's state of mind at that moment.

But God is gracious. Not only will He help our unbelief; He will also raise us out of any stupor that would cause us to stumble and miss our divine destiny. God knew that Boaz was a true man of integrity, so, in spite of his insecurities and uncertainties in the situation, God caused Ruth to speak the exact words that Boaz needed to hear in order to understand fully that this was in the plan of God. After Ruth spoke, Boaz once again affirmed his respect and adoration for her by giving her the greatest compliment any female could receive—that she was a virtuous woman.

As this blessed moment continued between them, more words were expressed, and certain plans were set. Then, after they had departed from each other's presence, God continued to work in their circumstances to finally join them together as man and wife.

The final chapter of the book of Ruth tells us:

> *So Boaz took Ruth, and she was his wife: and when he went in unto her, the* LORD *gave her conception, and she bare a son. And the women said unto Naomi, Blessed be the* LORD, *which hath not left thee this day without a kinsman, that his name may be famous in Israel. And he shall be unto thee a restorer of thy life, and a nourisher of thine old age: for thy daughter in law, which loveth thee, which is better to thee than seven sons, hath born him.*
>
> *And Naomi took the child, and laid it in her bosom, and became a nurse unto it. And the women her neighbours gave it a name, saying, There is a son born to Naomi; and they called his name Obed: he is the father of Jesse, the father of David.*
>
> *Now these are the generations of Pharez: Pharez begat Hezron, and Hezron begat Ram, and Ram begat Amminadab, and Amminadab begat Nahshon, and Nahshon begat Salmon, and Salmon begat Boaz, and Boaz begat Obed, and Obed begat Jesse, and Jesse begat David.* Ruth 4:13-22

Out of the mouth of two or three witnesses, let every word be established. Once more God has pulled back the curtain and showed us from His Word that when we do things according to His plan and submit ourselves to His leading and direction, nothing can hinder us from receiving a miracle. Ruth not only found peace with God; she married the man of her dreams, the one who was ordained by God to be her husband. She was honored with the privilege of being included in the linage of people who would bring forth Jesus into our world.

As a result of the faithfulness of Ruth, even Naomi was able to see her life blessed and restored exceedingly and abundantly beyond what she could have imagined. All of this and more proves beyond all doubt that the ways of God are always great, because they are always good.

I want to end this chapter with a testimony from the life of Dr. Lester Sumrall. Dr. Sumrall was a dynamic man of faith whose service for the Lord touched the world throughout the decades of the twentieth century. When he was a young man, already established in his ministry, he decided that he would remain a bachelor for the rest of his life and devote himself totally to Christian service. One day, he was attending a wedding in a certain country, and as he took his seat in the church, he noticed a very beautiful young woman playing the piano. He was instantly captivated by her, and all thoughts of remaining a bachelor instantly fled. After the wedding ceremony that day, the two of them struck up a conversation, and there was an instant connection that developed between them. The young woman was also a missionary who had a passion for winning lost souls to Jesus Christ.

Soon after that initial encounter, the two had to part ways because of their ministry schedules. Unlike today, there were no cell phones, no social media outlets, or other forms of modern communication that we enjoy today. However, they did decide to correspond by letter. As often as they could, they would write to each other, sharing thoughts about their goals, their passions and their desires. It was a sweet and loving courtship, because it grew from mutual admiration, tender affection, deep friendship, and joyous love.

Even though they had only experienced brief moments together in person, they realized that God had united their hearts as one. They were soon married, and Lester and Louise Sumrall lived many years together as a great soul-winning team for the Lord. They could have resisted God's leading or tried to rationalize things in their mind, but they knew that what God has in mind is always the best.

I share this testimony to reaffirm to you that if you live a life of purity before the Lord, consecrating your total being to doing His will, not only will your virtue be its own reward; it will continue to yield an ever-increasing harvest that will bless you in fulfilling all the desires of your heart.

CHAPTER 17

NEITHER MALE NOR FEMALE

"Eve was not taken out of Adam's head to top him, neither out of his feet to be trampled on by him, but out of his side to be equal with him, under his arm to be protected by him, and near his heart to be loved by him."

– Matthew Henry

One morning in August of 1588 a group of British soldiers gathered at Tilbury near the Thames river, to defend their nation from an invading foreign power. It was a daunting task that faced them, for on that fateful day they would be standing against the might of Spain, at the time one of the most powerful and influential nations in Europe. The Spaniards had gained great levels of control, not only over certain strategic parts in the continent, but also in the lands of the New World across the sea. Now they had set their sights on the tiny island nation of England, hoping to bring that country under their control as well.

The English troops who were gathered at the field of battle would soon have the enemy upon them, but before the battle commenced, they were given a boost of morale that strengthened them to the core of their being. Suddenly, across the field toward them rode Queen Elizabeth I, charging in on a great steed. She was dressed for battle, adorned in regalia that embodied the warrior spirit of the heroes of old. As she looked out over her troops, the virgin queen may have seen trepidation or maybe even fear in their eyes, or she may have felt the same emotions coursing through her own soul. Whatever her motivation, she decided to give a speech that would change the atmosphere and rally her army to stand fast in the day of battle.

Elizabeth raised herself up upon her horse, looked out over her army, then lifted up her voice and said to them:

> Wherefore I am come among you at this time but for my recreation and pleasure, being resolved in the midst and heat of the battle to live and die amongst you all, to lay down for my God and for my kingdom and for my people mine honour and my blood even in the dust. I know I have the body of a weak and feeble woman, but I have the heart and stomach of a king and of a king of England too .... Not doubting but by your concord in the camp and valour in the field and your obedience to myself and my general, we shall shortly have a famous victory over these enemies of my God and of my kingdom.

They were truly momentous words, spoken on a momentous day, and delivered by one of the greatest monarchs ever to sit upon the English throne. In spite of the rich cadence and rhetorical power of the speech, there is one aspect of it that, viewed from the lens of history, looks at the same time both profound and sad. The great queen, standing there before her army, felt it was necessary to say that even though she had the body of a woman, she had the heart of a king. If we were to change the vernacular of the words to fit our own time, we might interpret her words to say that, even though she was a woman, she had the inner strength of a man. This is instructive in both understanding her thinking and the thinking of the people of that day.

Queen Elizabeth I lived in an era when women were considered inferior to men, and therefore, could not be as effective as leaders, particularly in the role of commander-in-chief. Possessing that sense of pragmatism that is required of all successful leaders, Elizabeth knew that there might have been some concern over her ability to rule a nation, especially when it came to leading troops into battle. So she addressed the subject head on, saying that even though she was woman, she could do the job.

What is so sad about this is that she even had to address this issue in the first place. The fact that she was a woman should never have been a cause for concern, as to whether or not she could lead effectively. Because she lived in a day in which sexism was common, she felt she had no choice.

Now, as civilized, modern, sophisticated people, we can do what new generations always do when they look at the past. They scoff and ridicule those of past ages, wondering how those primitives could ever have harbored such barbaric notions. But human history does not progress as fast as we like to deceive ourselves into thinking. It seems that, for every step forward mankind takes, we seem to take two steps back. Even in this modern era, we have not traveled all that far in confronting the issue of sexism.

In 1972, the famed congresswoman Shirley Chisholm decided to seek the Democrat party's nomination for President of the United States. In spite of her impressive record in legislative achievements and obvious charisma on the national stage, in her heart of hearts she knew that hers was a long-shot candidacy. She was a person of color, which, sadly, has been the cause of many being denied rightful acceptance, a result of the evil of racism. But she was also a woman, and she once acknowledged that of these two things (which have both been used as forms of discrimination), the issue of her gender was a greater disqualifier than the color of her skin. In reflecting on her career, she made this statement: "I have certainly met much more discrimination in terms of being a woman than being black in the field of politics."

Congresswoman Chisholm lived long enough to discover that simply being born female caused her to face discrimination from white men, black men and every shade in between. She understood that even among other women there was, at times, a tendency to give deference and preference to the male over the female. That was in the middle of the twentieth century, and now, so many years later, we still have not come as far as we should on this issue. In certain parts of the world, women are still considered to be second-class citizens, not having rights equal to men. Some are still forced to wear oppressive clothing, making them cover their entire bodies in robes of sadness.

On the opposite side of that extreme, there are still companies and employers in the twenty-first century that require women to wear revealing clothing that demeans their personhood and their value. These maladies are severe. There are, on both sides of the examples I just cited, women who exist in those arenas and insist that they are happy and that they are not dehumanized at all. Even those women who have broken through and achieved success in business, politics, or any other meaningful profession have experienced their share of discrimination and sexism along their path to success.

It seems as if this is a problem that knows no boundaries – whether it be racial, social, or geographic, for it exists all over the world. And, while it seems that our society is beginning to address these issues in a real and meaningful way, unless the problem is dealt with at the root, the branches will just keep growing – no matter how much you trim them.

The world can never truly solve the ills of society because unregenerate men and women do not understand the source of the problems of society. This is why the Bible calls sin *"the mystery of iniquity"* (2 Thessalonians 2:7). So many people lack the spiritual perception to see things as they truly are. They do not understand the roots that Satan has planted so deep in the fabric of this world culture. No matter how much well-meaning people try to address the problem, they always fall short. Only the Church of the Lord Jesus Christ can deal with the ills of society, for we have the answer to all of society's troubles.

This is both uplifting and sobering to think about because it tells us that the reason sexual discrimination and gender prejudice exist in our world is because the Church has not only not addressed it, but it has even fostered and furthered it.

Let us consider the words of Jesus in the Sermon on the Mount:

> *Ye are the salt of the earth but if the salt have lost his savour, wherewith shall it be salted? it is thenceforth good for nothing, but to be cast out, and to be trodden under foot of men. Ye are the light of the world. A city that is set on an hill cannot be hid. Neither do men light a candle, and put it under a bushel, but on a candlestick; and it giveth light unto all that are in the house. Let your light so shine before men, that they may see your good works, and glorify your Father which is in heaven.* Matthew 5:13-16

In essence, Jesus was saying that if there is ever to be real social change in this world, it must be led by God's people. The Church was intended to guide the rest of the world toward truth. The Body of the Lord Jesus Christ is to salt the earth with the nutrients from the Scriptures that set people free from the powers of darkness. The House of God was meant to be a way-station that shines the light of revelation, to guide men and women toward the full counsel of the knowledge of God. But, it seems, the Church has either sat on the side-lines or led in the wrong direction. The reason women have been oppressed, demeaned, and discriminated against by society is that they have also experienced it in the House of God.

When Jesus spoke of the salt losing its flavor, He meant that if Christians fail to walk in the truth, then what hope is there for the world? And yet there are still religious leaders today who promote sexism and twist the Bible to justify their prejudices. Some preachers still shout from their pulpits that women should keep silent in church, covering their heads at all times, and not doing anything that even looks like usurping authority over men. So-called "Bible scholars" still teach that women cannot preach or hold certain ecclesiastical offices. I even heard a prominent minister on television stand and declare that a woman should never pastor a church because she would be usurping authority over a man, and that is forbidden by the Bible. This is the reason women find it so difficult to gain respect and equality in their homes, their jobs, and their communities – because they receive so little of it in church.

This world is crying out, groaning and travailing for justice and change, but the only way that true reform can happen is if and when it begins in the Church of the Lord Jesus Christ. The Bible puts it this way:

> *For the time is come that judgement must begin at the house of God: and if it first begin at us, what shall the end be of them that obey not the gospel of God?*
>
> 1 Peter 4:17

It is time to correct these things, time to realign our thinking to conform to the character of God. This is what judgment does; it tears the old waste places down, and, from the ashes of those demonic strongholds, it builds anew on the firm foundation of the Rock, Christ Jesus. The way in which the strongholds are broken is that you have to go down into the roots and pull up the weeds. Only then can new seeds be planted. This is what the Lord meant when He decreed these words through the prophet Jeremiah:

> *See, I have this day set thee over the nations and over the kingdoms, to root out, and to pull down, and to destroy, and to throw down, to build, and to plant.*
>
> Jeremiah 1:10

This is the work of reformation, to get rid of false teachings and expose ungodly prejudices. Then, once the serpent is crushed, you can raise a sure foundation and walk within God's anointed wisdom forever.

We will approach this task with the same foundation from which we have looked at other areas in this book, the standard that comes from the words of Paul to Timothy:

> *Study to shew thyself approved unto God, a workman that needeth not to be ashamed, rightly dividing the word of truth.* 2 Timothy 2:15

There is a right way to interpret the Bible and a wrong way, and we want to approach this subject by examining it the right way. It is, therefore, the responsibility of the seeker of truth to remove all forms of bias and prejudice and hear only what God says, adding nothing to it, nor taking anything away from it. Because wise counsel is like a well of deep water, let us gather our buckets, go to the well of the Bible and draw out the water of everlasting life that is found in the Word of our Lord.

To begin examining the root system of this problem, I want to start with Creation itself, as recorded in the book of Genesis. Not only is Genesis the account of the origins of all created things; it is the fountainhead upon which all other great truths in the Scriptures are built. If one misinterprets the information provided in the book of Genesis and presents those incorrect views to the public, everything else in the Bible that comes after it will be looked at from the prism of a faulty foundation. This is why certain preachers and Bible commentators have misinterpreted so many of the scriptures that deal with women's rights because the original passages that address these issues have been misunderstood and misapplied in the pattern of Christian living. When we go back to the origins and examine them carefully and correctly, the pattern of true revelatory knowledge will break forth.

In the beginning, we are told that God created all things, including the human race. Unlike other parts of creation, we are provided with a greater amount of detail as to how God actually constructed the human race, when He made the man Adam and his wife Eve. Concerning the creation of our original parents, the Bible records:

And the Lord *God formed man of the dust of the ground, and breathed into his nostrils the breath of life; and man became a living soul. And the* Lord *God planted a garden eastward in Eden; and there put the man whom he had formed.*
Genesis 2:7-8

And the Lord *God said, It is not good that the man should be alone; I will make an help meet for him.*
Genesis 2:18

And the Lord God caused a deep sleep to fall upon Adam, and he slept: and he took one of his ribs, and closed up his flesh instead thereof; and the rib, which the Lord *God had taken from man, made he a woman, and brought her unto the man.*
And Adam said, This is now bone of my bones, and flesh of my flesh: she shall be called Woman, because she was taken out of Man. Therefore shall a man leave his father and mother, and shall cleave unto his wife: and they shall be one flesh. And they were both naked, the man and his wife, and were not ashamed.
Genesis 2:21-25

This is how God brought our original parents into being, but these verses have been misinterpreted by some and used as a propaganda tool to promote the idea that women are inferior to men.

The Scriptures tell us that God constructed the body of Adam from the dust of the ground. He then put within this new vessel the essence of life by giving him a spirit, possessing a mind and all that came with it. Thus, man became a living soul.

Adam was unique from all the other creatures God had made, because he contained a dimension of vitality that only comes from words spoken by God. The Bible then goes on to inform us that because Adam required a companion to help him in life, God decided to make a female counterpart to and for Adam. To accomplish this, He performed a surgical procedure on Adam. Just as a surgeon puts a patient under anesthesia, God put Adam into a deep sleep. God then opened him up, removed a rib from him, and used the genetic materials from that organ to supernaturally fashion Eve.

After this surgical procedure was over, Adam awoke, and the Scriptures tell us that he joined himself to this woman, and the two became *"one flesh,"* man and wife.

Throughout the ages, as human beings examined this text, it seemed to many that Eve was a lesser being than Adam. Unlike him, she was not made from the earth, as Adam was; nor did the Bible say that God breathed into her the breath of life, as He had done for Adam. It was assumed that because of these factors, combined with the fact that she was made from material taken from the man, that Eve was an inferior creation, making all women inferior.

This interpretation, that has come down to us through history, is the root cause for gender inequality, not only in the world, but also in the Church. It has been adopted by many who have never given much thought to this account in Genesis, but when they hold these incorrect views, the ideas behind them originated from misreading this text.

This interpretation is completely contrary to the heart of God, and we know this because He tells us so in His Word. There is a principle of understanding Bible doctrines that is based on the following scripture:

> *But if he will not hear thee, then take with thee one or two more, that in the mouth of two or three witnesses every word may be established.*
>
> Matthew 18:16

Jesus made this statement to address the issue of settling disputes or disagreements between two parties. If someone has a case to be made against another, they should go directly to that person and present their argument. However, if the person fails to receive what is presented, then the person making the case should go and find one or more other persons who can corroborate their assessment of the matter and take them along for the next consultation. The principle to be extracted from this passage is this: Every case that is to be made should be established on at least two witnesses.

Take that same principle and apply it to the issue which we are addressing here, whether or not God considers men to be superior to women. As I have stated previously, some theologians have used the account of the creation of Adam and Eve and sought to interpret it from the point of view that promotes one gender being superior to the other. However, this is not God's point of view, and we will see this from the Scriptures.

There are two references in the New Testament given to us by two of the greatest apostles who have ever served in Christian ministry—Peter and Paul.

They both gave their declarations by the unction of the Holy Ghost, and these address God's view on how He looks at the human race.

When Peter was summoned by God to appear at the home of a Gentile named Cornelius and preach the Gospel to that man and his family, he said the following, which reveals God's views on equality:

> *Then Peter opened his mouth, and said, Of a truth I perceive that God is no respecter of persons: but in every nation he that feareth him, and worketh righteousness, is accepted with him.* Acts 10:34-35

Peter came to understand that there is no partiality with God. He judges people on the basis of whether or not they honor Him and do what is right, according to His Word. He does not place one group of people over another.

The words of the other witness, the apostle Paul, come from his letter to the Christians of Galatia as recorded in the book known as Galatians. Paul wrote these words to deal with issues of prejudice that had crept into the House of God. He wanted to put a stop to it immediately and succinctly, so he gave them God's position on the issue of equality:

> *For ye are all the children of God by faith in Christ Jesus. For as many of you as have been baptized into Christ have put on Christ. There is neither Jew nor Greek, there is neither bond nor free, there is neither male nor female: for ye are all one in Christ Jesus. And if ye be Christ's, then are ye Abraham's seed, and heirs according to the promise.* Galatians 3:26-29

In this passage, we are given further clarification on God's views on equality. Paul states that everyone who puts their faith in Jesus Christ by acknowledging Him as Savior and Lord is a child of God. And, just like any good parent, God loves all His kids equally, and none is preferred above another.

Paul went further by saying that if you have submitted your life totally to Jesus, then you *"put on Jesus Christ,"* taking on His nature and thinking like Him. Then, so that there could be no doubt on the issue whatsoever, Paul gave the thinking of Jesus regarding these issues. There is no racial or ethnic prejudice in Jesus (*there is neither Jew nor Greek*). There is no social or economic prejudice in Jesus (*there is neither bond nor free*). Then he put a crescendo on the arrangement by declaring that there is no gender prejudice in Jesus (*there is neither male nor female).* In the eyes of our heavenly Father, all His children are one because they are united by Christ Jesus. And, if that is the way God thinks, then we should think that way as well.

This takes us back to the beginning, when God made Adam and Eve. Because some theologians have taken the account of how the man and women were made and misinterpreted it to fit their prejudices, it has resulted in female oppression, both in the Church and in the world. But having seen from the Scriptures that there is no gender prejudice in God, we need to go back and examine the text in the light of God's point of view and not man's.

The original intention of the Father was to create a relationship that was based on absolute equality and mutual respect between the man and the woman. Although their roles might be different, there was not one superior or one lesser than the other. God did not intend for His people to take the fact that Eve was created from Adam's rib and look at it as the woman being of lesser value than the man. If we look at the thinking of the Creator and allow ourselves to think as He thinks, then the true nature of the male and female relationship will be made clear.

Before humanity came into existence, the Bible tells us that there was a conversation that took place between the members of the Trinity concerning the creation of the human race. God the Father, God the Son and God the Holy Spirit decided to create human beings, and the way in which they explained their intention and how the human race would exist shows us God's thinking regarding this subject. The Bible provides us with the details of their conversation:

> *And God said, Let is male man in our image, after our likeness: and let them have dominion over the fish of the sea, and over the fowl of the air, and over the cattle, and over all the earth, and over every creeping thing that creepeth upon the earth. So God created man in his own image, in the image of God created he him; male and female created he them. And God blessed them, and God said unto them, Be fruitful and multiply, and replenish the earth, and subdue it: and have dominion over the fish of the sea, and over the fowl of the air, and over every living thing that moveth upon the earth.*
>
> Genesis 1:26-28

Here we can clearly see God's point of view regarding His creation. The Trinity said that They would create the human race in Their image, for in verse 26, the word *man* refers to humankind as a whole. Then the Godhead got more specific, and we read that with the idea of creating the human race, They would make of that race both males and females. So, from God's point of view, the male and the female were equal as created beings. The way God went about making Adam was different from the way He went about making Eve, but that was because of the difference of components between the man and the woman. Also, the difference in the way the two were made was to symbolize their distinction from one another, not one being lesser or greater than the other, but rather equals, just different in gender.

The equality issue is even further settled by the Scriptures, and it came from the mouth of God Himself. The Trinity declared that both the male and female were blessed, both of them were to be fruitful, and both were called to multiply. God gave both the male and female dominion over the earth and over all the creatures and elements of the earth. He specifically said,*"Let them have dominion"* (verse 26).

Man was not meant to have dominion, while woman sat on the sidelines. It was always meant to be a mutual understanding of equality between the two. Man is not greater than woman. In the eyes of God, they are equals. In fact, God said that it was the man who could not be alone and, therefore, needed help. Not the woman, the man! With this proper understanding of the Scriptures, we see the true nature of the mind of God. God made both male and female, and He destined them both to be prosperous and blessed.

This is another great aspect of revelation that the virtuous woman understands. Not only does she know her value, and not only does she glean in the right field, but she knows that there is no inequality between herself and her male counterparts – whether those counterparts are in business, ministry, or in the home (her husband). She understands that God has not oppressed her, but rather, freed her to walk in her calling and exercise her gifts.

We see in the life of the Proverbs 31 woman that she is gifted and free to use her gifts for God's glory. She is not oppressed by her husband; nor is she oppressed by the elders of the city. She and her husband are a team, and they respect each other deeply.

Let us look once more at some of the verses in that powerful chapter:

Who can find a virtuous woman? for her price is far above rubies. The heart of her husband doth safely trust in her, so that she shall have no need of spoil. She will do him good and not evil all the days of her life.

Proverbs 31:10-12

She is not afraid of the snow for her household: for all her household are clothed with scarlet. She maketh herself coverings of tapestry; her clothing is silk and purple. Her husband is known in the gates, when he sitteth among the elders of the land. She maketh fine linen, and selleth it; and delivereth girdles unto the merchant.

Strength and honour are her clothing; and she shall rejoice in time to come. She openeth her mouth with wisdom; and in her tongue is the law of kindness. She looketh well to the ways of her household, and eateth not the bread of idleness. Her children arise up, and call her blessed; her husband also and he praiseth her. Many daughters have done virtuously, but thou excellest them all. Favour is deceitful, and beauty is vain: but a woman that feareth the LORD, she shall be praised. Give her of the fruit of her hands; and let her own works praise her in the gates.

Proverbs 31:21-31

This is the picture of the woman God wants all of His daughters to become. This woman is blessed to have gifts and talents, and she uses them for the glory of God. The great blessing in her life is that the men around her recognize her gifts, and value the fact that she uses them.

This scripture tells us that her husband has confidence in her and her abilities. He is famous in his community because he has connections with the elders of the land. So, here we see a marriage of two prominent people, and the woman is blessed to have a husband who is not intimated by her success. The Bible declares that he always sings her praises, and he is grateful for the person she is.

This point is valuable to glean from, particularly in the area of women in leadership positions. This Proverbs 31 woman is the owner and chief officer of her own company, and the Bible gives no indication that this was a problem for her husband or the other leadership of her city. Too many women have been oppressed by their husbands and by religious leaders when it came to holding leadership positions and using their gifts and talents. Women have been told that they could not preach, nor could they stand in ministerial offices. And, because they have been held back in the Church, this has caused women to hold back in other areas of leadership.

As with all false views that exist in the Body of Christ, these oppressive mindsets come from taking certain scriptures out of context, building whole doctrines around them, and then using them to hurt people and shame the Church. As with the scriptures that deal with makeup and jewelry, the verses that some have used to suppress the idea of women in leadership have, in large part, been ignored by the modern church. The attitude has been: "Because we cannot explain it, let's just ignore it and focus on the parts of the Bible we find more suitable to the thinking of the times." And, because there has been such a great increase in the number of women rising up and taking their place in leadership roles, some in the Body of Christ have chosen just to focus on that positive trend and not deal with the scriptures that were once used to hold women back. This is a dangerous and defeatist point of view. Avoiding the issue only allows it to continue to fester below the surface.

Although it is not as popular and mainstream as it once was to say publicly that women cannot preach or be in leadership, many people still secretly hold these views. And, while these views are not expressed as loudly or as often as they once were, some still believe and practice them. I could never stress enough the fact that God does not want any of His Word to be ignored. It is there for a reason, and we, as Christians, cannot be afraid to examine what the Bible says. I have stated it before, and I will express it again. When the Body of Christ takes the time to study the Word of God fully, by looking at scriptures in the right context, based upon God's thinking, then we can know and understand the truth. Jesus said that when we know the truth, the truth will set us free (see John 8:32), and God wants us all, not just women, but men as well, to be free from any ungodly form of bias and/or prejudice.

The devil has been very skillful at holding the Church back from being as effective as it should be in winning lost souls to Jesus. For every woman throughout history who has used her gifts and talents to serve the Lord, there have been countless others who, because they were told that women could not preach, did not preach. As a result, the Church has not had the impact in the world it should have. God is calling His people to maturity and saying to us that we need to rightly divide the word of truth by studying it correctly.

The false doctrines that have held women back have existed for too long. It is time to cast down every stronghold that exalts itself against the knowledge of God. To start on this journey, we must go straight to the root of the problem by looking at the passage of scripture that has been, from the beginning, twisted and distorted to promote claims against women in ministry and leadership.

The text of which I speak comes, once again, from the first letter the apostle Paul wrote to Timothy. It is interesting how one verse or one chapter can be so misconstrued that an entire doctrine is built around it. There is a series of verses from the same chapter in which Paul addressed the issue of proper attire for women, and he also shared thoughts concerning women and men and how they should relate to one another. Here are the verses in question:

> *Let the woman learn in silence with all subjection. But I suffer not a woman to teach, nor to usurp authority over the man, but to be in silence. For Adam was first formed, then Eve. And Adam was not deceived, but the woman being deceived was in the transgression. Notwithstanding she shall be saved in childbearing, if they continue in faith and charity and holiness with sobriety.*
>
> 1 Timothy 2:11-15

These five verses have been used over and over again to promote the idea that women should not preach, teach, or hold any position in the church that has a level of influence over the congregation. They have been used to suggest that women cannot be apostles, prophets, evangelists, pastors, or teachers. And they have been used to indoctrinate the church with the notion that women are weak, second-rate citizens in the eyes of God and in the laws of nature. This is not so. All those misconceptions are lies from the devil. And we are going to see from the Bible that God is truly *"no respecter of persons."*

We begin with the question: Can women serve as ministers of the Gospel? To answer this question, let us establish, once again, that the Bible will never contradict itself. If something that someone says is a revelation from the Scriptures, it should be in agreement with the entirety of God's Word. If it really came from God, it will be. Otherwise, it is just the opinion of men, and not the counsel of God.

If God used Paul to make a statement that was meant to establish a doctrine to be followed by an entire gender, and that decree was set in stone for all time, then God would not let the same man tell women to participate in anything that would contradict what he had been used to establish. Paul was too intelligent to contradict himself. And, most definitely, God is too intelligent to contradict Himself. Therefore, we must deduce that these scriptures cannot be interpreted to suggest that women cannot preach, for there is much evidence in the Bible that suggests that they can.

In making my case for this, the first witness I wish to call to the stand is none other than the great apostle Paul himself. One of the greatest theological treaties that has ever been written is Paul's letter to the Christians at Ephesus, otherwise known as the book of Ephesians. Contained within that book is a wealth of knowledge concerning the great truths of the Christian faith. It is a book that is both scholarly profound and passionately spiritual in its content. Not only does it include great insight into the work that Jesus did in His ministry both in earth as well as in Heaven; it also contains information regarding the ministerial offices that were put in place to lead the Body of Christ.

These offices, also known as the five-fold ministry gifts, are positions that were established by Jesus, to guide and instruct the Body of believers through the teaching and preaching of God's Word. These titles represent the highest levels of leadership roles in the Body of Christ, and every person who is called by God to serve full-time as a minister of the Gospel will be in at least one, if not more, of these offices.

Looking at how Paul defined these offices and looking at what he said and did not say is instructive for the purpose of disproving the lie that women cannot serve as ministers. Paul began his teaching by looking at the ministry of Jesus and what He did for us in the plan of salvation. He said:

> *There is one body, and one Spirit, even as ye are called in one hope of your calling; one Lord, one faith, one baptism, one God and Father of all, who is above all, and through all, and in you all.*
>
> *But unto every one of us is given grace according to the measure of the gift of Christ. Wherefore he saith, When he ascended up on high, he led captivity captive, and gave gifts unto men.*
>
> *(Now that he ascended, what is it also that he descended first into the lower parts of the earth? He that descended is the same also that ascended up far above all heavens, that he might fill all things.) And he gave some apostles;*

and some, prophets; and some, evangelists; and some, pastors and teachers; for the perfecting of the saints, for the work of the ministry, for the edifying of the body of Christ: till we all come in the unity of the faith, and of the knowledge of the Son of God, unto a perfect man, unto the measure of the stature of the fulness of Christ.

That we henceforth be no more children, tossed to and fro, and carried about with every wind of doctrine, by the sleight of men, and cunning craftiness, whereby they lie in wait to deceive; but speaking the truth in love, may grow up into him in all things, which is the head, even Christ. Ephesians 4:4-15

Let us think about this text and both what it says and what it does *not* say. The apostle here was writing to explain the importance of understanding sound doctrinal truth. He stated that there is one body of Christ, thus signifying one family of God. Then he declared that there is only one true Lord, one true faith, and one way of being immersed, or baptized, into that faith. Then he changed his focus and began speaking directly of Jesus and explaining how Jesus redeemed us from the power of sin by leading captivity captive.

Next we learn that after Jesus fulfilled His assignment on the earth, He then gave gifts to His Church. These ministry gifts were offices that were placed in the Church to help the saints mature in their understanding of God and His Word. They were established to execute the duties and tasks that are required to keep the ministry functioning properly. They were put in place to help make the Body of Christ strong in God and strong in faith. This work would be accomplished through leading the people into proper alignment with the will and purposes of God, and by speaking the truth, or what we would term "teaching and preaching," so that God's people can grow into spiritual adulthood.

Paul then defined these ministerial gifts as apostles, prophets, evangelists, pastors, and teachers. He was very specific in emphasizing that God made some in the Church to stand in these offices and not all of the Church. Not everyone in the Body of Christ is called to stand in the five-fold ministry, but (equally as important to point out) Paul placed no gender restrictions on who could stand in these offices. He did not say that God placed some men to be apostles, some men to be prophets, some men to be evangelists, some men to be pastors, or some men to be teachers. He simply said *some,* so that would infer that there is no stipulation as to gender. This tells us that a woman can be an apostle, she can be a prophet, she can be an evangelist, she can be a pastor, and she can be a teacher. Although some men have placed stipulations on women by telling them that they could not preach the Gospel, God never got that memo. When we read the words from His Bible, He does not place any restriction based on gender, and if God doesn't, who is man to say anything different?

Also, we can rightly deduce that if Paul, when writing to Timothy about women keeping silent in church, meant for that to be a concrete prohibition against women preaching the Gospel, he certainly would have made that clear when listing the five-fold ministry gifts. Paul did not put any gender restrictions in his explanation because his heavenly Father did not, and he was going to believe what his Father believed.

The main reason the idea that women should not preach or lead in Christian ministry has existed so long in the church is that too many Christian people just don't know their Bible. If we would just take God at His Word, we would see there has never been any such prohibition put in place anywhere in His Word, from Genesis to Revelation. With that said, let us go through the Bible, and look at some key examples of women preaching, teaching, and serving as spiritual leaders. Since Jesus said that out of the mouth of two or three witnesses, every word was to be established, let's find some witnesses and dispel these silly notions once and for all.

One of the greatest events that took place in the history of this planet was the momentous occasion when God delivered His people from the Egyptians at the Red Sea. When the Lord parted the waters and allowed His people to cross over onto dry land, it truly was a miracle like no other. And when the mighty host of Pharaoh's army drowned in the midst of the waters, as they attempted to pursue their prey, Israel rejoiced, knowing that God was truly on their side. As the children of Israel looked out over the waters and realized that they would never see their oppressors again, they begin to sing and rejoice before the Lord, Who had so graciously saved them.

One of the people who took part in that great celebration was a woman named Miriam. She was the sister of the prophet Moses, the man who was the leader of the people at the time. Miriam has become famous in her own right, not just for being the sister of a great prophet, but for being a minister who stood in the office of a prophet as well. The Bible tells us her story:

And Miriam the prophetess, the sister of Aaron, took a timbrel in her hand; and all the women went after her with timbrels and with dances. And Miriam answered them, Sing ye to the LORD, for he hath triumphed gloriously; the horse and his rider hath he thrown into the sea.

So Moses brought Israel from the Red Sea, and they went out into the wilderness of Shur; and they went three days in the wilderness, and found no water.

Exodus 15:20-22

It is obvious that the people of God in that day did not have a problem with a woman being a prophetess. Not only was Miriam a minister; she led what was probably the first women's fellowship, and all the women followed her lead and began to praise the Lord for the great things He had done. She even delivered a prophetic declaration in song that day, to commemorate the auspiciousness of the occasion.

Some preachers today might have told Miriam to sit down, and they might have said that she could not be a prophet. However, Moses, the leader at the time, seemed to have no problem whatsoever with her role. He did not rebuke her, nor did he attempt to stifle her. He just kept on leading the people on their journey.

If there ever was a preacher who had the authority to rebuke a woman for being a minister, it was Moses. The Bible says that he was the greatest prophet in all of Israel's history, and he was a man who knew God *"face to face"* (Exodus 33:11). If God had a problem with women preachers, surely Moses would have known it, and he would have rebuked his sister for stepping outside of her calling. Since God saw fit to call Miriam a prophetess and affirmed her calling, I plan to stick with Him rather than with the preachers who fail to read their Bibles.

One of the more craftier tactics that are being used by certain preachers to suppress women is to promote the idea that God allows women to preach, but that He prohibits them from serving in positions which require them to lead congregations (such as an apostle or a pastor). Because of the great increase of women ministers in the world today, these theologians know that they cannot put a stop to women in the ministry. They are determined to maintain male domination, so they use the old, cheap wine, but try to sell it in a new wineskin. They use the text I referenced from 1 Timothy, that speaks about a woman usurping authority over a man, and then twist it to promote the doctrine that a woman should not be a pastor because she would be leading both women and men, thus usurping male authority. Even though their teachings are cloaked in fanciful theological language, it is apparent that the Bible teachers who promote this garbage simply do not like a woman telling a man what to do. So they pervert the Bible to make God's Word seem as biased and sexist as they are.

For those who seek to rightly divide the word of truth, the question then becomes: Is that what the Bible is really saying? In order to answer that question with absolute certainty, we have to find another scriptural reference that would support the interpretation of the claims of these ministers who preach such things.

To begin seeking an answer to this question, we must first define the terms *apostle* and *pastor*. The term *apostle* means "a sent one," and it usually refers to one who is sent to establish churches. The term *pastor* means "a shepherd, one who is called to lead a congregation into the paths of righteousness." Both of these positions involve leading a group of people made up of men, women, and children. The main difference between the two is that, while a pastor will stay in one church and lead the congregation, the apostle will go from place to place establishing churches, pastoring them for a season, and then moving on to start another work, after installing someone to continue pastoring in their stead. Both of these offices involve leadership positions over a congregation. Because some men do not wish to be led by a woman, and also because some of the men who hold these views happen to be preachers, they contend that a woman should not be a pastor.

In the New Testament, there are several words that are used in reference to a pastor. The terms *shepherd, elder, bishop,* and *overseer* all are synonymous with the term *pastor*. We find very few examples of pastors in the New Testament other than the apostles. In fact, there are only two primary examples of pastors in the New Testaments, and they were Timothy and Titus, who both happened to be men. Even though we are not provided with information regarding a woman who served as the pastor of a church in the New Testament, this does not mean that there were not any who served in that office. Also, based on the manner in which the ministry gifts were described in Ephesians 4:11, there was nothing in that verse to indicate that a woman could not lead a congregation.

To prove beyond a doubt that God is *"no respecter of persons,"* He did not leave us without a witness. There is a woman the Bible speaks of who served as a leader of her people, and her name was Deborah. During the time of the Old Testament, there was a period in Israel's history in which they were not governed by kings, nor were they led by Moses or Joshua. During this transitional period, the nation of Israel was governed by what the Bible calls "judges." The individuals who served in this office administered justice in trying cases, acted as military leaders in protecting or delivering God's people from foreign invasion, and stood in the role of the spiritual leader of the nation.

The book of Ruth tells us that her story took place *"in the days when the judges ruled"* (Ruth 1:1), meaning they were the leaders over the congregation of believers known as the children of Abraham. So, in a sense, they were the pastors of their day, leading and guiding the people in the ways of righteousness. Most Christians know of the two most famous judges—Samson and Gideon—but there was another of equal stature, and she was a woman. Deborah also achieved great renown among her fellow countrymen, for she was their spiritual mother, their governor, and the commander-in-chief for the entire nation.

God made sure to record the story of Deborah for our posterity, because He knew that one day wolves would come in sheep's clothing spreading lies in God's vineyard. The Lord put Deborah's history in His Book to show us that, not only can a woman become a leader, but to show us that a woman did successfully lead a nation. And, what God did in the past He can still do today.

I want to let the Bible speak for itself from the book of Judges:

> *And Deborah, a prophetess, the wife of Lapidoth, she judged Israel at that time. And she dwelt under the palm tree of Deborah between Ramah and Bethel in mount Ephraim: and the children of Israel came up to her for judgement. And she sent and called Barak; the son of Abinoam out of Kedeshnaphtali, and said unto him, Hath not the* LORD *God of Israel commanded, saying, Go and draw toward Mount Tabor, and take with thee ten thousand men of the children of Naphtali and of the children of Zebulun? And I will draw unto thee to the river Kishon Sisera, the captain of Jaban's army, with his chariots and his multitude; and I will deliver them into thine hand.*
>
> *And Barak said unto her, If thou wilt go with me, then I will go: but if thou wilt not go with me, then I will not go.*

And she said, I will surely go with thee: notwithstanding the journey that thou takest shall not be for thine honour; for the Lord *shall sell Sisera into the hand of a woman. And Deborah arose, and went with Barak to Kedesh.*

Judges 4:4-9

Every time I read this passage of scripture, I laugh to myself, because it always makes me think of a comment I heard from a famous Christian minister. This gentleman stood behind his pulpit and boldly proclaimed to his congregation and also to his television audience that a woman can preach, but that she cannot pastor a church, because, in doing so, she would be usurping authority over a man. Whenever I read these verses in the Bible and think about what the minister said, I laugh and think that he must have cut these verses out of his Bible. This is God's record about a woman who served in both of those positions.

The Scriptures say of Deborah that she was a *"prophetess"* (Judges 4:4), which meant that she was a preacher of righteousness. Not only was she a preacher, but we are told also that she was the judge of the entire nation of Israel, which was the spiritual equivalent of what we would define as a pastor in our time. She was able to do all of this, and God did not strike her with fire from Heaven, nor did He throw her out of the country. No, God appointed her to those offices, and He even blessed her with a husband who was secure enough in his own manhood not to hinder his wife from fulfilling the call of God upon her life.

The Bible tells us also of a man who was chosen to be the military commander who would lead the mighty warriors to battle against the enemies of God's people. This mans name was Barak, and he was anointed and appointed to go forth and conquer every foe by the Word of the Lord. In spite of this blessed assurance, he determined in his heart that he would not go forth to battle unless Deborah was at his side. It seems that he did not mind being led by a woman, nor did he give a thought to being usurped by her. And, in spite of what I heard from that preacher, God was not offended by Deborah's leadership and Barak's submission to it. In fact, God, as if to stress the point that women are qualified for Christian service, spoke through Deborah and said that He would give His people victory, but that it would come through the hands of a woman, not a man.

This woman that was spoken of was a lady by the name of Jael. The Bible tells us that she was just a housewife, married to a man named Heber. When Deborah and Barak led the fight against the enemy, they prevailed in battle, but the captain of the opposing army, Sisera, somehow escaped. He fled, probably believing that no man could catch him, but God had other plans. God had a woman at the right place at the right time, and this woman was brave and willing to fight for the Lord her God. Let us read what became of this cowardly enemy commander and who it was that did him in:

> *Howbeit Sisera fled away on his feet to the tent of Jael the wife of Heber the Kenite: for there was peace between Jabin the king of Hazor and the house of Heber the Kenite.*
> *And Jael went out to meet Sisera, and said unto him, Turn in, my lord, turn in to me; fear not. And when he had turned in unto her into the tent, she covered him with a mantle.*
> *And he said unto her, Give me, I pray thee, a little water to drink; for I am thirsty. And she opened a bottle of milk, and gave him drink, and covered him.*
> *Again he said unto her, Stand in the door of the tent, and it shall be, when any man doth come and enquire of thee, and say, Is there any man here? that thou shalt say, No.*
> *Then Jael Heber's wife took a nail of the tent, and took an hammer in her hand, and went softly unto him, and smote the nail into his temples, and fastened it unto the ground: for he was fast asleep and weary. So he died.*
> *And, Behold, as Barak pursued Sisera, Jael came out to meet him, and said unto him, Come, and I will shew thee the man whom thou seekest. And when he came into her tent, behold, Sisera lay dead, and the nail was in his temples.*
> *So God subdued on that day Jabin the king of Canaan before the children of Israel. And the hand of the children of Israel prospered, and prevailed against Jabin the king of Canaan, until they had destroyed Jabin king of Canaan.*
> Judges 4:17-24

God always has the right person in position to carry out His divine will for any particular moment in history, and the amazing ways in which He chooses to carry out His will is used to teach us lessons concerning how He thinks and what we need to focus our attention on. The Bible here described how after fleeing the battle, Sisera sought shelter with a household that was on good terms with his king. Unbeknownst to him, however, the lady of this house had been chosen by God to prevent this enemy of His people from escaping to fight another day. This story not only confirms the fact that God uses women to carry out His will, but show us that they are also strong enough to do what is necessary to ensure that the mission is accomplished.

This woman, Jael, was both skillful and decisive in the manner in which she dealt with her adversary. First, she drew his attention toward her home and invited him to come in for shelter. Then, she lulled him into a false sense of security by making him feel both at ease and also comfortable. He was so soothed by her charming hospitality that he soon fell asleep. Then, very quickly, she, like a fierce warrior queen out of the ancient myths, took her weapon of choice and carried out his execution, insuring that he would never rise again. When Barak arrived, Jael met him at the door and informed him that the enemy was already defeated.

Just think of how many souls could be saved, how many churches could be built, and how much progress could be made in the Body of Christ if all the women who have been called by God were no longer restrained, having to wait on men, to do what God has put in their hearts to do. It is time for the shackles to come off and for all God's chosen vessels to rise up and take their place in the army of the Lord.

If there was ever a minister who was familiar with the events recorded in the Old Testament, it would have been the apostle Paul. He quoted from the Old Testament quite frequently in his writings and, as a trained Pharisee, he would have been well versed in all the great historical figures of Israel's glorious past. He would have certainly been aware of the life of Miriam and Deborah, and how God had blessed their lives and their ministries. And, having been aware of that, he would not have made an outright statement condemning women from preaching the Gospel, for in doing so, he would be attacking the very same God Who called him into the ministry—just as He had called women. Also, Paul would have understood that having lived in the time of the Old Testament, Miriam and Deborah were living under the Old Covenant. When Jesus came to earth and gave His life to take away the sin of the world, He instituted a New Covenant based upon better promises. If God used women in the ministry under the Old Covenant, how much more would He use them under the New!

Paul was certainly aware of the Day of Pentecost, when the Holy Ghost poured out His Spirit upon the disciples in the Upper Room. He had surely heard about the moment when Peter stood up and preached that day, taking his text from the words of the prophet Joel. He must have known and heard those words many times. And we cannot forget what Peter spoke on that day, because the Bible records it for us:

> *But Peter, standing up with the eleven, lifted up his voice, and said unto them, Ye men of Judea, and all ye that dwell at Jerusalem, be this known unto you, and hearken to my words: for these are not drunken, as ye suppose, seeing it is but the third hour of the day. But this is that which was spoken by the prophet Joel; And it shall come to pass in the last days, saith God, I will pour out of my Spirit upon all flesh: and your sons and your daughters shall prophesy, and your young men shall see visions, and your old men shall dream dreams: and on my servants and on my handmaidens I will pour out in those days of my Spirit; and they shall prophesy.* Acts 2:14-18

This prophetic word concerning the days we are now in was given to us by God's servants, and it was crystal clear. God said that He would put His Word in the mouths, not just of men, but of women as well, and that they both would prophesy. Then He repeated Himself and said again, that He would pour out His Spirit upon His servants and His handmaidens, meaning both mean and women. The prophecy was fulfilled in scriptures such as Acts 21:

> *And the next day we that were of Paul's company departed, and came unto Caesarea: and we entered into the house of Philip the evangelist, which was one of the seven; and abode with him. And the same man had four daughters, virgins, which did prophesy.* Acts 21:8-9

If Paul believed that women should not speak God's Word, then he would have rebuked those young women on the spot. But He knew God, and He knew God's Word. Because God pours out His Spirit upon women as well as men, then Paul was determined to enjoy the blessing of that moment, and let God use whomever He chose to use.

We also have another example from the book of Acts, of a woman being used to share the Gospel. This woman, named Priscilla, along with her husband Aquila, were close friends of Paul and were great supporters of his ministry. The couple was used nightly for a time to instruct a man who became one of the greatest preachers of that era. This man was Apollos, and he was already an astute scholar of the Scriptures, but he did not yet have a knowledge of the full gospel of Jesus Christ. The Bible tells how the couple met Apollos and what they did for him:

> *And a certain Jew named Apollos, born at Alexandria, an eloquent man, and mighty in the scriptures, came to Ephesus. This man was instructed in the way of the Lord; and being fervent in the spirit, he spake and taught diligently the things of the Lord, knowing only the baptism of John. And he began to speak boldly in the synagogue: whom when Aquila and Priscilla had heard, they took him unto them, and expounded unto him the way of God more perfectly. And when he was disposed to pass into Achaia, the brethren wrote, exhorting the disciples to receive him: who, when he was come, helped them much which had believed through grace: for he mightily convinced the Jews, and that publicly, shewing by the scriptures that Jesus was Christ.* Acts 18:24-28

Just think of it! One of the greatest ministerial careers to ever arrive on the stage of history began through the agency of a husband and wife team, a man and woman joined together to share the truth of the Gospel to a yielded vessel. All of this confirms to us that all of our biases and prejudices would fade away if we would simply open our Bibles and take God at His Word.

All of these witnesses should be more than enough to close the case, but I have one more person to call to the stand. This witness' character and reputation are beyond reproach. His credentials are impeccable, and His theological brilliance and keen philosophical mind are unmatched by any other person who has ever lived. He stands as the Author and the Finisher of the Christian faith, thereby giving His testimony preeminence above any other. This witness is none other than Jesus Christ, the Son of the Living God.

When we think of trying to answer the question of whether or not a woman can preach, we have to look at the first person Who was commissioned by the Messiah, to go and tell the Good News that He was risen. If Jesus saw fit to call a person to preach His Word, who are we to argue with the Master? When we examine the Scriptures, we discover that the first person Jesus commissioned was a woman.

After our Lord had risen from the grave, several of His most devoted followers went to visit His tomb. To their great amazement, the stone that had been placed over the entrance had been rolled away, and the sepulchre was empty. John, the beloved disciple, very eloquently described the events that followed:

> *The first day of the week cometh Mary Magdalene early, when it was yet dark, unto the sepulchre, and seeth the stone taken away from the sepulchre. Then she runneth, and cometh to Simon Peter, and to the other disciple, whom Jesus loved, and saith unto them, They have taken away the Lord out of the sepulchre, and we know not where they have laid him.*
>
> *Peter therefore went forth, and that other disciple, and came unto the sepulchre. So they ran both together: and the other disciple did outrun Peter, and came first to the sepulchre. And he stooping down, and looking in, saw the linen clothes lying; yet went he not in. Then cometh Simon Peter following him, and went into the sepulchre, and seeth the linen clothes lie, and the napkin, that was about his head, not lying with the linen clothes, but wrapped together in a place by itself. Then went in also that other disciple, which came first to the sepulchre, and he saw, and believed. For as yet they knew not the scripture, that he must rise again from the dead.*
>
> *Then the disciples went away again unto their own home. But Mary stood without at the sepulchre weeping: and as she wept, she stooped down, and looked into the sepulchre, and seeth two angels in white sitting, the one at the head, and the other at the feet, where the body of Jesus had lain.*
>
> *And they say unto her, Woman, why weepest thou?*
>
> *She saith unto them, Because they have taken away my Lord, and I know not where they have laid him. And when she had thus said, she turned herself back, and saw Jesus standing, and knew not that it was Jesus.*
>
> *Jesus saith unto her, Woman, why weepest thou? whom seekest thou?*
>
> *She, supposing him to be the gardener, saith unto him, Sir, if thou have borne him hence, tell me where thou hast laid him, and I will take him away.*
>
> *Jesus saith unto her, Mary.*
>
> *She turned herself, and saith unto him, Rabboni; which is to say, Master.*

Jesus saith unto her, Touch me not; for I am not yet ascended to my Father: but go to my brethren, and say unto them, I ascend unto my Father, and your Father; and to my God, and your God.
Mary Magdalene came and told the disciples that she had seen the Lord, and that he had spoken these things unto her. John 20:1-18

This moment in time that John has so beautifully recounted for us settles once and for all the issue of whether or not God calls women to preach, even as He calls men to do the same. John began his story by pulling back the curtain and laying out before us the tomb where Christ was buried. The sun had not yet risen, so the sky was still dark, and a cool morning breeze could still be felt in the air. In spite of the atmospheric conditions of the hour, one devoted follower came to pay her respects to her fallen Lord. She came with a mixture of pain and passion that consumed her heart and propelled her forward to the spot where Jesus had been laid in state.

Then John moved quickly forward in his narrative, showing that Mary ran to Peter to inform him that the body of Jesus was gone. With swiftness, the men now ran back to the gravesite to investigate this situation. Then, John became part of the story. He, along with Peter and Mary, made their way to the tomb to see what had happened. Upon their arrival at the site, they could find no sign of Jesus' body, only empty grave clothes. Because of their disappointment, Peter and John gave up and walked away, perplexed and in despair, perhaps thinking that all hope was now lost.

But even though the men had left, the woman stayed. There is something about us not growing weary in well doing and never giving up that moves the heart of God. Even in our times of grief and despair, if we can hold fast to the Word of the Lord and wait patiently upon Him, we will see the salvation of our God. This is what Mary did, and she was rewarded for her faith.

Suddenly, Mary saw two angels, and they asked her why she was weeping. She told them she was looking for her Lord. As soon as these words left her mouth, she looked up and saw the Man Who had changed her life. Her grieving state was so intense that she did not recognize the Master at first. After Jesus questioned her, and she answered, He then revealed Himself in a way that could leave no doubt that He was Jesus and that He was alive.

Although, at that moment, Mary probably could have spent an eternity at the Lord's feet, there was work that needed to be done. There was a world that needed a Savior, and laborers that needed to be prepared to go forth and gather the harvest. So, when Jesus needed to send out the first person to proclaim the Gospel, He chose the best candidate for the job. He chose the one who stayed waiting for her Lord, the woman called Mary.

If Jesus saw fit to send a woman to preach His resurrection message, then who is any man to say anything contrary to that mandate? Jesus is Lord, and this means He is Lord over everything. Whatever He says is the first word and also the final word on any matter.

Paul wrote to the Galatian believers, summarizing Jesus' opinion on this issue:

> *There is neither Jew nor Greek, there is neither bond nor free, there is neither male nor female: for ye are all one in Christ Jesus.* Galatians 3:28

Paul wrote these words because he knew that we are all equal in the eyes of Jesus, and we must all humble ourselves at the foot of the cross. Paul agreed with his Bible. He agreed with his Lord. And so should we.

This brings us back to the verses in question in 1 Timothy:

> *Let the women learn in silence with all subjection. But I suffer not a women to teach, nor to usurp authority over the man, but to be in silence. For Adam was first formed, then Eve. And Adam was not deceived, but the woman being deceived was in the transgression. Notwithstanding she shall be saved in childbearing, if they continue in faith and charity and holiness with sobriety.*
> 1 Timothy 2:11-15

Now that we have established what these verses are *not* saying, let us proceed to discover what they *are* saying. In order to gather full insight into these words, I want to draw your attention to the comparison that Paul made, as he started to bring this exhortation to a close.

After he made his statement regarding women and men, he then pivoted to speak on Adam and Eve, who were not only our original ancestors, but they were also the first married couple the Bible speaks of. So, then, the apostle Paul, was making his comments about women not usurping authority over men, not in the context of a church or business setting, but within the covenant of marriage. This particular teaching is dealing directly with the relationship between a husband and his wife. Understanding this not only helps us to be free from archaic and unsound doctrine; it also provides insight into the issues that couples of that day dealt with and allows revelation to come forth from seeing the spiritual application that is contained within the text.

One of the great challengers the early Church had to confront was the issue of maintaining discipline and order in congregational worship and in times of corporate Bible study. As God began to pour out the gifts of the Spirit upon His people, and men and women began to feel an unction to speak out and prophesy or shout and testify, they would do so. The problem occurred when more than one would speak at a time, or someone would say something when it was not their moment to speak. This is an area that Paul dealt with very strongly in his ministry to the church at Corinth, and this is the reason there is a great deal of time devoted in his letters to that church on establishing proper order in the service, particularly in the area of when a person should speak out during the meeting and when they should remain silent.

If problems such as these were allowed to continue, it would cause both division and disorder in the church, and thhis had the potential of affecting the homes of the Christians as well. If husbands and wives chose to speak out of turn, this could lead to a breakdown in the marriage. Through many years of public ministry, Paul saw that it was best that within the confines of the marriage relationship, both husband and wife felt that they had something to contribute to their service, whether it was a song, a prophecy, or a testimony, and if there was a disagreement about who should speak, it was best to let the husband speak on behalf of both, him being the spiritual head of that union.

This was the reason Paul specifically said, *"I suffer not a woman to teach, nor to usurp authority over a man."* He was writing to Timothy from the perspective of a seasoned minister counseling one with lesser experience, and he presented his best advice, sometimes based on things he had learned. It was not as much from spiritual revelation as it was from practical experience.

When Paul said, *"I suffer not ... ,"* what he was saying, in our twenty-first century vernacular, was: "I think it best," or "I advise you to take this course of action." God allowed Him to include that advice in His Word, because it was sound wisdom that came from the heart of a man inspired by the Holy Ghost. This exhortation was not in any way directed to all women, only to those who were married.

In the original Greek, the word translated here as *woman* was used interchangeably for both single and married females. So to know which category of woman Paul was referring to we have to look at the full context. Certain scriptures in the Bible were addressed to certain groups of people, and one cannot place universal restrictions on the Church based on texts that were directed solely at a certain class of people. The prohibition was not for all woman to be silent, but, rather, for married woman to allow their husbands to speak. If both felt an unction to bring forth a message, and there was a schism as to who should deliver it, Paul's preference was to defer to the husband, given the fact that he was the head of the household. This was the reason Paul directly connected his advice to Adam and Eve, not only to provide his words with a scriptural subtext, but also to drive home the point that he was dealing with husbands and wives in this particular passage.

Paul stated that because God Himself laid out the pattern of Adam being made first and then Eve coming after him, they should apply that same principle to who in the marriage should bring forth whatever message they both felt led to deliver. Given the fact that Adam came first, then let the husband speak first. That way, order would be maintained, and the conflict would be settled.

Paul then turned his attention to the wives and admonished Timothy to encourage them not to feel inferior because of giving this deference to their husbands. As a way to encourage the married women, Paul exhorted Timothy to encourage them in the fact that they alone in the union had the ability to bear children, which, in the culture of that day, was considered one of the greatest honors bestowed by God upon human beings.

Paul was working to address a problem on multiple fronts. First, he was advising Timothy on how to maintain order in his church. Second, he was addressing a cultural problem of the day that existed between husbands and wives. And finally, he was providing spiritual insight into the inner workings of a godly marriage. When a person studies the Bible, they must take all of these historical, cultural and spiritual applications into account and allow the Holy Spirit to help them understand these factors in order to see the full truth.

The same methodology can also be applied to the issue of whether or not women should cover their heads when they pray and when they attend church services. This is another one of those issues some have built an entire doctrine around. If, they insist, a woman fails to cover her head when she prays, her prayers will go unanswered. This has been a major issue of contention for decades in the church, causing many schisms in the Body of Christ and much oppression of women, some of whom just did not want to wear a covering when they prayed. Once again, the modern church has chosen to simply ignore this issue altogether, and this is not a valid solution for addressing it. There are still some theologians, particularly of the older generations, who believe the Bible insists that all women cover their heads when they pray. Whether one ignores the issue or promotes the teaching, both approaches are unscriptural and represent two extremes.

I have stated before (and it is worth stating again): we cannot just ignore the parts of the Bible that do not seem to be fashionable according to modern standards. Nor can we misinterpret the Bible, to make it say what we want it to say. We have to search out the truth, embrace the truth, and allow the knowledge of the truth to set us completely free from our fears, our prejudices, and ourselves. In that spirit, I want to turn our attention to the passage of scripture that has been used to promote this unscriptural doctrine and discover what the Bible is actually saying to us.

This issue of whether or not women should cover their heads in prayer comes out of a teaching Paul gave to the Corinthian church. It is amazing how, throughout the centuries, the apostle Paul has been accused of sexism or bias toward women. But, as with all great writers, people tend to project into their words the things they want to see, rather than what the author is actually saying. Here are the words in question, just as they were written by the great apostle himself:

> *Be ye followers of me, even as I also am of Christ.*
> *Now I praise you, brethren, that ye remember me in all things, and keep the ordinances, as I have delivered them to you. But I would have ye know, that the head of every man is Christ; and the head of the woman is the man; and the head of Christ is God. Every man praying or prophesying, having his head covered, dishonoureth his head. But every woman that prayeth or prophesieth*

with her head uncovered dishonoureth her head: for that is even all one as if she were shaven. For if the woman be not covered, let her also be shorn: but if it be a shame for a woman to be shorn or shaven, let her be covered. For a man indeed ought not to cover his head, forasmuch as he is the image and glory of God: but the woman is the glory of the man. For the man is not of the woman: but the woman of the man. Neither was the man created for the woman; but the woman for the man. For this cause ought the woman to have power on her head because of the angels. Nevertheless neither is the man without the woman, neither the woman without the man, in the Lord. For as the woman is of the man, even so is the man also by the woman; but all things of God. Judge in yourselves: is it comely that a woman pray unto God uncovered? Doth not even nature itself teach you, that, if a man have long hair, it is a shame unto him? But if a woman have long hair, it is a glory to her: for her hair is given her for a covering. But if any man seem to be contentious, we have no such custom, neither the churches of God. 1 Corinthians 11:1-16

If one were to read this passage quickly and casually, it might seem as if Paul was putting a stipulation upon all women to cover their heads every time they pray. However, let us examine the text and use the same methods of deduction that we applied to other scriptures, to root out what is *not* being said, and embrace the truth of what remains.

The key to understanding this text is to start with the beginning and the end of it. Paul began his teaching with these words:

But I would have you know, that the head of every man is Christ; and the head of the woman is the man; and the head of Christ is God. 1 Corinthians 11:3

Paul concluded his teaching with these words:

But if any man seem to be contentious, we have no such custom, neither the churches of God. 1 Corinthians 11:16

Both the beginning and the end inform us that this is a message for married couples, and it is addressing certain social customs that existed in that time. Just as in the passage from 1 Timothy, when the terms *man* and *woman* are used in this context, it is referring to married men and married women. Paul is putting forth a divine order for Christian marriage and comparing it to the divine order, the sovereign nature, of the Godhead.

Paul stated that the head of the woman is the man, and the head of the man is Jesus Christ. He then declared that the head of Christ is God. Paul made a similar comparison when writing about marriage in his letter to the saints at Ephesus. The language is quite similar, and it reinforces the fact that Paul was dealing with married couples. The similarities are clear:

> *For the husband is the head of the wife, even as Christ is the head of the church: and he is the saviour of the body. Therefore as the church is subject unto Christ, so let the wives be to their own husbands in every thing.* Ephesians 5:23-24

Viewing the similarity of the language in these two texts provides us further evidence that we are dealing with Paul speaking to married couples in his first letter to the Corinthians. The last verse of the teaching, which speaks about certain customs, shines further light on our study.

In the days of the early church, it was a custom for women to wear veils and other types of coverings as symbols of their deference to their husbands. It was a cultural custom of that day, just as when men would enter a room and immediately remove their hats, to symbolize their deference and respect for the people in that environment. Paul here was acknowledging the custom and using it to make a spiritual point: a married woman should feel the comfort and spiritual covering of a husband who loves her and prays for her. Then Paul brought this within the context of how Christ covers His Church through prayer and love. To finalize his teaching, Paul stated that although other churches did not have such customs and he respected them, he saw the opportunity to use the custom to make a spiritual analogy.

In short, God does not require all women to keep their heads covered when they pray or go to church, but He does want us to understand that Christian women who are married to Christian men should expect her man to cover her spiritually through love and prayer, just as Jesus Christ covers His Church.

This brings the matter to an even larger context, the issue of the roles of women and men in marriage. The biblical teachings on marriage may be the doctrines most misunderstood and misrepresented by the Christian Church.

Of all of the institutions in the world today, it is the most unique and the most special, because it is the first institution that God placed on earth. Before any government, any military force, and even any church ever came into being, God established marriage to be the fountainhead upon which all society is built. This institution, more than any other in the world, was meant to be the clearest expression of Christ and the Church. In spite of the sacredness of this institution, however, secularists and atheists have often accused the Christian idea of marriage of being an institution that oppresses women and keeps them in bondage.

When others hear such terms as *"head of the woman,"* or *"being in subjection to a man,"* they cringe and ultimately mock the institution and call it archaic and idiotic. It is unfortunate that these accusations often gain credibility, because some religious men have twisted the Scriptures to tear down their wives and belittle them, all the while justifying their behavior by saying that they are the *"head"* of the marriage. God's desire is that both of these false views be torn down, never to rise again. And the only way to do this is to go back to the Bible, and rightly divide the word of truth.

To begin, we must establish a clear distinction between the institution of marriage and all other institutions in the world. Unlike marriage, God places no restrictions upon women serving in a leadership capacity. A woman can be a preacher, a CEO, or the leader of a government, and there is nothing in the Bible that puts any restrictions upon her. The institution of marriage is different. Within the order of rank and command, God is the head of the man, and the man is the head of the woman. Even though there is an order of leadership between the man and the woman, they are still considered equal in the marriage in the eyes of God. The key to understanding this is understanding God Himself.

The Bible has always compared a marriage to the union of Christ and the Church, and in a passage of scripture I referenced earlier from 1 Corinthians, we gain some further insight into this point. As a reminder, I want to quote the verse again:

> *But I would have you know, that the head of every man is Christ; and the head of the woman is the man; and the head of Christ is God.*
>
> 1 Corinthians 11:3

Paul was teaching us the nature of Christian marriage. He stated that the ideal of equality within the marriage was comparable to the union of Christ and His Father. Within the communion of the Trinity, God the Father, God the Son, and God the Holy Spirit are all equal because they are all one. They are all equally God. Still, God the Son, in the person of Jesus, humbled Himself and submitted to the will of God the Father. This is what Paul meant when he said that God is the head of Christ, because Jesus' role in the earth was to do the will of His Father. Although they are equally God, because the Father comes before the Son, the Father is the head of the Son.

The Bible shows that this same concept is applied to a marriage. When a man and a woman come together in holy matrimony, the two become one flesh. They are equal in worth and quality because they are one. Yet, in terms of the roles and offices executed in the home, because God formed Adam first, and then Eve afterward, the pattern is that the man is the head of that home.

This term *head* does not mean "dictator," "owner," or "boss." It means "leader" of the home. Even though the Bible gives this office to the husband, he and his wife are still equal, just as Jesus and the Father are equally God. A Christian marriage is not an institution in which one person is subordinate to the other, but a relationship in which there are two very different roles, and yet the two are equal because they are one.

Now I want to quote once again from the passage in Ephesians that I referenced earlier. This time I want to include the entirety of Paul's teachings concerning marriage:

> *Giving thanks always for all things unto God and the Father in the name of our Lord Jesus Christ; submitting yourselves one to another in the fear of God. Wives, submit yourselves unto your own husbands, as unto the Lord. For the husband is the head of the wife, even as Christ is the head of the church: and he is the saviour of the body. Therefore as the church is subject unto Christ, so let the wives be to their own husbands in every thing.*
>
> *Husbands, love your wives, even as Christ also loved the church, and gave himself for it; that he might sanctify and cleanse it with the washing of water by the word, that he might present it to himself a glorious church, not having spot, or wrinkle, or any such thing; but that it should be holy and without blemish. So ought men to love their wives as their own bodies. He that loveth*

his wife loveth himself. For no man ever yet hated his own flesh; but nourisheth and cherisheth it, even as the Lord the church: for we are members of his body, of his flesh, and of his bones. For this cause shall a man leave his father and mother, and shall be joined unto his wife, and they two shall be one flesh. This is a great mystery: but I speak concerning Christ and the church. Nevertheless let every one of you in particular so love his wife even as himself; and the wife see that she reverence her husband. Ephesians 5:20-33

Here is the divine portrait of a godly marriage.

Paul began by stating that we, as believers, should be subject unto each other. This word *subject* or *submit* is used in the original Greek to signify rank, as in a military unit. Within a military unit, every officer is equal in humanity, but different in rank. So, too, in the relationship in a marriage. The two are equal, but different in rank.

The Bible says that the husband is the head, and that the wife is to honor that headship. However, the key for every husband to understand is that his leadership of the home is only carried out in the same way that Christ leads His Church. When we study the gospels, we see a Jesus Who led by serving His disciples, by loving them, protecting them, praying for them, and covering them spiritually. Christ did not use His headship to oppress His Church, but, rather, to nourish and cherish it. You, as a virtuous woman, deserve a man who will lead you and love you in the same way.

Understanding this idea of Christian love makes scriptural passages such as the following much easier to comprehend:

Even as Sara obeyed Abraham, calling him lord: whose daughters ye are, as long as ye do well, and are not afraid with any amazement. Likewise, ye husbands, dwell with them according to knowledge, giving honour unto the wife, as unto the weaker vessel, and being heirs together of the grace of life; that your prayers be not hindered. 1 Peter 3:6-7

Often these scriptures have been used to promote gender inequality, but the true light of revelation shows their clear meaning. God said that Sara, setting a pattern for all virtuous wives to follow, gave honor to her husband as the head of the family, calling him lord. This was not a sign that he was her master, but her leader. Abraham was a man of God who spent time in the presence of the Lord, and Sara could rest in the fact that when Abraham led his family, he was taking his orders from the Lord Himself.

Abraham also set the pattern for all godly men, by loving his wife and treating her as a valued treasure, not weaker by being inferior, but being valued and treated with tender, loving care. This is what God desires for the virtuous woman, a life in which she has fellowship with God, equality with her man, and freedom to be all that her Maker has called her to be.

You might be reading these words and are discovering that you have allowed yourself to be held back by the lies of the devil. Maybe you know that there is a call of God upon your life, to pastor a church, start a business, or have the type of family life that will bring you joy and contentment. Whatever the dream is, God has shown you in His Word that you are not limited by who you are and that you are just as anointed by the Holy Ghost as any other person who has accomplished great things for God's Kingdom. Where the Spirit of the Lord is, there is liberty to be all that He has called you to be.

When Jesus met the woman of Samaria at Jacob's well, she could not have imagined at that moment how influential and pivotal that seemingly-chance encounter would be for her. That moment not only changed her individual life, but the cultural life of an entire city. After she met the Master, she went forth, and the Bible says of her:

> *The women then left her waterpot, and went her way into the city, and saith to the men, Come, see a man, which told me all things that ever I did: is not this the Christ? Then they went out of the city, and came unto him.*
> *And many of the Samaritans of that city believed on him for the saying of the woman, which testified, He told me all that ever I did.* John 4:28-30 and 39

Just think of it! An entire city was transformed because of the testimony of one woman. How many people are waiting for your testimony, your sermon, your book or your song? In Christ, there is neither male nor female, for we are all equal in God's sight, and we all have been given a word to share. Rise up and do what He has told you to do. Rise up, and say what He has called you to say. As you obey, you will see your world change—for your good and for His glory *In Jesus' name. Amen!*

AFTERWORD

DAUGHTER, THY FAITH HATH MADE THEE WHOLE

Our revels now are ended. – William Shakespeare

This book was written for the purpose of serving as a journey of self-discovery. Very often, in this great theater of the universe called life, we fall short of achieving our highest potential. We sway back and forth from one meaningless journey to the next, at the cost of wasting years chasing things that never come to fruition. The reason this tragedy takes place is that so many people really never discover the part they were born to play. By missing the role that was tailor-made for you, you miss your divine appointments, and when the lights come up and the curtain closes, you are left on a bare stage, and the rest is awful silence. I hope that after reading this book, you have discovered some things about the Lord, some things about His Word, and some things about yourself.

After looking at yourself through the lens of the holy Scriptures, maybe you have discovered some things about yourself that are not pleasing in God's sight. Maybe, after looking through a clear mirror and no longer seeing through a shattered glass, you might not like the person you have become. The good news is that this is a new moment, and there is an opportunity for you to become the virtuous woman God wants you to be.

There is one more scriptural reference that I want to use in closing. It tells the story of a woman, who, after careful reflection, discovered that she did not like the person she had become. However, she did not stay in the shadows; she pressed her way to the light and found redemption at the feet of Jesus. Here is her story:

And one of the Pharisees desired him that he would eat with him. And he went into the Pharisee's house, and sat down to meat. And, behold, a woman in the city, which was a sinner, when she knew that Jesus sat at meat in the Pharisee's house, brought an alabaster box of ointment, and stood at his feet behind him weeping, and began to wash his feet with tears, and did wipe them with the hairs of her head, and kissed his feet, and anointed them with the ointment.
Now when the Pharisee which had bidden him saw it, he spake within himself, saying, This man, if he were a prophet, would have known who and what manner of woman this is that touched him: for she is a sinner.
And Jesus answering said unto him, Simon, I have somewhat to say unto thee. And he saith, Master, say on.
There was a certain creditor which had two debtors: the one owed five hundred pence, and the other fifty. And when they had nothing to pay, he frankly forgave them both. Tell me therefore, which of them will love him most?
Simon answered and said, I suppose that he, to whom he forgave most.
And he said unto him, Thou hast rightly judged.
And he turned to the woman, and said unto Simon, Seest thou this woman? I entered into thine house, thou gavest me no water for my feet: but she hath washed my feet with tears, and wiped them with the hairs of her head. Thou gavest me no kiss: but this woman since the time I came in hath not ceased to kiss my feet. My head with oil thou didst not anoint: but this woman hath anointed my feet with ointment. Wherefore I say unto thee, Her sins, which are many, are forgiven; for she loved much: but to whom little is forgiven, the same loveth little.
And he said unto her, Thy sins are forgiven.
And they that sat at meat with him began to say within themselves, Who is this that forgiveth sins also?
And he said to the woman, Thy faith hath saved thee; go in peace.

Luke 7:36-50

Here was a woman who had a past mired in sin, but despite all her failings, she knew that the Messiah had come to take away the sin of the world. So she pressed her way to Jesus. She moved past the animosity of the crowd, the guilt of her shameful life, and all the voices that tried to tear down her worth, just so she could touch the Master. As she began to anoint His feet, and wash them with her tears, she was pouring out of her being all of the sin, all the mistakes, all the regrets, and all the shame.

We are told that the master of the house looked on in wonder, for he knew what manner of woman she was, and she was not one of virtue. But what he did not understand was that in that moment, the strange woman removed all the uncleanness from her life, the silly woman renewed her mind to the obedience of Christ, and the person who was lost was found and discovered the virtuous woman within her, the woman Jesus had caused her to be. Like the master teacher He was, Jesus told His host a story of forgiveness that brought clarity and crystallization to the beauty of that moment.

As Jesus ended His parable, He looked at the woman and told her that she was forgiven. When the other guests stared in doubt and bewilderment, Jesus confirmed the change that had taken place within her, speaking out these words for all to hear: ***"Woman, thy faith hath saved thee, go in peace."***

No matter where you are today and no matter what you have done, Jesus can change your life. You do not have to be the strange woman, standing outside the household of faith. Nor do you have to be the silly woman, fully connected and bound by the spirit of this world. You can be free and can become the virtuous woman, cleansed and made whole by the blood of the Lamb.

If you do not know Jesus as your Savior and Lord, I invite you to welcome Him into your heart right now by saying this prayer:

Dearest Lord Jesus,

I come to You in this moment,
To acknowledge that I am a sinner,
And that I need a Savior.
I believe that You are the Son of the Living God.
I believe You died and rose again.
And I believe that all of what You have said is true.
So, I repent of my sins.
I turn from my wicked ways.

I renounce Satan and all his works.
I reject the powers of darkness,
And I embrace the power of the light.
I confess You as my Lord and Savior.
I give my heart to You,
And I dedicate my life to serve You
Today, tomorrow, and forever.
So. Lord I now thank You for saving me,
And I give You praise for it.

In the name of the Father, the Son and the Holy Ghost,
Amen!

If you prayed that prayer from your heart, you are now born again. So arise, and go forth in peace. Like the woman who touched Jesus, your faith has made you whole.

www.ingramcontent.com/pod-product-compliance
Lightning Source LLC
Chambersburg PA
CBHW021219090426
42740CB00006B/282

* 9 7 8 1 9 5 0 3 9 8 2 3 2 *